Learning that Transfers is a rare combination of practical and in... together concepts from psychology, neuroscience, and the learning sciences, the authors mount a case that transfer is one of the keys to designing curriculum that can produce deep and durable learning for the 21st century. Educators everywhere will welcome the book for its clarity, use-value, and timeliness.

Sarah M. Fine
Director of the San Diego Teacher Residency at the
High Tech High Graduate School of Education

Accessible. Reflective. Timely. Inspiring. Engaging. By asking all of the right questions, this book enables teachers to navigate overwhelming numbers of outcomes by creating/ uncovering complex relationships between concepts and extending learning through real-world transfer. I want education to help develop deep thinking, compassionate humans, and this book supports this aim fully.

Charlie Kraig
Designer of Professional Learning/
Learning Network Educational Services

There is so much I love about this book. *Learning That Transfers: Designing Curriculum for a Changing World* provides a step-by-step process that allows readers to connect their learning and transfer it to the work they do. It is based in research and practice.

Peter DeWitt, Ed.D.
Author/Consultant Finding
Common Ground Blog (Education Week)

This is a serious and ambitious book that makes explicit connections from a model of learning right through to curriculum design and implementation. In doing so, it provides the reader with an explicit structure that supports their progress as they acquire, connect and transfer what they learn, demonstrating the efficacy of their model of learning.

Oliver Caviglioli
Designer, Illustrator, Author

The authors have brilliantly captured the purpose of instruction today. Our students MUST be able to acquire, connect and transfer knowledge and, as educators, we must be intentional in our curriculum design to ensure that happens. This book is a great resource for ALL 21st Century educators.

Dr. Jeff Bearden
Superintendent of Schools, Forsyth County, GA

How might we design agile curriculum that prepares learners for a wildly unpredictable world? How might we design learning experiences for a silo-free system, even as we continue learning inside of them? The practical wisdom and tangible tools tucked into every nook and cranny of this ground-breaking text make this the right book for the right time, and these are the right people to learn from.

Angela Stockman
Author and Professional Learning Facilitator

The book guides you from "what to WOW" in a clear and concrete way, offering a multitude of strategies as a primer to design learning that transfers. Everything in it has been tested with diverse students around the globe by educators like you. This work is a promise for transformation in education with an abiding focus on student ownership, complex thinking, and relevant learning.

Alena Zink
Professional Learning Specialist/Forsyth County Schools

The authors have advanced a critically important new synthesis of the science and art of effective teaching. By focusing on the practical methods teachers can use to help students engage deeper conceptual understanding, this book helps keep the big questions about life, humanity, and sustainability in mind, even as we structure the fine-grained details of everyday classroom lessons.

Dr. Susan Hanisch & Dustin Eirdosh
Co-Founders of GlobalESD.org and education
researchers at the Max Planck Institute for Evolutionary Anthropology

We live in a world of often bewildering particularities. Children begin thinking, Vygotsky says, by assembling their immediate world into mental complexes where particularities understood by their juxtaposition. With schooling, children learn to organize the world by concepts or transferable patterns of meaning. The authors of this important new book masterfully explore the way these two pivotal ideas— concepts and their transfer—play out in educational practice.

Dr. Bill Cope
Professor, College of Education, University of Illinois

In an increasingly neoliberal world of performance and accountability, this book is a call-to-arms for anyone passionate about real learning. The "Try Next Day" strategies would enhance any classroom because they complement what you do already.

Gregory Anderson
Teacher of English www.thequillguy.com

Learning That Transfers articulates the interconnected relationships between past and present knowledge, offering a framework for future learning that will stand strong as education evolves. As a teacher educator, I value the fusion of theory combined with practical "Next-Day Strategies" that make this book a valuable addition to any teacher preparation program.

Michele Dugan
Alternative Certification & Induction
Coordinator (Forsyth County Schools)

Imagine an education system that "empowers teachers and students to tackle the problems facing us in the 21st century and beyond". It's possible and this book shows us how. With equal parts inspiration and practical implementation, the authors detail the strategies, tools and supports they use in their own classrooms to enable their students to thrive in an unknowable future. HIGHLY recommend!

Julie M Wilson
Founder & Executive Director,
Institute for the Future of Learning

As educators, we constantly strive to prepare our learners to navigate the complexities of their world. Drawing on latest research, the authors articulate a compelling visual model that enables students to apply their understanding to new contexts. *Learning that Transfers* is a must for teachers who are seeking ways to provide opportunities for authentic learning.

Richard Healy
Head of Senior - British School Manila

Our world is increasingly complex and preparing our students for tomorrow depends on our teacher's ability to teach more than just curriculum. *Learning That Transfers* is a thoughtful and essential guide for any educator concerned with preparing students to meet challenges through deep, powerful thinking and learning.

Katie Graham
Assistant Superintendent,
Learning Services, Grasslands School Division

What a fantastic resource! This book is loaded with concrete examples of how to design meaningful and engaging learning experiences for students. I felt empowered as I read each chapter, thinking the ideas could easily be integrated into my practice immediately. This book should be a mandatory resource in every school and in teacher education programs.

Jenni Donohoo
Author/Educational Consultant

In a connected and complex world, our ability to navigate myriad contexts becomes paramount. What's essential in that world? Learning transfer. Immediately practical, drawing on diverse scholarship and rich classroom experience, this book reveals the what, why, and how of learning transfer, for teachers of all types. This is a must-read for anyone striving for equity and excellence in education.

Michael Crawford, PhD
CoFounder/EdSpace

No one today would suggest that we live in a stable world with little change, little need to adapt as individuals, to meet the challenges of the next several months let alone the next 10, 20 or 30 years. Ch 4 Modern Literacies alone is why every educator should read this book. Like never before we must teach and lead our students not for a final exam, but for life. This book will help.

Dr. Rick Gilson
Executive Director: Southern Alberta
Professional Development Consortium

It's a uniquely human trait to make deep meaning out of knowledge, giving it significance and context. Through the ACT mental model, practical examples of shifts in practice, guidance in curriculum planning and more, Learning That Transfers is a text that empowers readers to reframe learning and build in that deeper level of meaning that makes all the difference in revolutionizing education.

Caitlin Krause
Author, Mindful by Design and Designing Wonder

Learning That Transfers

Learning That Transfers

Designing Curriculum for a Changing World

Julie Stern

Krista Ferraro

Kayla Duncan

Trevor Aleo

Foreword by John Hattie and
Afterword by Yong Zhao

FOR INFORMATION:

Corwin

A SAGE Company

2455 Teller Road

Thousand Oaks, California 91320

(800) 233-9936

www.corwin.com

SAGE Publications Ltd.

1 Oliver's Yard

55 City Road

London EC1Y 1SP

United Kingdom

SAGE Publications India Pvt. Ltd.

B 1/I 1 Mohan Cooperative Industrial Area

Mathura Road, New Delhi 110 044

India

SAGE Publications Asia-Pacific Pte. Ltd.

18 Cross Street #10-10/11/12

China Square Central

Singapore 048423

Associate Editor: Eliza Erickson

Production Editor: Megha Negi

Copy Editor: Diane DiMura

Typesetter: C&M Digitals (P) Ltd.

Proofreader: Theresa Kay

Indexer: Integra

Cover Designer: Lysa Becker

Marketing Manager: Margaret O'Connor

Printed in the United States of America

Library of Congress Cataloging-in-Publication Data

Names: Stern, Julie Harris, author. | Ferraro, Krista Fantin, author. | Duncan, Kayla, author. | Aleo, Trevor, author.

Title: Learning that transfers : designing curriculum for a changing world / Julie Stern, Krista Ferraro, Kayla Duncan, Trevor Aleo.

Description: Thousand Oaks, California : Corwin, [2021] | Includes bibliographical references and index.

Identifiers: LCCN 2020052681 | ISBN 9781071835890 (paperback) | ISBN 9781071835883 (epub) | ISBN 9781071835876 (epub) | ISBN 9781071835869 (pdf)

Subjects: LCSH: Curriculum planning. | Instructional systems—Design. | Transfer of training. | Concept learning.

Classification: LCC LB2806.15 .S746 2021 | DDC 375/.001—dc23

LC record available at https://lccn.loc.gov/2020052681

This book is printed on acid-free paper.

21 22 23 24 25 10 9 8 7 6 5 4 3 2 1

Contents

CHAPTER 4

CHAPTER 5

CHAPTER 6

CHAPTER 7

CHAPTER 8

Visit the companion website at
learningthattransfers.com
for downloadable resources.

Foreword

THE PLEASURES OF TEACHING TRANSFER

For two hundred years, one of our dirtiest secrets is that while we know the importance of transfer from one problem to another or from one situation to another, it has been notoriously hard to know how to teach students to transfer. Often we turn the tables, and say Student X can transfer, they must be smart; but this hides that we are less able to teach other students to also transfer and become smart. Finally, along comes this book dedicated to the core issues of teaching transfer.

There are skills involved in transferring knowledge and understanding from one situation to a new situation. This can be to near (problems somewhat similar to the one just completed) or far (problems quite different but relating to similar processes of thinking), or transfer of knowledge and transfer of problem-solving methods. This book introduces similar or dissimilar transfer that captures these variations on transfer, and outlines optimal teaching methods for both. Such methods require deliberate choices of learning strategies, knowledge, and ideas, detecting similarities and differences between the current and new situation, and building higher conceptual understanding that sits above specific problems. Marton (2006) argued that transfer occurs when the learner learns strategies that apply in a certain situation such that they are enabled to do the same thing in another situation when they realize that the second situation resembles (or is perceived to resemble) the first situation. He claimed that not only sameness, similarity, or identity might connect situations to each other, but also small differences might connect them as well. Learning how to detect such differences is critical for the transfer of learning. As Heraclitus claimed, no two experiences are identical; you do not step into the same river twice.

In one of the pioneering studies of transfer, Gick and Holyoak's (1983) classic work showed how students who could successfully be taught to solve a problem failed to transfer that knowledge to a similar problem, if the latter had a different context and occurred a mere two pages later. But, if the students are invited to see connections between the two problems then their chance of success is increased. They need to be taught to "see the old in the new." Similarly, students can overgeneralize and apply strategies even when the new problem does not require them to do so or indeed requires alternative strategies to be successful. Such negative transfer primarily occurs because students are unaware that there was something different required. Thus, students need a set of skills to help students to not overgeneralize but pause and spot the difference—the difference in the task demands of two similar or seemingly dissimilar tasks and task requirements.

Throughout this book there are many exemplars of how to detect similarities and differences and to employ pattern recognition skills; there is emphasis on teaching students to use their learning to unlock novel scenarios. They adopt the language of adaptability, organizing our world so we can understand it, and build from a model of cognitive complexity that moves from ideas to concepts to pattern detection between these ideas and concepts. By overlearning the skills of pattern detection, we have the beginning of the skills of transfer. Hence their three steps: acquire, connect, transfer.

This skill of seeing patterns is core to our skills in learning. When we first encounter new ideas, such as sitting in an anatomy class and listening to hundreds of bones being cited, we often look for patterns based on our prior knowledge. At this phase, summarizing and outlining to build patterns and "hang" new ideas and facts is necessary, otherwise the incoming is just that—incoming soon not to be retained, learned, appreciated, and often then discarded. As we build these coat hangers, or schema, they help us to build relations between ideas, accommodate new ideas, and make predictions and hypotheses. There can be too many students who do not see the connection to past ideas, fail to summarize and build initial schema and often are soon left behind as more ideas are then provided, and we wonder why they cannot transfer. Teaching pattern recognition is the core skill of learning, and especially of transfer. The claim is that there are four important attributes to organizing curricular outcomes that facilitate teaching transfer—**prioritize** thoughtfully, **arrange** effectively, **supplement** strategically, and **flow** cohesively.

The book is full of many examples as to how to teach for transfer across a multitude of curricula domains. I love their analogy to building a barbed-wire fence (and having lived on a farm for many years, they still scare me particularly when the top strand is electrified; but they work brilliantly). The story is about the posts, which need to be sturdy so that they can support the wire and give it shape. Then the wires are strung, and the barbs can catch the ideas and build them into a more coherent pattern that becomes the whole fence. It is not one big idea that makes the wire, but the overlapping of the many strands of knowledge (Wittgenstein, 1953). We must teach the fundamental principles (the posts), situate new ideas between these posts, and then teach the student how to weave the many ideas into a coherent picture, such that when new ideas and problems are encountered, they can use these bigger picture skills to decode what is required, understand the strategies needed, and bring new ideas into the coherent whole (or even question whether the coherent whole is optimal).

It is pleasure to have a full length treatise on this most important topic. May this focus on transfer become much more debated, taught, and valued in our schools.

John Hattie

REFERENCES

Gick, M. L., & Holyoak, K. J. (1983). Schema induction and analogical transfer. *Cognitive Psychology, 15*, 1–38.

Marton, F. (2006). Sameness and difference in transfer. *The Journal of the Learning Sciences, 15*(4), 499–535.

Wittgenstein, L. (1953). *Philosophical investigations*. Wiley.

Preface

WHERE ARE WE IN PLACE AND TIME? WHY DO WE NEED TO RETHINK CURRICULUM DESIGN?

How long have we educated children the way we currently do? Surprisingly, we have separated students according to age, frequently rotating them through distinct subject areas, and assessing specific content knowledge for only a tiny fraction of the time humans have lived on earth, less than half of 1 percent.

As a species, we have discovered and created astonishing feats such as fire, language, religion, the arts, mathematics, medicine, sports, democracy, and agriculture *without* teaching the way we currently do. We are comforted by this realization, because change is hard. Change is complex. Change is risky. Nevertheless, we must change the way we design schooling because *not* attempting to change is the most significant risk of all. The COVID-19 crisis shined a spotlight on significant flaws in our current ways of teaching, such as how dependent our students have become on adults to direct their learning and how damaging our assessment practices are for intrinsic motivation for learning.

We must rethink curriculum and instructional design because of the scale and pace of change taking place in our world. The speed and degree to which technology, economics, information, politics, climate, and population patterns are changing is deeply affecting human interaction and behavior, with potentially devastating consequences (Bostrom, 2019). While the anatomy of our brains has remained relatively stable in the last few thousand years, the tools and technology that we use to make meaning of our lives and our world have had a major impact on how we think and interact. Much like the advent of oral language or large-scale literacy, the rapid increase in technological development is causing a massive shift in the way humans communicate and relate to one another. We are sharing and processing more information than ever before and require new cognitive tools to tackle the increasingly complex, transdisciplinary problems of 21st-century life. Rote learning and isolated outcomes will become increasingly less useful in the world our children will enter upon completion of high school.

Exponential change often leads to feelings of chaos and a loss of control. These feelings bring about all sorts of negative consequences such as addiction, rise of conspiracy theories, and political polarization (Friedman, 2016). Mental illness among young people is increasing at a concerning rate (Twenge et al., 2019). We've entered an era when the stories, structures, and norms that hold society together are being called into question. It's times like these when we need a spirit of inquiry and innovation to help us better understand ourselves and navigate our complex, interconnected world. We need to provide students with new sense-making tools so that they can understand complexity and then act in an informed way.

All these drivers lead to an overwhelming need to teach our children to be adaptable, flexible, lifelong learners. But how, exactly, do we do that? Should we seek more open-ended methods like project-based learning, personalized learning, and authentic assessments? Are soft skills such as critical thinking and creativity the answer? How does each of these relate to job readiness and career education?

These initiatives hold promise, but they can be dramatically enhanced by **learning transfer**, that is, explicitly helping students to understand the deeper structural patterns of the world so that they can use their learning beyond the situation at hand. We can harness research from the science of learning to ensure our students are prepared for lifelong learning. This book will detail a framework and principles to help teachers and other educators integrate ideas from many fields and perspectives to answer the question we all seek to answer: *How can we best enable our students to live meaningful lives?*

> As educators, we need frameworks that allow us to respond to changes without constantly overhauling or reinventing everything that we do.

Teachers of the past knew what children needed to know and be able to do. That is changing rapidly. How do we prepare students for a future that we can't quite see? And how do we do this without exhausting ourselves? Many teachers feel caught between competing pulls for their time and attention. Even if they want to be innovative, they feel boxed in by their learning objectives or lack the tools to facilitate more divergent, self-directed learning. As educators, we need frameworks that allow us to respond to changes without constantly overhauling or reinventing *everything* that we do.

What if we selected the most powerful, transferable, organizing ideas from our curricular documents, and anchored everything we explored in those concepts? Could this help educators turn off the conveyer belt of "covering" an endless list of objectives while also ensuring students are prepared to tackle topics they encounter without a teacher's guidance? Yes, it can. We can both teach less *and* prepare our students to tackle more.

Learning transfer: Using our previous learning to understand or unlock a completely new situation.

Mental models: A formulation—usually through words and visuals—that helps us to make visible the invisible, often subconscious frameworks that we use to think through complex situations.

Concept: An organizing idea with distinct attributes that are shared across multiple examples.

Mental models are the frameworks that we use to think through complex situations—we often use them automatically and without inspection. We believe that a new mental model that helps us make sense of increasing complexity will be key to helping our students become adaptable, flexible, lifelong learners. Research from cognitive science and neuroscience point to the notion that every area of expertise can be viewed through the lens of its most fundamental elements, called **concepts**, and the ways in which those elements interact. We can view our curricular aims through a model of *acquiring, connecting, and transferring conceptual relationships* to new situations, thereby expediting our students' abilities to apply their learning to new situations.

We can harness the power of long-standing disciplines such as mathematics, science, and the arts to help our students become innovative problem-solvers. Even as the world changes and technology advances, the key disciplinary ways of knowing, thinking, analyzing, and communicating will still serve us as we solve complex problems. But as the demands of our civic, social, and work lives evolve, so too must our pedagogy. Knowledge is readily available via the internet; therefore, knowledge consumption is no longer the sole priority of education. Application of understanding and skills to new situations, learning transfer, must become the priority. Learners must be able to use their learning to unlock novel scenarios.

We can organize curriculum in a way that harnesses the key concepts of traditional disciplines as students work to solve complex modern problems. This approach can help us work toward systemic equity. It can even be an essential part of the solution to the looming mental health crisis. Curriculum design can help our young people make sense of these complicated issues, find their passions, and solve complex problems in their communities. It won't be easy, but it will be rewarding. We are hopeful and encouraged by our experiences in schools that are already piloting these ideas.

This book is not a prescriptive set of rigid routines that limit teacher autonomy. Nor is it a catalog of inspirational phrases that lack detail in exactly how to implement them. The framework and principles that we describe in the next seven chapters will empower teachers, and their students, to tackle the problems facing us in the 21st century and beyond. We'll still need facts and knowledge to succeed in the Information Age and Fourth Industrial Revolution. However, we must center our ability to navigate, interpret, and transfer our learning if we want education to keep pace with our rapidly changing world.

The mental model at the heart of this book empowers students to become adaptable, lifelong learners by teaching them how to intentionally and relatively expeditiously grasp the structures of mathematics, science, language, and more. And then students can apply this same way of learning—acquire understanding of single concepts, connect them in relationship, and transfer those relationships to new situations—to increasingly essential fields such as digital literacy and ethical reasoning. The most in-demand skillset of the future will be the ability to combine long-standing expertise with new fields in order to innovate to solve the world's toughest challenges (Gardner, 2006).

If we see how the world is organized, we can understand it. If we can understand it, we can impact it for the better and lead meaningful lives. This belief lies at the heart of our work and is the guiding principle for this book.

About the Authors

Julie Stern is the best-selling author of *Tools for Teaching Conceptual Understanding, Elementary* and *Secondary, Visible Learning for Social Studies,* and *Learning That Transfers*. She is the thought leader behind the global workshop series Making Sense of Learning Transfer and is a certified trainer in Visible Learning Plus. Her passion is synthesizing the best of education research into practical tools that support educators in breaking free of the industrial model of schooling and moving toward teaching and learning that promotes sustainability, equity, and well-being. She is a James Madison Constitutional Fellow and taught social studies for many years in Washington, DC and her native Louisiana. Julie moves internationally every few years with her husband, a US diplomat, and her two young sons.

Krista Ferraro is a history teacher and department head at Thayer Academy in Braintree, Massachusetts. Her passions include civic education, social justice, and preparing students for effective global citizenship. Previously, she served as deputy director of public policy and curriculum innovation at Chavez Schools in Washington, DC, where she also taught history and public policy courses. Her published works include the bestselling *Tools for Teaching Conceptual Understanding, Elementary* and *Secondary*. Krista holds bachelor's degrees in American studies and Spanish from Cornell University and a master of arts in teaching from American University. She is also an alumna of Teach for America.

Kayla Duncan is a personalized instruction coach for Forsyth County Schools in Cumming, Georgia. Her passion centers around empowering student voice through meaningful, authentic experiences and increased ownership. Kayla currently supports personalized learning schools in creating their new vision for education through the design thinking process. She believes the voices of students and the community should drive what happens in the school building. Before her coaching role, Kayla taught elementary physical education and middle grades mathematics. She holds a bachelor of science in kinesiology from the University of Georgia, a master of arts in mathematics education from Western Governors University, and an educational specialist in learning, design, and technology from the University of Georgia. Kayla is pursuing a doctor of education in school improvement from the University of West Georgia and hopes to use this new knowledge to propel schools toward innovative visions for education. Kayla resides in Georgia with her husband, a fellow educator, and their fourteen-year-old dog Georgie.

Trevor Aleo is a middle school English teacher in Wilton, Connecticut, where he designs meaningful learning experiences while reading and writing alongside his students. Prior to his current position, he taught high school and was a grade-level lead in Prince William County, Virginia. In addition to leading teams at his own school, he's drafted curriculum at the district level, created instructional resources for the Virginia Department of Education, and presented at local, state, and national conferences. He believes education should help people become better sense makers and story tellers and is a passionate believer in pedagogies that align with those values. Growing up in a house of teachers, he developed a love of learning that continues to serve as the driving force behind all his work. He holds a bachelor of arts in English and a master of arts in teaching from James Madison University and is currently pursuing a doctorate in learning design and leadership at the University of Illinois Urbana-Champaign. Trevor currently resides in Fairfield, Connecticut, with his amazing wife Lindsey and will be welcoming a son into the world somewhere around the release of this book.

Chapter Overview and How to Use This Book

This book is intentionally designed to begin with an understanding of how transfer works, key shifts in practice that set the foundation for learning that transfers, and then a series of concrete steps for planning courses, units of study, assessments, and instruction that facilitate learning transfer to new situations. We follow an overall **backward design** approach, which begins with the end in mind. We start with curricular goals, then move to assessment and how we will measure those goals, and finally, we plan for instruction.

Features that help to guide the application of the ideas in this book include **Thinking Prompts** that offer important moments of reflection to inform curriculum design, **Next-Day Strategies** that suggest practical ideas to be implemented immediately in the classroom, and **Design Steps** that are the critical moments of creating curriculum for learning that transfers. A glossary at the end also provides definitions for most key terms throughout the text.

CHAPTER OVERVIEW

The Learning Transfer Mental Model. Chapter 1 of this book outlines the learning transfer mental model—a way of making sense of new topics and fields that help us to grasp the overall structure of our world. We explain what learning transfer is and how it works, and how we can use this relatively simple model to think about and design curriculum and learning experiences. Most importantly, we can teach our students how to use the mental model so that they can become their own teachers—especially so they can effectively draw upon their previous learning when they encounter completely new and different situations or challenges.

Shifts in Practice. Chapter 2 directs attention to explicit shifts in practice that are necessary to truly harness the power and potential of learning that transfers. We do not have to throw everything out that we are currently doing. Often, simple reframing can produce profound results. But without shifts in some key areas, attempts to teach for transfer will fall flat.

(Continued)

Backward design: Starting with the end in mind. First, establish goals of learning, then design assessment that will measure those goals, and then design learning experiences.

1

(Continued)

Disciplinary Literacy. Chapter 3 compels us to view individual subjects, topics, or standards as part of a larger discipline of study—or a way of making sense of our complex world. Disciplinary literacy is a powerful way to think about how each subject area helps us to understand, communicate, and take knowledgeable action. This chapter will inspire you to use standards in a nonstandardized way, embrace the power of concepts in your classroom, and to articulate the big picture of your course that will facilitate learning that transfers. We offer several reflection protocols and considerations for articulating the most essential elements of each course that empower students to transfer their learning to new situations.

Modern Literacies. Chapter 4 seeks to place a growing body of important competencies under one large umbrella, *modern literacies*. We all know that teaching science, mathematics, and all the other traditional disciplines is not enough to prepare students to navigate today's complex world. Students must learn to be digitally literate, communicate across cultures and modalities, and make ethical decisions. We can apply the learning transfer mental model to these same competencies. And we can mix them with more classical disciplinary literacy in order to solve multifaceted problems.

The Story of Your Course. Chapter 5 synthesizes the previous chapters into an overall vision for the course that you teach.

Unit Planning. Chapter 6 sets up the steps for unit planning. We outline the critical steps for planning a transfer-focused course that ensures students can use their learning in new and increasingly different situations. Then we offer a series of exercises and templates to choose from as you and your team of teachers map out the story of each course.

Assessments. Chapter 7 provides the building blocks of 21st-century assessment design. We want to measure more than students' recall of knowledge. This chapter provides guidance and strategies for using novel situations, providing authentic value beyond school walls, and creating comprehensive assessments that give all stakeholders a picture of students' ability to transfer their learning.

Instructional Design. Chapter 8 brings everything together with tools for creating robust lesson plans designed to help students move between surface, deep, and transfer levels of learning. We explain how to utilize concept attainment, conceptual questions, and novel scenarios to ensure students can apply their knowledge to any situation. We provide strategies, tools, and examples from the classroom to help support the planning process.

The conclusion describes additional food for thought to prepare students for an unprecedented world. We outline some key drivers of change, such as artificial intelligence and the rise of China as a global superpower, to forecast what might be in store for formal schooling. We include considerations that push our thinking beyond the recommendations in the main sections of this book.

HOW TO USE THIS BOOK

In order to truly harness the power of learning that transfers, we need to consider some key shifts in our practices to ensure that many of our actions are aligned to maximize results for our students. The first two chapters of the book are designed to promote these shifts in practice with a series of **Thinking Prompts,** to promote reflection and provide intentional planning, and several important **Next-Day Strategies** that offer tips for practical, immediate application in the classroom. We want readers to observe the key ideas in action—so that you are excited and ready to design powerful transfer-focused learning experiences. Chapters 3 and 4 set up big picture goals for a course including a **Course Overview** as well as **Vertical** and **Horizontal Alignment**, and Chapter 5 begins sequencing and planning specific units.

Scan the QR codes throughout the book to access examples and templates, or visit learningthattransfers.com.

The Learning Transfer Mental model, or ACT model, at the heart of this book, is simply a way of thinking about how to facilitate and design learning that can be applied to multiple situations or contexts. It is not a rigid procedure that has a "right way" of following or implementing.

At the same time, without a crystal-clear, long-term view, all efforts to improve teaching and learning occur in a haphazard way. Teachers can often get bogged down in the details of learning outcomes or standards of learning. Before we dive into these details and jump into unit planning, we need to zoom out and consider the larger aims of schooling and the disciplines that we teach. A key reflection question that we will pose a number of times throughout the book is this: *What do we want our students to understand and do as adults, as a result of our teaching?* In other words, what are we really trying to achieve? This question will guide us through the first half of the book so that we can plan powerful learning experiences for our students through the design steps in the second half of the book.

FOUR LEVELS OF ENGAGEMENT FOR DESIGNING LEARNING THAT TRANSFERS

Depending on availability of time and commitment, we put together four levels of engagement with this text. While we don't advocate for anyone to try to only design a lesson—as this goes against backward design of beginning with the goals, then moving to assessment, and then moving into instruction—we are also realists and know that perhaps if you start with Level 1, you will see the value and return to the book to move toward Level 2.

Level 1: Design a Lesson

- Read Chapter 1 for an overview of the purpose and model for learning that transfers.

- Read Chapter 2 for the key shifts needed to set the foundation for learning that transfers.

- Then head over to Chapter 6 and read the section on anchoring concepts to select at least a couple of focus concepts and create questions of conceptual relationship with these concepts.

- Use Chapter 8 for daily instructional strategies for learning that transfers.

Level 2: Design a Unit

- Read Chapter 1 for an overview of the purpose and model for learning that transfers.
- Read Chapter 2 for key shifts needed to set the foundation for learning that transfers.
- Turn to Figure 3.15 in Chapter 3 (and read the accompanying section) to select two or three disciplinary lenses that you want students to apply to nearly every situation in your course.
- Then, head over to Chapter 6 for specific unit planning steps.
- Next, we suggest turning to Chapter 7 for assessment design.
- Finally, use Chapter 8 for daily instructional strategies for learning that transfers.

Level 3: Design a Course

- Read Chapter 1 for an overview of the purpose and model for learning that transfers.
- Read Chapter 2 for key shifts needed to set the foundation for learning that transfers.
- Complete at least one exercise from Chapter 3 to think about the larger picture of the discipline(s) that you teach. Turn to Figure 3.15 in Chapter 3 (and read the accompanying section) to select two or three disciplinary lenses that you want students to apply to nearly every situation in your course.
- Complete at least one exercise from Chapter 4 to select a couple of modern literacy concepts.
- Take an extended look at Chapter 5 for sequencing the standards and concepts of your course, then Chapter 6 for unit planning.
- Next, we suggest turning to Chapter 7 for assessment design.
- Finally, use Chapter 8 for daily instructional strategies for learning that transfers.

Level 4: Design a Curriculum

- Gather a team of talented educators and other community members and move through this book step by step.
- Scan the QR code to review tips for how specific roles—such as district or state level curriculum leads, instructional coaches, school administrators, grade level leads, or department heads—can approach this book.

We provide a number of reflection protocols, templates, and flexible options (or ways you can adapt your current curriculum documents) throughout the book and on the companion website. If you ever feel like you are "box ticking" or complying, please pause and try to grasp the larger purpose of what the section intends to achieve. If you cannot figure out the purpose of the thinking prompt, design step, overall template, or specific box and how it will be useful in classroom practice, we fully support skipping it. We believe teachers should have authorship and autonomy over their curriculum planning documents. We trust you, your professional judgment, and we are honored that this book ended up in your hands.

Scan this code for tips on specific roles.

This book provides frameworks, principles, and strategies to guide teachers in creating classrooms that foster deep, transferable learning. We hope that it serves to transform our schools into places of connection, meaning-making, and innovation, so that our innate desire for understanding can keep up with our changing world. As a result, we envision a healthier, more sustainable, and peaceful world, led by our current generation of children who will transfer their learning to solve today's complex problems.

CHAPTER ONE

Learning Transfer
What Is It and How Can It Transform Teaching and Learning?

"Grasping the structure of a subject is understanding it in a way that permits many other things to be related to it meaningfully. To learn structure in short, is to learn how things are related."

—Jerome Bruner

Why does this chapter matter?	We need to teach students how to use their learning to unlock new situations.
What will I be able to do by the end of this chapter?	I will be able to explain how learning transfer works and begin to reframe how I think about teaching.

We have yet to encounter a teacher whose aims for students stop at the classroom wall. At the end of each lesson, each unit, each school year, teachers hope their students carry with them an arsenal of new knowledge and skills that will help them better understand and impact the world in which they live. They hope that studying the water cycle will help students care for the environment, that studying government will help them take part in civic life, that studying proportions will help them double a recipe when the time comes. In short, they want students to *transfer* their learning to the real world.

Transfer of learning is at once incredibly simple and incredibly complex. At its most fundamental level, it simply means applying our past learning to a new situation. Humans are wired to do this. A young child who has been bitten by the neighbor's chihuahua may cry or retreat to the safety of a parent's arms when they encounter grandma's golden retriever. We instinctively use our past experiences to help us navigate new circumstances. Yet, when it comes to school, students struggle mightily when asked to apply Monday's math lesson to the word problems on Friday's test. Why does our natural ability to transfer our learning break down when that learning occurs in the classroom?

Perhaps the problem is that most classroom learning is divorced from students' lived experience. We run through lists of standards or chapters in a textbook, covering required content in a vacuum and rarely asking students to draw out lessons that can be transferred to and from other aspects of their lives. We plan engaging activities to keep their attention but rarely plan ways for students to use their learning to impact the real world. Therefore, most kids have learned that school learning stays at school. They have not been taught to see the applicability of their learning and, so, their brains have stopped trying to apply it.

At its most fundamental level, transfer of learning simply means applying our past learning to a new situation. Humans are wired to do this.

The challenge we face as teachers, then, is to break down the paradigm of what school is. We must reorient our classrooms so that learning transfer is the heart of all we do. Surprisingly, this shift is not that hard to make. We don't have to throw out our current curriculum or restructure the entire school to make it happen. In fact, we've found that once teachers understand the building blocks of teaching for transfer, they're better able to plan and implement exciting, valuable lessons for students *and* feel more energized and less burnt out.

Before moving on, stop to consider the following questions. Every chapter will provide a set of reflection questions at the beginning and again at the end of the chapter, which will prompt you to activate the organizing ideas and pathways in your brain and call attention to the ways in which your thinking has expanded or deepened, to optimize your reading journey. We suggest you take a moment to jot down your ideas. Then, at the conclusion of the chapter, you can come back to these thoughts and add to them.

THINKING PROMPT

- How do you currently help your students to organize their understanding?

- What are some of the strategies you use to motivate your students?

_____

_____

_____

_____

_____

> Once teachers understand the building blocks of teaching for transfer, they're better able to plan and implement exciting, meaningful lessons for students *and* feel more energized and less burnt out.

CHAPTER STRUCTURE

This chapter provides a foundation for understanding transfer and how we can organize our curriculum and instruction through a powerful and flexible model that can be applied to any subject, course, skill, or hobby. We will use this model to design curriculum and learning experiences that prepare students for a complex world. The chapter is organized around the following sections:

- The Role of Concepts in Promoting Transfer

- ACT: The Learning Transfer Mental Model

- Putting It All Together

- Envisioning the Possibilities

THE ROLE OF CONCEPTS IN PROMOTING TRANSFER

Comprehending the organizational structure of an area of study is a hallmark of both expertise and the ability to transfer our learning to new situations (Bransford et al., 2000). For our students to get better at transfer, we must help them both pay attention to the deeper structures of their learning and organize knowledge into these structures the way experts do. This means helping students build these arrangements in their brains, too. Let's look at how this works.

Concepts are organizing ideas with distinct attributes that are shared across multiple examples. Like mental file folders, they are words we use to organize and categorize our world. They help our brains organize examples into meaningful groups based on shared attributes. Whether we're looking at a chihuahua or a golden retriever, our brains are able to notice the distinct attributes of each—fur, snout, four legs, tail, and so on—and place them into our "dog" file folder despite their differences. Consider the visual in Figure 1.1 as an illustration of concepts as mental file folders.

Figure 1.1 Concepts as Mental File Folders

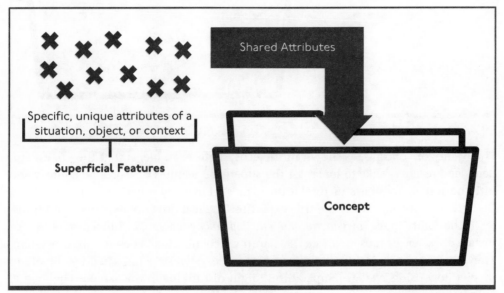

This organizing process is what helps us to make meaning. By connecting novel experiences, objects, or contexts to preexisting cognitive frameworks we are able to make sense of our world. Consider this explanation:

> Fortunately, even novel things are usually similar to things we already know, often exemplifying a category that we are familiar with . . . Concepts are a kind of mental glue, then, in that they tie our past experiences to our present interactions with the world, and because the concepts themselves are connected to our larger knowledge structures. (Murphy, 2002, p. 1)

Whether a scientist on the cutting edge of their field or a toddler navigating their living room, concepts are the connecting point between old knowledge and new learning. Importantly, the more knowledge we gain and assimilate into our schema, the more capable we are of learning increasingly abstract and complex concepts. This is especially true once we begin to develop expertise in a particular domain or discipline.

For instance, scientists use the concept *ecosystem* to understand different communities of life on the planet, such as coral reefs and rainforests. When a scientist learns about a new ecosystem—a desert or tundra—they connect their new learning to the other information in their mental ecosystem "folder." Instead of starting anew, trying to memorize all the superficial features of life in the desert, they build upon their prior understanding of the deeper attributes of ecosystems in general. The visual in Figure 1.2 helps to illustrate this point.

Figure I.2   Conceptual File Folder of Ecosystems

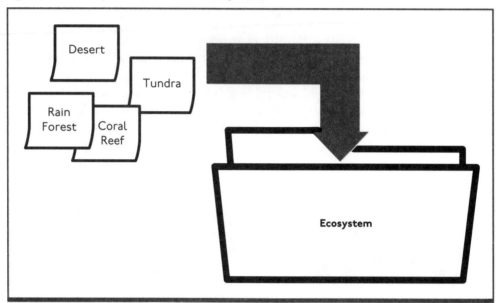

The beauty of concepts, as shown in the ecosystems example, is that they point students and teachers alike to look past the superficial features of a specific context and into the deeper, invisible structural features present in every situation. Concepts alone, though, do not suffice to create true expertise. The real driver of expertise, and transfer, is the ability to see the *patterns of interaction among concepts* within a discipline. For instance, a scientist must do more than simply recognize that a desert is an ecosystem. They need to use their understanding of how ecosystems are impacted by climate to predict how rising average temperatures might disturb life in the Sahara. The mental "file folders"—concepts like ecosystem and climate—need to be organized in relation to one another to create a **conceptual framework** in the expert's mind (Donovan & Bransford, 2005). Figure 1.3 demonstrates how those conceptual file folders are organized, connected, and structured in the mind of an expert.

> The real driver of expertise, and transfer, is the ability to see the *patterns of interaction among concepts* within a discipline.

The ability to transfer understanding to new situations is a hallmark of expertise in any field. Imagine, for instance, that a professional chef and a novice cook are both presented with a basket of unfamiliar ingredients and instructed to create a meal. Even if the professional chef has never worked with the specific meats, vegetables, and spices given, they can draw on their understanding of flavor, texture, and balance to create a tasty dish. The novice, on the other hand, would be lost without a recipe for guidance.

Research shows that one of the reasons experts can engage in this type of transfer is the way knowledge is organized in their brains and the ways that experts access that knowledge in the new situation (Anderson et al., 2001; Vendetti et al., 2015). Novices often place their attention on the superficial features of a new situation, not on the

Conceptual framework: The ways ideas are organized in the brain.

Figure 1.3   Patterns of Interactions Among Conceptual File Folders

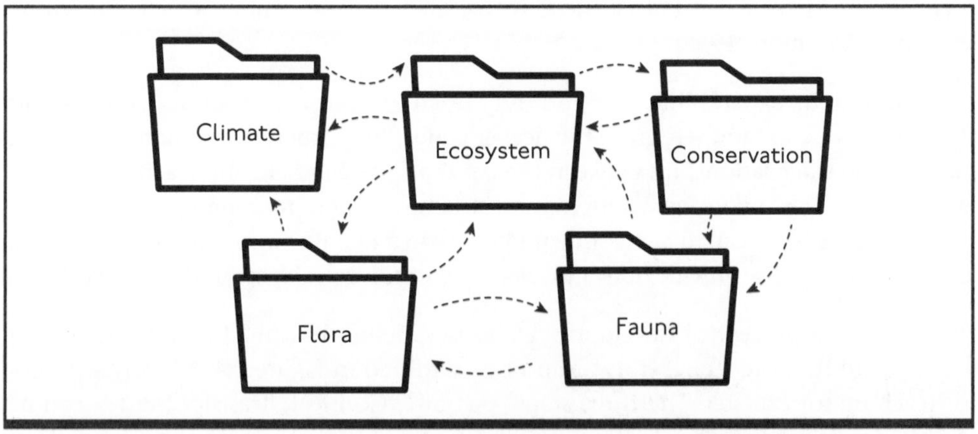

deeper, underlying structures. Beginners, therefore, tend to see bits of information as separate, unconnected facts, while experts see new, fact-rich situations as part of a larger system of ideas that exists in their minds. They mentally organize the concepts in their field into frameworks that help them quickly assimilate new knowledge, retrieve prior knowledge, and interpret problems (Bruner, 1977; Donovan & Bransford, 2005; Mehta & Fine, 2019).

ACT: THE LEARNING TRANSFER MENTAL MODEL

Every field, hobby, or complex skill can be viewed through this model of fundamental elements, or concepts, and the predictable ways those elements interact. Basketball players understand that the goal of offensive plays is to ensure at least one player is "open" (unguarded by an opponent) so they can take a shot. And, reciprocally, they understand that the goal of defense is to prevent the opponent from getting open. The fundamental concepts of offense, defense, and openness are connected in a web of interaction in players' brains, which they use to adapt to new situations as a game plays out. If a play breaks down, players can use this understanding to improvise effectively.

Musicians understand that dissonant chords, which have harsh sounds, are usually resolved by consonant chords, which have more stable, harmonious sounds, in the typical musical progression. The fundamental concepts of chord, dissonance, consonance, and progression—each its own mental "file folder"—are linked together in a predictable pattern to help the musician sight read a new piece of music or compose a new song.

As teachers, we often assume that our students are creating the right file folders in their brains and that they see how each element of our curriculum relates to the others. We assume that as they learn they develop frameworks of knowledge in their minds. This often occurs because a teacher's expertise in any given subject area creates blind spots, meaning they see the content so clearly and understand it so deeply that they forget how that content might appear to their students (Wiggins & McTighe, 2005). They gaze into the night sky and immediately see constellations that give shape and meaning to each star—they see ursa major and Orion's belt—whereas their students gaze upon the same stars as random points of light. Forgetting what it is like to *not* see the connections, teachers teach each star—each standard or topic or bit of information—and assume that kids are creating the right constellations in their minds. Then, when kids struggle with transfer, they wonder what went wrong (Perkins & Salomon, 1992).

To overcome the expert blind spot and truly teach for transfer, we must first teach our students to look for and recognize the deeper conceptual structure in any situation. We make visible the relationships between the concepts in each field and teach students to intentionally draw upon these patterns and structures when interpreting new phenomena. If we do this, we can increase students' ability to remember information, apply skills, and transfer their learning flexibly and creatively to solve problems in the real world.

Of course, the process of developing expertise is complex and time intensive. But we've found that the straightforward process outlined in Figure 1.4 is a powerful tool for teaching for transfer. The three steps—Acquire, Connect, Transfer (ACT)—can be used to design learning experiences that ensure that students attain the *constellations* as well as the *stars*, and that they can create and apply new patterns when they look out upon an unfamiliar quadrant of the sky.

Figure I.4   ACT: The Learning Transfer Mental Model

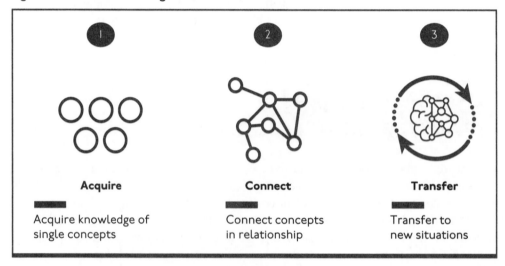

Step I: Acquire

If we want students to be able to transfer their knowledge to new situations, we must be intentional about how they acquire and store that knowledge in their brains in the first place. Thus, the first step in teaching for transfer is helping students understand the most important organizing concepts in each discipline and ensuring that they use these concepts to categorize key details of their learning. Or, to continue our previous analogy, we start by helping students look beyond the superficial features of a situation and create distinct file folders in their minds.

Let's consider one of the key concepts in baking: leavening. Leavening refers to the process of adding gas to a dough or batter to make it rise when baked. This can occur through a variety of ingredients or methods. For instance, baking soda, a base, can be combined with an acid, such as buttermilk or lemon juice, to produce tiny air bubbles that contribute to the fluffiness of a pancake. Whipping egg whites to form an airy foam, and then folding the whipped egg whites into a batter, can do the same. Yeast, a single-celled living organism, can also produce gas in baked goods and cause them to rise when it is combined with water and sugar.

To the novice, baking soda, whipped egg whites, and yeast are all distinct, unrelated ingredients. Novice bakers can easily follow a recipe to produce a loaf of properly risen sourdough, or an adequately puffed pastry, but they may find it difficult to make substitutions for a leavening agent they don't have, or to modify a recipe to make it rise more or less to meet their taste. But, once they have created a mental file folder for the concept of *leavening* and organized these seemingly unrelated ingredients accordingly, they move one step closer to expertise and the ability to use their knowledge flexibly in response to novel situations.

This is true for students in the academic disciplines as well. Just because they have studied the international agreements that ended World War I and World War II does not mean they have gained any larger understanding of the concept of treaties. Calculating measures of center and measures of spread does not mean they automatically have expertise in the concepts of scale, bias, and data representation. As students move through the particulars of our content—the historical events, works of literature, mathematical algorithms, scientific facts—it is up to us to help our students recognize the concepts at play and to organize their learning in conceptual terms (Bransford et al., 2005; Bruner, 1970; Perkins & Salomon, 1988).

Because all new learning requires some degree of transfer, usually by comparing our prior learning to new situations, we can more powerfully harness the existing knowledge and experiences all of our students bring to the classroom—by looking past the superficial features and into the deeper structures of every situation. When our students struggle to comprehend new situations, it is a good indication that they are stuck on the superficial features of the situation.

For instance, students may struggle to understand complex texts such as *To Kill a Mockingbird*, because they are focused on the prose and the customs of the time period, which may seem foreign to them. But they likely have experience with concepts such as fairness, injustice, courage, belonging, social pressures, culture, and racism. They also likely understand the value of concepts such as word choice, setting, character development, and suspense when thinking about their favorite songs, music videos, movies, tv series, and more. Organizing concepts bring students into the situation and help them more easily comprehend the unique details of the new situation.

As teachers, we often have to train ourselves to look past the superficial features of what we are teaching to find the organizing ideas or concepts. If we focus only on those specific details without helping students to organize them in terms of concepts, we reduce our classrooms to rote learning, which will not be useful to our students in other contexts and likely easily forgotten (Bruner, 1977). Figure 1.5 depicts a visual of how we often have to look past the superficial features of the topics we are teaching in order to identify the organizing concepts embedded in the deeper structure of the discipline.

Take a look at the list of common topics (Figure 1.6) taught in schools today for examples of corresponding organizing concepts. The list of potential concepts is certainly not exhaustive and is meant to illustrate how we want to direct student attention to finding the organizing concepts in each new learning situation. The topics on the left are what we often hear teachers saying they are teaching. We must train ourselves and our students to see those topics through organizing concepts.

Once we have identified organizing concepts ourselves, we can help to point student attention to the features that define those concepts. To help students acquire knowledge of concepts, teachers can use activities like those described in Figure 1.7.

The first step in teaching for transfer is helping students understand the most important organizing concepts in each discipline and ensuring that they use these concepts to categorize key details of their learning.

Scan this QR code for additional examples of organizing concepts.

Figure 1.5   Identifying Deep, Structural Concepts in Our Curriculum

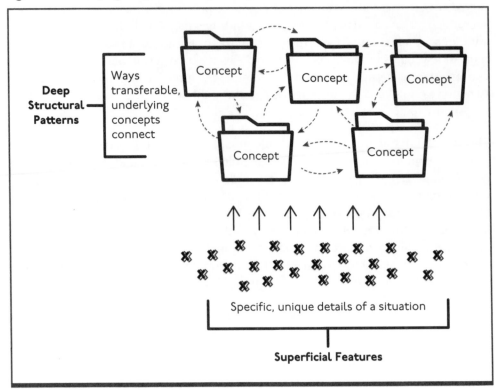

Figure 1.6   From Topics to Organizing Concepts

Subject Area	Common Topics: Facts, Skills, Examples, Details	Potential Organizing Concepts
Science	Crawling and flying animals	characteristics, interaction, living things, environment
	Rocks and minerals	change, earth's processes, cause and effect
	Genetics	patterns, code, relationship, reproduction, sequence, identity, mutation, inheritance, characteristics, trait
	Electricity and magnetism	connection, flow, attraction, repulsion, energy
Math	Skip counting	strategy, number sense, order, quantity, pattern
	Multiply with arrays	multiplication, pattern, structure
	Commutative property	equivalence, relation, manipulation, flexibility
	Chain Rule	derivative, function, rate of change, interdependence

Subject Area	Common Topics: Facts, Skills, Examples, Details	Potential Organizing Concepts
English	Stories, fairy tales	life lessons, friendship, imagination, kindness, struggles, decoding, phonics, vocabulary
	Nonfiction texts	informative, literary, text features, structure, medium, audience, context, purpose
	Romeo and Juliet	love, hate, loyalty, identity, rivalry, tragedy, figurative language, dramatic elements
	The Bluest Eye	identity, whiteness, blackness, beauty, racism, narratives, symbolism, characterization
Social Studies	Rivers, lakes, prairies, mountains	location, place, natural resources, human-environmental interaction, settlement
	Ancient Greece	civilization, resources, systems, governance, social structures
	World War II	conflict, power, competition, cooperation, alliance, nationalism
	Macroeconomics	supply, demand, scarcity, deficit, debt, budget, inflation, growth, policy, stimulus

Figure 1.7 Acquiring Knowledge of Single Concepts

Strategy	Example
Identify shared attributes across examples.	Science students examine a variety of *physical changes* in the lab in order to write their own definition for this concept.
Sort examples and non-examples of each concept.	Math students sort a series of graphs into two piles to show which are *functions* and which are not.
Explain each concept in their own words.	Literature students turn to their partner and explain *irony* in as many different ways as they can.
Illustrate each concept through non-linguistic representation.	Government students draw images and diagrams to explain the idea of *checks and balances*.

The key to each of these strategies is making sure that students are *organizing* their learning of specific details or examples using concepts, not just memorizing definitions for concepts or lists of facts. Let's compare rote learning about numbers and addition to conceptual learning about the same topic. Examine the differences between Classroom A and Classroom B in Figure 1.8.

Figure 1.8 Rote Learning vs. Surface Learning in Mathematics

Classroom A	Classroom B
Teacher A informs students that in order to become good mathematicians, they must be able to recall basic math facts quickly and easily. Students then make flashcards with basic addition facts on them (1 + 2 = 3, 2 + 3 = 5, etc.) and practice with their partners. Periodically, the teacher challenges the class to a "mad-minute" activity where students answer as many basic addition questions as they can in sixty seconds.	Teacher B explains to students that numbers can be composed of other numbers. They show students how a pile of five apples can be broken up into two smaller piles of two and three apples, or one and four apples. Students practice breaking the number five down into other sets of numbers as many ways as they can. The teacher tells students that when mathematicians see the number 5 they also see a group of three with a group of two, and a group of four with a group of one, and even two groups of two with a group of one. Then students create flashcards with different ways of composing (or decomposing) the number 5 and then practice these addition facts with a partner.

In Classroom A, students may gain automaticity with math facts (and might have fun doing so!), but they are unlikely to gain the type of conceptual understanding of numbers or addition that students in Classroom B would acquire. In Classroom B, the teacher is helping students organize their learning of math facts in terms of important concepts of the discipline.

Of course, there is still room for some of the memorization and practice described in Classroom A; students need to have basic math facts readily available in their brains in order to focus mental effort in solving more complex problems. But the foundation of conceptual learning must be in place for all that practice to pay off. Yes, the type of learning described in Classroom B will take more time. But redesigning learning with transfer in mind requires that we "go slow to go fast"; taking the time to help students organize new learning conceptually will enable them to interpret and retain new information much more quickly in the future.

Imagine a classroom where surface level learning occurs without conceptual organization. For instance, eighth-grade civics students may be asked to memorize the three branches of American government—legislative, executive, and judicial—and a list of ways the branches check and balance each other. However, if students go about building this foundational knowledge in a haphazard way, without organizing the examples around key concepts such as *limited government* and *separation of powers*, they will not be ready for the deep or transfer phases of learning. In fact, as they progress through the curriculum, they will keep asking questions such as, *Why doesn't the president just make a law to accomplish X?* or *Why doesn't the president just send people to jail for Y?*—both of which are disallowed due to the separation of powers among the branches—because they do not actually understand the larger principles at play. Teachers must then go back to re-teach old material to compensate for students' poor learning the first time around. All the time spent memorizing definitions for these terms will not have helped students apply their learning to new situations and, in the long run, is time wasted.

Step 2: Connect

The first step in our model involved students acquiring knowledge of single concepts—filing essential details and examples into the correct mental folders as they engage in surface learning. The second step builds on this foundation by asking students to draw connections among the conceptual folders they've been building in their brains. The result is a web of linkages between and among concepts. In the end, the step of *connecting concepts in relationships* is what allows students to use the concepts for more than just categorization of new information.

The most straightforward way to help students construct these webs of meaning is to ask questions that prompt student attention to conceptual relationships. We can plug concepts into the following conceptual question stems to achieve that:

- How are _____ and _____ connected?

- What is the relationship between _____ and _____?

- How does _____ impact/affect/influence _____?

- What effect do _____ and _____ have on _____?

- How do _____ and _____ interact?

- What is the role/purpose of _____ in _____?

For example, disciplinary ideas in music involve the relationships between concepts such as tone, rhythm, harmony, and expression. By investigating questions about the relationships among these concepts such as, *What is the role of tone and rhythm in creating harmony and expression?* and *What happens to the musical expression when the rhythm changes?* students are better able to analyze the impacts of new musical genres without explicit teacher instruction. A student who understands these complex interactions can more easily select, edit, or even create an original score for a multimedia presentation that communicates a certain message.

This music example illustrates a simple yet powerful method for designing learning that transfers. We can use a cycle with two main components as a broad way to think about curriculum design:

1. Teachers pose abstract questions about how concepts relate in order to call attention to the deeper structures of a situation.

2. Students explore a specific context—for example, a mathematical problem, scientific experiment, historical moment, or passage of text—in which the concepts play a major role.

After students have a chance to explore a specific context and answer the conceptual question, the cycle should continue, allowing students to apply their understanding to increasingly dissimilar contexts. See Figure 1.9 for a visual of this cycle. We will show you exactly how to design your curriculum using these steps in the subsequent chapters in this book. For now, we just want you to see the overall picture.

Consider the example in Figure 1.10 from an elementary school socioemotional curriculum. Students are exploring the concepts of empathy and conflict. To begin, of course, teachers help students understand each concept on its own. They give students a quick definition of each concept and have students categorize a series of scenarios

> Once students understand certain concepts, teachers can pose simple questions about the relationship between those concepts.

Figure I.9   Learning Transfer Cycle Deepens Learning

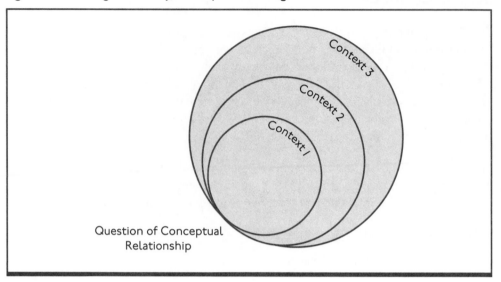

SOURCE: Stern (2017)

Figure I.10   Learning Transfer Cycle Example

How Are Empathy and Conflict Related?

Abstract Conceptual Question	Context for Investigation
How can a lack of empathy lead to conflict?	Students read a short story about a younger brother who always feels left out by his older siblings. Then they discuss the role a lack of empathy played in this sibling conflict.
How can conflict make it difficult to empathize with someone else?	Students brainstorm instances in which they have had a conflict with someone else and write a journal entry about how the conflict made them feel. Then they discuss how the feelings associated with conflict—anger, frustration, resentment, sadness—can make it difficult to put yourself in another person's shoes to practice empathy.
How can empathy help resolve a conflict?	Students watch a video in which a girl overcomes a feeling of anger during a fight with her best friend by imagining things from her friend's point of view.
How are empathy and conflict related?	Students reflect on their learning through the previous three contexts and respond to the overall question of how empathy and conflict are related.

and images as representing either empathy or a lack of empathy. Students brainstorm as many types of conflict as they can and create a nonlinguistic representation of what conflict means to them. These activities help direct students' mental effort to the shared characteristics of empathy in new situations, which is essential for learning (McTighe & Willis, 2019).

Once students understand the meaning of each concept, the teacher poses a simple question about the relationship between them: *How are empathy and conflict related?*

Then, students work through the learning transfer cycle to deepen their understanding of the concepts and understand how the concepts relate to each other.

Notice that with each new book, video, or exercise, students are not only looking beyond the unfamiliar, superficial features to recognize the familiar, organizing concepts, they are using the unique features of the situation to explore the deeper patterns involved in the relationship between empathy and conflict in order to build a complex web of connections between the two ideas in their minds. This aids in both memory retention and in transfer of learning, as strong patterns in relationships allow predictions when confronting a new situation (McTighe & Willis, 2019).

The beauty of this cycle is that each new context also helps students strengthen their understanding of each concept individually. After investigating the relationship between empathy and conflict in these various iterations, students will have many examples of each concept in their respective mental file folders and can draw upon those examples when investigating the relationship between, say, conflict and peace, or empathy and resilience, down the road. And, just as important, each new context provides fertile ground to practice learning transfer, the third step of our model.

Step 3: Transfer

Ultimately, we hope that students' understanding of important concepts and their connections will help them navigate new situations. Although transfer is the final step of our learning model, students who have investigated the relationships among concepts through a variety of distinct contexts have already engaged in learning transfer with each new context introduced to them. As they approach each new scenario—each new math task, text, lab experiment, work of art, or historical development—they are charged with applying their previous understanding of the concepts and then refining that understanding in light of new information. This is why we often remind teachers that transfer is both the *means* and the *end* of our approach.

Transfer works because our brains are designed to seek patterns (Gentner, 2010). We naturally look for similarities and differences in order to evaluate new information or situations and assimilate this into our existing network of thoughts and experiences. The network or patterns of thought is called **schema**. This inborn tendency not only aids us in basic processes such as the fight or flight response, but this connection making and pattern seeking increases the brain's capacity to learn and retain information (Sousa, 2017). Not only do patterns help us retain information better, but they help us predict and respond to new phenomena as well. For instance, once we internalize the pattern that "good triumphs over evil" in most fairy tales, we can easily predict the ending of stories we've never read before. Understanding that "to the victor go the spoils," we can recognize the underlying motives of war even when other justifications are given.

Our brains seek patterns because we have a bias for organizing information into systems, meaning we prefer to see our world as predictable and coherent instead of haphazard or random (Gentner, 2010). However, most classroom learning fails to take advantage of the brain's power to recognize and apply patterns. In fact, most classrooms remain at the factual and topical levels, which do not transfer to new situations (Erickson & Lanning, 2014). Whenever we try to apply our insights from one situation to another, we look beyond the superficial details and abstract to the conceptual level,

Schema: Patterns of interaction or networks of thoughts between concepts and ideas.

generalizing from a specific instance to a broader rule, before our knowledge helps us unlock the new situation. If instruction is stuck in the specific instances, rather than focusing on the deeper principles and patterns that bring coherence to the world, students will struggle to transfer what they learn in school to real-life scenarios.

All transfer is achieved through comparing what we already understand to a new situation. So obviously, the more closely a new situation matches students' prior learning experiences, the more easily they can transfer what they know. Students who learn to graph a linear equation given in the format $y = mx + b$ will more likely transfer their learning when asked to graph a new equation given in this same format than, say, one in the format $Ax + By = C$. And we can imagine that students will struggle even more when asked to transfer their graphing abilities when a word problem is posed. Similarly, students who can identify the theme of a story may struggle when asked to apply that skill to a poem. This is because transfer occurs at different levels.

In the 1980s, researchers Perkins and Salomon (1988) coined the terms "near" and "far" to describe these different levels of transfer. Transferring knowledge or skills from one task to another very similar task is known as near transfer; we refer to it as **similar transfer** for ease of use. When students are just starting out, similar transfer tasks can help them gain independence and confidence working with new material. A math teacher might model the process for graphing a linear equation and then pose a very similar equation (near transfer) to allow students to practice graphing on their own. Eventually, though, we want students to engage in **dissimilar transfer** (what Perkins and Solomon call "far transfer"), which requires them to apply their learning to tasks that are *not* similar to the original situation.

We usually want to begin with transfer between similar tasks. It is a good place to start as students need practice in abstracting to the conceptual level and transferring their learning to increasingly dissimilar tasks. Transferring to scenarios that closely match each other can serve as training wheels for more challenging transfer tasks (Gentner, 2010). We can gradually increase the dissimilarity of the transfer tasks so that students can gain insights from very different situations.

Consider the premise used in one of the most iconic studies done on learning transfer. Researchers presented subjects with a story about a military general and a fortress. The general's goal is to capture a fortress located at the convergence of several roads, each of which has been booby trapped so that large armies cannot proceed to the fortress unscathed. However, smaller numbers of people can travel the roads safely. Since the general cannot send the necessary number of troops down any one road to capture the fortress, he divides his soldiers into smaller groups and has each group traverse a different road in order to simultaneously reach the target.

After being taught the story, subjects were asked to imagine they were a doctor trying to save a patient who had been diagnosed with a malignant tumor. The tumor was inoperable but could be destroyed using rays. However, rays that were intense enough to destroy the tumor would also destroy healthy tissues and cause great damage to the patient. Lower-intensity rays would leave the healthy tissues intact but would not be strong enough to treat the tumor. What should they do? Although the solution to the doctor's problem—to use many lower intensity rays that converge on the tumor at the same time—bore a strong resemblance to the general's strategy in capturing the fortress, few of the subjects in the study could transfer their learning from the story

The more we can coach students to apply general patterns and conceptual insights to dissimilar, real-world contexts, the more flexible and creative their problem-solving abilities will be, and the more primed they will be to innovate.

Similar transfer:
Applying learning to a different, but quite similar situation to the original learning context.

Dissimilar transfer:
Applying learning to a completely new scenario that is very different from the original learning context.

to the tumor dilemma without being explicitly told to do so (Gick & Holyoak, 1983). Consider the visual in Figure 1.11 and see if you can identify the shared concepts present in both situations.

Figure 1.11 Dissimilar Transfer Example

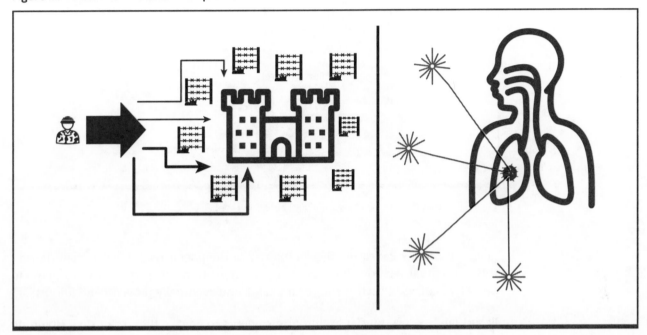

This is a prime example of dissimilar, real-world transfer and illustrates nicely the connection between this type of transfer and innovation. Study participants were being asked to look beyond the surface details of the situation and transfer their understanding of a larger principle—perhaps summarized as "divide and conquer" or "diffusion of force" and "convergence of force"—from the domain of military strategy to the domain of medicine, two very dissimilar situations. Yet, once they recognized the analogous features of each problem, an insight from one realm could be applied to create a breakthrough in another. The more we can coach students to apply general patterns and conceptual insights to dissimilar, real-world contexts, the more flexible and creative their problem-solving abilities will be, and the more primed they will be to innovate.

Students need to understand conceptual relationships within and across disciplines to tackle our world's most pressing problems. Every conceptual structure that students recognize can become a new tool on their problem-solving utility belt. How it's used will depend on the situation at hand, but it's adaptable enough to work in many different contexts and alongside other discipline specific skills. Having a combination of broad interdisciplinary structures and more focused, disciplinary structures will ensure students are equipped to navigate complex academic and real-world contexts.

Figure 1.12 illustrates how a teacher might use an intentional sequence of contexts to guide students to increasingly dissimilar acts of transfer. The abstract conceptual question asks students to explain the effects of the concepts of rhyme, repetition, imagery, and word play on texts. We can start exploring this question with short and simple

Figure 1.12   Example of Similar to Dissimilar Transfer

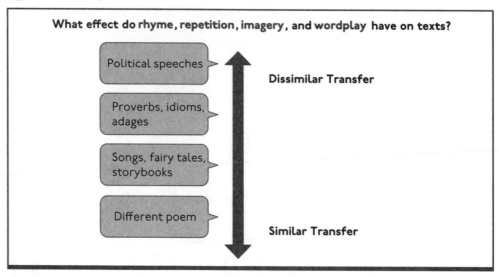

SOURCE: Visual inspired by the work of Perkins & Salomon, 1988

poems, gradually increasing the complexity of the poems read. We can then transfer this conceptual relationship—about rhyme, repetition, imagery, and word play—to other types of texts, such as songs, fairy tales, and eventually proverbs and idioms.

Each time that we transfer, we prompt students to engage their prior understanding and monitor their thinking along the way. Remember, our goal is to rise above the topical or factual level of thinking and see the larger patterns that hold true across many examples of texts. With each new text, students strengthen their understanding of those patterns and train their brains to see these patterns more clearly. That way, by the time we transfer to something such as political speeches, such as Martin Luther King Jr's "I Have a Dream" speech, students will recognize the deeper conceptual connections at play and, therefore, be adept at the act of transferring their learning to unlock new situations.

The **ACT model** is a synthesis of our understanding of how learning happens, particularly learning that transfers, as opposed to inert knowledge or simple memorization. Our review of research spans cognitive science, educational psychology, neuroscience, and meta-analyses on student learning and achievement such as those conducted by Robert Marzano and John Hattie. Importantly, the ACT model is simply a mental model, or a visual to help us and students think about how to effectively learn and transfer our learning to new situations. It is *not* an education model and is *not* a rigid formula that competes with other pedagogies or curriculum models. It is flexible enough to be adapted to many contexts, which we hope you will notice by the variety of examples provided in this book and accompanying digital resources.

ACT model: The process of acquiring, connecting, and transferring concepts and their relationships to new situations.

Readers familiar with Visible Learning or Professor Hattie's work may recognize some of the often-discussed influences, such as engaging students' prior knowledge, as well as some that are underrepresented in curriculum and instruction methods, such as conceptual change and transfer strategies. Through the steps of acquiring, connecting, and transferring conceptual relationships, students are engaging in the following influences on learning, all of which are in the category of "potential to considerably accelerate learning" according to the synthesis of research conducted by John Hattie (Visible Learning MetaX, 2020). This means that if done well, they have the potential to more than double a year's worth of growth within a single academic year:

- Integration with prior knowledge

- Conceptual change programs

- Elaboration and organization

- Self-judgment and reflection

- Transfer strategies

PUTTING IT ALL TOGETHER

Now that we have examined each step of the ACT model—acquire, connect, transfer—consider how this process might transform teaching and learning in a typical English language arts classroom. Let's contrast a more common approach, which we'll call "teaching a list of standards," with the approach we just described, *teaching for transfer*. We want to note there is nothing about the standards themselves that prevents teaching for transfer. It's all about how one approaches, organizes, and frames them.

In the teaching a list of standards approach, teachers use the content standards or a textbook to plan lessons, breaking up larger chunks of content into more digestible pieces. The result is a progression of learning experiences that unfold much like episodes of a television series. Each topic or chapter is treated somewhat in isolation from the others, perhaps with a few pauses to step back and admire the bigger picture. In an English language arts course, the class might spend a few weeks on short stories, examining the key ideas, details, craft, and structure of a few important stories. First, they read "The Gift of Magi," followed by "Everyday Use," and finally, "To Build a Fire." Along the way there would be tests and quizzes, perhaps some papers or projects, to assess students' understanding of each story. The unit is bookended by a summative assessment that measures students' knowledge of each particular short story. Even if each lesson plan is perfectly aligned to the test and delivered in an engaging manner, the understanding students develop is limited to the group of short stories they examined.

In the teaching for transfer approach, teachers approach the content by asking the following:

- What organizing concepts bring coherence and meaning to this content?

- How do the connections among these concepts produce transferable insights that will help students navigate the complexities of their world?

- Where can the lessons learned from this content be applied in the real world today?

Instead of breaking information down into digestible chunks—episodes to be consumed and remembered—they devise conceptual questions and a series of contexts in which to explore those questions. They seek out a novel real-world situation to use as a means of assessing students' ability to transfer their learning. They organize and frame their standards in ways that move students toward conceptual understanding and learning transfer.

This does not mean that you have to throw away your curriculum, abandon your standards, and start from scratch to begin teaching for transfer. When one of the authors of this book, Trevor, was teaching English at a public high school in Virginia, he still followed the curriculum outlined by his district. He still taught many of the same texts. He still worked in a department with teachers who had a variety of philosophies and approaches.

By organizing and orienting his standards in creative ways, he developed new frames for old units. What was previously his Short Story Unit became The Power Paradox Unit. Instead of dragging students through a random sequence of short stories, he curated texts that all explored the concepts of power, control, class, and status. Each short story was also paired with nonfiction articles, podcasts, TED Talks, or other videos to build the background knowledge necessary to interpret the story effectively. Students still read short stories, analyzed characters, deduced themes, and wrote paragraph responses. But, instead of treating each text as an isolated learning experience, he selected stories that explored two conceptual questions:

1. What's the relationship between power, control, class, and status?

2. How do plot, setting, characters, and conflict impact theme?

Students explored the relationship between those concepts in each text, refining their understanding after each new text. Most importantly, the understanding they developed along the way wasn't locked to those individual stories. They were able to transfer their understanding of the relationship between plot, setting, characters, conflict, and theme to every text they read or composed for the rest of the year. Similarly, since each story's content, and its paired nonfiction piece, grew student schema around the concepts of power, control, class, and status, they were able to leverage that knowledge when encountering future texts.

This simple reframing of an old unit helped students connect more meaningfully with the content, invest deeply in their learning, and even begin to transfer their understanding to their own lives and experiences. It didn't require a curricular revolution, tons of technology, or countless hours of creation and implementation. All it required was a new way of thinking about, relating to, and organizing his content.

ENVISIONING THE POSSIBILITIES

Imagine what would happen if students were encountering this type of learning at every grade level and across all disciplines. Instead of viewing school as a series of hoops to jump through—vocabulary lists to memorize, worksheets to complete, tests to study for—students would get the message that the purpose of education is to prepare them to tackle the complex challenges that each of us must navigate in real life. Instead of feeling intimidated by complicated issues like conflict in the Middle East or curing cancer, they would feel empowered to jump right in, form their own opinions, and take action.

Just as exciting is the potential for this type of teaching to bring coherence to the otherwise jolty school experience most kids endure each day. Consider the following list of topics taught in the first month of school for ninth graders:

- Art—line, shape, color in one-dimensional art

- English—poetry and short stories

- Science—ecosystems

- History—Islam in the Middle Ages

- Math—solving one-step equations

With a traditional approach, students are expected to contemplate the theme of a poem in first period and then head next door to solve for *x*. After lunch, they'll examine the teachings of Muhammad and then run off to a lecture about rainforests. No wonder students have trouble organizing what they've learned into meaningful frameworks of knowledge.

But, when the whole school is teaching for transfer, some simple changes can have a profound impact. What if we trained students to recognize similarities and differences among the deeper structures of situations, through transferable concepts, like this:

How Does Changing One Part of a System Impact the Other Parts?

- Art—How does a change in color/line/shape impact our perception of a work of two-dimensional art? Students create three different versions of the same image by altering color, line, and shape accordingly. Then they discuss how a change in one element impacts the overall piece.

- English—Can one word change the meaning of a poem? Students consider the specific connotation of words in short poems and discuss the implications of alternate word choice. Then they write their own poems and give a presentation to the class to explain their own word choice.

- Science—What happens when one part of an ecosystem is disturbed? Students study the impacts of pollution on a local watershed and map out the ripple effects on all living things that belong to the system.

- History—How do economic and religious expansion reinforce each other? Students investigate how the expansion of Islam was intertwined with the expansion of trade between Islamic societies and their neighbors in the Middle Ages. They look for ways that economic expansion paved the way for religious conversion, and how religious expansion paved the way for trade relationships to flourish.

- Math—How can we change an equation to make it easier to solve? Students learn to manipulate equations to isolate variables, distinguishing between changes that maintain the original balance of the equation (e.g., subtract 7 from both sides, or multiply both sides by 2) and changes that disrupt the equation (altering one side but not the other).

This is an example of analogical reasoning and transdisciplinary learning, which we will explore more in future chapters. Since nearly all new learning involves transferring our previous understanding to new situations, we can expect student learning to deepen with each new situation they encounter. Imagine the power of a student who, at the conclusion of these units, now understands that

> *Because all the elements of a system are related in complex and often invisible ways, changes to one part of a system often results in unintended "side effects" in other parts of the system.*

and

When we understand the relationships in a system we can manipulate them to produce a desired change.

By the end of this unit, students would have investigated the nature of change in a system in many different ways. They would come to understand interdependence. Insights from one discipline could easily be tested out in another. And, ultimately, a project requiring students to apply these principles of change to a new scenario would reveal their ability to use the concepts in flexible ways.

Think about how this type of learning would lend itself to some possible projects and performance tasks. Here's a simple example:

Our school is a system of interdependent parts. Think of a change you would like to make in our school community. Then analyze the ways in which your desired change might impact the entire system of the school. Create a display, with careful attention to visual elements and word choice, that communicates this analysis to students, faculty, and parents. Afterward, write a reflective piece that explains how your understanding of change, systems, and interdependence influenced the course of your project.

The moral of the story? Teaching for transfer is exciting, relevant, and has the power to transform schools into vibrant laboratories of learning and problem solving. And we do not have to throw out the entire infrastructure of our schools to make it happen.

CONCLUSION

The goal of Chapter 1 was to demonstrate that this book, and our broader vision for curriculum and instruction, is anchored in research and shaped by classroom experience. The idea of learning that transfers is not a buzzword we invented to dazzle readers and sell books. It is a well-established and researched phenomenon studied by cognitive scientists. We have read the scholarship and know the related challenges, but we also know that rote knowledge and decontextualized skills are not enough to prepare students for our increasingly complex world. If we want to truly help evolve students' capacity to make sense and make meaning in school and beyond, we need to integrate all the best elements from past and present pedagogies (and add new ones as well) to help them develop conceptual understanding that transfers.

The tools, frames, and moves we have previewed and will share over the course of this book are not things we simply hope or assume will work either—we have used them ourselves in our classrooms, with our colleagues, and alongside educators around the world. Of these tools, frames, and strategies, we believe the ACT model to be the most powerful. It is an infinitely adaptable tool that can be used to guide and sequence learning experiences. Though it is a relatively simplified model of how we learn, we believe it should be used as a heuristic to conceptualize, organize, and scaffold all the other complex moves, frameworks, and tools that shape teaching. Not a rigid model or prescriptive form that attempts to replace them. It is not a fill in the blank template or a paint-by-numbers protocol. Like the learning processes it is meant to represent, it is a dynamic and open-ended process that can, and should, be adapted and adjusted to suit your learning context and objectives.

To help you better envision how we can create schools and classrooms focused on learning that transfers, Chapter 2 will detail essential shifts in practice and mindset that will set the stage for more meaningful and transferable curriculum and instruction. Though we might not need to throw out the entire infrastructure of school to implement the ideas shared in this book, we will need to think deeply and deliberately about the relationship between our pedagogies, practices, and beliefs as educators, administrators, and community members.

THINKING PROMPT

Let's reflect on how our thinking has expanded, deepened, or evolved over the course of this chapter.

- How do concepts and patterns impact transfer of learning?
- What is the relationship between learning transfer and student motivation?

_____

_____

_____

_____

_____

CHAPTER TWO

Shifts in Practice

How Can We Set the Foundation for Learning That Transfers?

"For me, the child is a veritable image of becoming, of possibility, poised to reach towards what is not yet, towards a growing that cannot be predetermined or prescribed. I see her and I fill the space with others like her, risking, straining, wanting to find out, to ask their own questions, to experience a world that is shared."

—Maxine Greene

Why does this chapter matter?	Shifting certain practices accelerates and increases the power of learning transfer.
What will I be able to do by the end of this chapter?	I will be able to reflect on my teaching habits and apply strategies that facilitate shifts in practice.

Picture a classroom where students are busily editing proposals for ways to make the school campus a more inclusive and supportive community. They are in small groups giving and receiving feedback on the latest draft of their proposals. There's a palpable buzz in the air as students swap ideas and offer insight. Most of the walls are being used as visual thinking spaces, covered in sticky notes, connecting lines, and sketches of their early ideas. The classroom looks like a design studio in full swing of a new project.

The students' body language is a picture of engagement. They're leaning forward, moving sticky notes around, jotting notes in their individual notebooks, using animated gestures and excited voices, and actively listening to their peers. Groups are combining concepts from a variety of fields: restorative justice, civil rights, home design and décor, scale drawings, and mental health. Students are using design thinking and problem-solving protocols to enhance their proposals—just like their professional counterparts would. Next week, they will present their ideas at the local school board meeting. Their excitement is electric.

They began with this compelling question: *How can we make the school campus a more inclusive and supportive community for all?* They applied different disciplinary concepts to this question, pausing to think like a historian, scientist, mathematician, and artist, with the help of guest speakers and mentors from the local community. Then, each student pursued a specific aspect of the project that appealed to their interest and passions. Now, each small group is coming together to synthesize their findings into a single proposal.

This is just one example of what learning looks like when transfer is the focus. Although most of this book is centered on curriculum design, many areas need reframing—in some cases dramatically—in order to truly unleash the power of teaching for transfer. This chapter provides explicit shifts and considerations to set a strong foundation for learning that transfers.

THINKING PROMPT

Before we move on, let's reflect on the following questions:

- What do you think is the primary role of the **student** in your classroom? The role of the **teacher**?

- What is the role of **curriculum, instruction, and assessment** in your classroom?

- What is the role of **parents, leaders**, and the **larger community** in your classroom?

My current thinking:

_____

_____

_____

_____

_____

CHAPTER STRUCTURE

This chapter focuses on seven key shifts in practice that are necessary for learning transfer to take hold in formal schooling. Several Next-Day Strategies assist in immediate application of these shifts, and the rest of the book takes a closer look at each shift for more comprehensive adjustments in teaching routines and habits.

- The Roles of Students and Teachers
  - Fostering Self-Directed Learning
  - Establishing Teacher Credibility
- The Roles of Curriculum and Instruction
  - From Subjects to Disciplinary Literacy
  - Expansive Framing to Facilitate Transfer
  - Mental Organization Aided by Iterative Learning
- The Role of Assessments
- The Roles of Leaders, Parents, and the Community
  - The Learning Transfer Spectrum
- The ACT Model in Action

The list in Figure 2.1 lays out the essential shifts in practice necessary to lay the foundation for learning that transfers. As you read each one, consider how well your current practice matches up, and where you might have room for growth.

Figure 2.1   **Essential Shifts in Practice**

Shift #1: Students	1. The role of the students is directors of their own learning.
Shift #2: Teachers	2. The role of the teacher is designer of transfer-focused lessons.
Shift #3: Curriculum	3. The goal of curriculum is to build transferable, organizing schema of both disciplinary and modern literacies.
Shift #4: Instruction	4. Instruction honors students' prior knowledge and experiences to foster conceptual connections that transfer.
Shift #5: Assessments	5. Assessments are a system of feedback about the quality of teaching and learning.
Shift #6: Leaders and Parents	6. Parents and school leaders partner with teachers on the long-term growth of students so that they can live meaningful lives.
Shift #7: Community	7. Community members collaborate with teachers so that students can transfer their learning to real-world situations.

SHIFTS #1 & #2: THE ROLES OF THE STUDENT AND THE TEACHER

Each section of this chapter begins with a comparison between a *non*-transfer-focused classroom (Classroom A) and a transfer-focused classroom (Classroom B). Comparison between two contrasting scenarios points attention to the unique features at hand, which is why we so frequently ask students to sort examples and non-examples of concepts in the acquire phase of learning, and why this chapter uses this technique through each section to demonstrate the shifts necessary for learning that transfers.

We'll begin by comparing the roles of students and teachers in the two classrooms. What do you notice about the differences between Classroom A and Classroom B in Figure 2.2? Jot down your thoughts in the column on the right.

The first difference refers to the key shift toward *student ownership* of learning. Classroom B highlights the importance of students clearly understanding how learning works and how to monitor their understanding along the way. It also highlights the value of students setting goals and transferring their learning to situations that interest them, all of which contribute to student ownership of learning.

Through the massive school closures and shift to online learning due to COVID-19, we saw vividly that many students had become dependent on the teacher standing over them or guiding their every physical and intellectual move. We can help our

Teacher credibility:
Students' beliefs in the teacher as knowledgeable, trustworthy, enthusiastic, and accessible, has the power to significantly increase student learning (Fisher, Frey, & Smith, 2020).

students find joy in the learning journey and to become the directors of this journey with important shifts in practice.

Shift #2 highlights the tools that teachers can leverage in motivating students beyond games or scores. Our true powers lie in establishing credibility, strong teacher–student relationships, a trusting classroom and school culture, and high-quality curriculum and instruction, as shown in Classroom B. **Teacher credibility**, that is, students' beliefs in the teacher as knowledgeable, trustworthy, enthusiastic, and accessible, has the power to significantly increase student learning (Fisher, Frey, & Smith, 2020). Let's briefly explore concrete ways to build both student ownership and teacher credibility in the following sections.

 Figure 2.2 Key Differences About the Role of the Student and Teacher

Key Differences	Classroom A	Classroom B	What Do You Notice?
Shift #1: Students	Students enter this classroom and wait for the teacher to give them instructions on what to do. When they get stuck, they sit quietly until the teacher is available to help direct them on what to do next. They believe that learning is about collecting bits of information and proving they have retained them on an assessment task.	Students in this classroom know what it means to acquire, connect, and transfer their understanding to new situations. They set their own goals and determine their next steps in the learning journey. They monitor their understanding and know specific steps to take when they get stuck.	
Shift #2: Teachers	The teacher in this classroom spends a lot of time thinking about how to engage students, such as setting up elaborate games, decorations, or hands-on activities to sort of trick students into learning while they are having fun. She sometimes feels frustrated that her students lack motivation and uses grades or scoring as motivators for students to put in effort on assignments.	This teacher establishes credibility by demonstrating competence and dynamism. She articulates high expectations, creates a culture of thinking and collaboration among her students, and builds strong relationships with them. She curates powerful learning experiences that allow students to transfer their understanding to novel situations that interest them and impact the world.	

Fostering Self-Directed Learning

In today's complex and changing world, students must learn how to learn, as they will have to continue learning far into their adult lives (Davies et al., 2011). Three critical pieces for fostering self-directed learning include a classroom culture of collaboration, risk-taking, and intellectual growth. Students must be open to learning with and from their peers, learning from mistakes, and monitoring their thinking.

The table in Figure 2.3 is one that we currently use to think about our roles and one that we share directly with students. As you read through the table, picture what that might look like in your classroom.

A common theme across the examples in Figure 2.3 is the importance of centering intellectual growth in the classroom. Everything that we do should aim to engage students' brains. This is achieved through establishing a culture of thinking, risk-taking, a sense of safety where mistakes are embraced as moments to grow and learn. Teachers can also empower students by demonstrating our own thinking, how we learn from our mistakes, and ways our thinking evolves as a result of monitoring, questioning, and yes, even changing or revising our understanding.

Figure 2.3 Student and Teacher Roles in a Transfer-Focused Classroom

Student Role	Teacher Role
DIRECTOR of their own learning **DETECTIVE** of their own thinking **COLLABORATOR** with peers and teachers **PATTERN SEEKER** through diverse ideas and experiences	**DESIGNER** of empowering lesson plans **DETECTIVE** of student thinking **EVALUATOR** of their own impact on learning **CURATOR** of diverse resources and experiences

Might look like
- Co-constructing success criteria
- Setting goals
- Monitoring their thinking
- Self-questioning
- Self-regulating
- Selecting among strategies
- Providing self- and peer-feedback
- Applying feedback
- Deciding what to investigate next
- Adjusting learning behavior

Might look like
- Establishing a collaborative, safe culture
- Establishing credibility
- Making thinking routine
- Modeling thinking
- Modeling risk-taking
- Modeling learning from errors
- Cognitive coaching students
- Providing and soliciting feedback
- Adjusting instruction

NEXT-DAY STRATEGY

Facilitate a short discussion with your students about what "learning" means and what it looks like to learn. Ask them to think of a time when they have figured something out or had a light-bulb moment, when something suddenly became clear, and have them share their experience in small groups. Perhaps share an example of your own learning journey with a particular topic—such as learning how to bake, paint a room, or learn a language. Share the habits of mind you had—such as goal-setting, determination, reflection, collaboration, planning ahead—and how each influenced your learning. Then, ask your students which habits of mind they would like to apply to learning in the classroom.

A high level of peer collaboration doesn't always come naturally to students. It must be fostered, nurtured, and afforded time to evolve. Peer coaching protocols require students to give and receive feedback and provide opportunities for cognitively demanding thinking. By requiring a partner to process input from a peer, analyze their work, and provide a suggestion to help their partner move forward, students are able to build confidence and autonomy as learners.

NEXT-DAY STRATEGY

Peer Coaching

Partner A	Partner B
• Explain what you understand about the concept or skill. • Ask for specific feedback so that your partner knows where to give the most attention. • Listen to your partner's feedback without interruption and write it down. • Reflect and tell your partner what your next step is.	• Listen to your partner without interrupting. • Write down the feedback they would like to receive to ensure your feedback is helpful and wanted. • Analyze your partner's work and provide thoughtful feedback based on their request. • Acknowledge your partner's reflection and direct them to any resources that will assist in their next step.

Once we establish a positive, collaborative community, we turn attention to encouraging risk-taking and learning from mistakes in the classroom community. Students need to know it is okay to make mistakes, ask questions, and explore different perspectives—that learning is valued over scores or class rank. This starts with shifting the mindset that not being perfect is okay. We can build this by introducing the concept of a "yet" mindset. This mindset stems from Carol Dweck's work around growth mindset (Dweck, 2016).

When students have a yet mindset, they know their first attempt is only a baseline measure from which they will improve. Students believe they have potential and will be successful if they prioritize goals and put in the effort toward those goals. Students with a yet mindset do not let struggle hold them back; they persist and identify resources and supports to help them overcome any challenge they face.

Like collaboration, this mindset might not come innately for students. It takes practice, sometimes reprogramming of the mind, and a conscious effort on the part of the teacher to help students embrace the power of the yet mindset. We can start by shifting the language we use (shown in Figure 2.4) when a student shares their frustration and that they don't understand; remind them they don't understand *yet*. Provide opportunities for students to stop and reflect on how their thinking has grown. Continuously reinforce what knowledge and skills students bring to the table (an asset-based approach) rather than pointing out the gaps in their knowledge or skills (a deficit-based approach).

Figure 2.4   Simple Shifts in Language for a "Yet" Mindset

Hindering Mindset	Yet Mindset
I can't do this . . .	I don't know how to do this yet . . .
I made a bad grade . . .	I have a starting point for progress to be made . . .
I didn't do as well as . . .	I improved my personal goal . . .

Another essential step for shifting the ownership to students is to focus on having students monitor their thinking and learning. **Metacognition** is an explicit way of monitoring what we are thinking about as we move through the learning journey. We want students to think about their own learning more explicitly, usually by teaching them to set goals and monitor and evaluate their own academic progress (Muijs & Bokhove, 2020).

Of course, this is much easier said than done. Just asking students to monitor their thinking or providing opportunities for reflection isn't enough. One powerful strategy is to engage in the metacognitive processes ourselves, aloud and in front of our students (Frey & Fisher, 2010). Although metacognition is often framed as a way to make classes more learner centered, it's clear that teachers and their expertise still play a vital role in the classroom.

NEXT-DAY STRATEGY

Post a new problem, text, or situation related to what you are teaching and think aloud to your students. Share what goes through your mind. Use first person statements such as *I notice* . . . and other ways to demonstrate the moves and considerations you engage in while exploring a new situation. Then ask students to articulate what they noticed and share ways in which they already make similar cognitive moves, and how they might enhance their thinking the next time they encounter a new problem or situation.

The process of metacognition isn't an easy or natural one, so students need to see us model it, ask questions about it, and practice it themselves to become proficient. If students don't know what it means to "think about their thinking," or are unsure how to do that, simply creating opportunities to practice metacognition won't be of much use. On the flip side, simply asking students to mimic the expert moves of the teacher leads to dry, decontextualized, and inauthentic instruction. If learners are merely parroting the thinking of their teachers, their understanding will remain at the surface level, rendering them unable to transfer to new contexts.

Treating metacognitive instruction as an apprenticeship can resolve this tension. When someone becomes an apprentice, they must spend some time listening to and learning from an expert to learn the basics of their desired skill. No blacksmith hands their apprentice a hammer and asks them to start banging on molten steel! It takes time, practice, and patience to build up one's skills.

Metacognition: Monitoring what we are thinking about as we move through the learning journey.

The purpose of apprenticeships is to help students eventually become experts themselves, so we must give students opportunities to apply their learning and engage in meaningful, authentic work. That is why frequent transfer to increasingly authentic tasks is another key shift in a transfer-focused classroom. We want to model how we deepen our own understanding, and question what we believe to be true, with each new situation that we encounter.

There are two universal truths embedded in the shifts required for a transfer-focused classroom. First, we can have the most beautiful curriculum in the world, but if we do not establish credibility and positive relationships with our students, learning will likely be stunted. On the flipside, we can have strong relationships with our students but if the curriculum is not vibrant and instruction does not actively engage students intellectually, learning will be restricted. This leads us to the next two key shifts necessary for a transfer-focused classroom.

Establishing Teacher Credibility

Professor Hattie (2009) defines teacher credibility as a teacher who is perceived by students to be competent, trustworthy, and caring. When students are determining if a teacher is credible or not, they are really determining if they want to invest in the class or learn from the person. Teacher credibility, or student perception of the teacher as an authority, has an effect size of 1.09, meaning it has the potential to considerably accelerate student learning, nearly tripling an average year's worth of growth in a single academic year (Visible Learning MetaX).

NEXT-DAY STRATEGY

Reflect on how well you demonstrate the key traits of teacher credibility. Are there ways you can appear more knowledgeable, trustworthy, enthusiastic, or accessible to your students? Perhaps think of one or two students who typically struggle in school and make it a point to connect with them, joke around with them, and show your concern for their growth and well-being. The other students will notice, and it will likely increase your credibility with them, too!

An additional layer that forms with teacher credibility is strong classroom cohesion. When students have faith in their teacher and their classroom is a community working toward positive learning goals and is perceived as equitable, there is a sense of unity or cohesion.

Students often enter our classes with preconceived notions about their abilities or interests. These notions can harm their experience even if we design amazing lessons. We can build strong relationships with students who need it the most by remaining curious about them and thinking about how we can motivate them to believe in themselves.

When students inevitably get overly excited, give up on a problem or task, or don't want to participate in class, rather than passing judgment, we like to ask ourselves, *Why might this student be acting this way?* When we become curious, we can learn a lot about past experiences that shape our students' mindsets and behaviors. Students often want our attention or need our help with learning self-regulation skills. Once we have tapped into our curiosity, we are in a much more productive place of reaching and meeting the needs of our students.

Figure 2.5 illustrates a few next-day strategies that can be implemented easily to support teacher credibility, positive student–teacher relationships, and strong classroom cohesion.

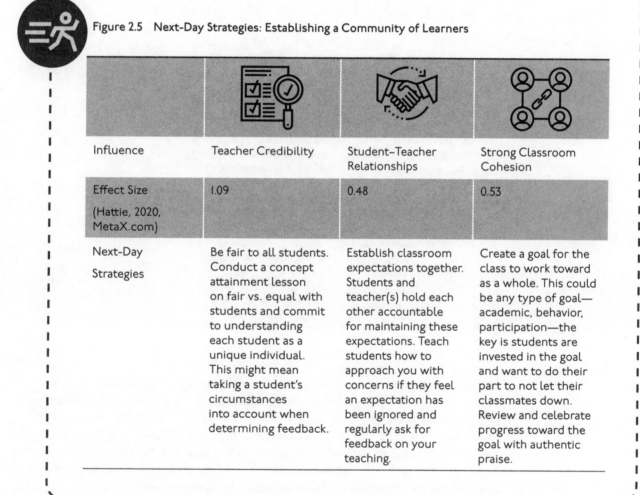

Figure 2.5   Next-Day Strategies: Establishing a Community of Learners

Influence	Teacher Credibility	Student–Teacher Relationships	Strong Classroom Cohesion
Effect Size (Hattie, 2020, MetaX.com)	1.09	0.48	0.53
Next-Day Strategies	Be fair to all students. Conduct a concept attainment lesson on fair vs. equal with students and commit to understanding each student as a unique individual. This might mean taking a student's circumstances into account when determining feedback.	Establish classroom expectations together. Students and teacher(s) hold each other accountable for maintaining these expectations. Teach students how to approach you with concerns if they feel an expectation has been ignored and regularly ask for feedback on your teaching.	Create a goal for the class to work toward as a whole. This could be any type of goal—academic, behavior, participation—the key is students are invested in the goal and want to do their part to not let their classmates down. Review and celebrate progress toward the goal with authentic praise.

SHIFTS #3 & #4: THE ROLES OF CURRICULUM AND INSTRUCTION

Once we shift our practice around the specific roles that students and teachers play in the classroom, we are ready to think about the roles of curriculum and instruction. What do you notice about the differences between Classroom A and Classroom B in Figure 2.6? Jot down your thoughts in the column on the right.

Figure 2.6   Key Differences About the Role of Curriculum and Instruction

Key Differences	Classroom A	Classroom B	What Do You Notice?
Shift #3: Curriculum	This teacher moves through the standards, teaching them one by one. She often feels there are just too many and not enough time to teach them all. The end of the unit, and especially the end of the year, is often a harried race to cover as much as possible.	This teacher views curriculum design as a way to build organizing patterns of thought in students' brains. She reads through the standards of learning to determine the most transferable, organizing concepts that lie at the heart of the disciplines she teaches.	
Shift #4: Instruction	This teacher delivers lessons mostly as predetermined information and skills that he wants students to know and be able to do. He rarely pauses to ask his students what all of the parts add up to and rarely considers the long-term value of each standard in students' lives beyond the classroom.	This teacher connects learning to students' prior knowledge and recognizes that students must revisit their learning in multiple situations in order to deepen their understanding. He considers complementary competencies that students need, such as digital citizenship, and layers these on as students transfer their learning to new situations.	

The main difference between the two classrooms is that the teachers in Classroom A view standards or outcomes of learning as the *ceiling*, or the sole and ultimate goal, of all learning and leave little room to look beyond individual, discrete standards. A simple yet powerful shift is to view standards of learning as the metaphorical *floor*, an important foundation but not the ultimate goal of learning. We can anchor our units in the most *powerful, transferable concepts* within our standards documents that give students the tools to unlock new situations, even those we have not covered in class. Less is truly more if we plan well.

From Subjects to Disciplinary Literacy

Disciplinary literacy: The specialized ways of knowing and doing that characterize a particular field of study (Shanahan & Shanahan, 2012).

Many teachers struggle to determine the most essential concepts and skills—we often read our lists of standards or learning outcomes as though they are all equally important. A shift to disciplinary literacy is a powerful way to figure out what is most important and how to help students see how the world is organized. Although the meaning of the word "literacy" is usually associated with the ability to read and write, disciplinary literacy refers to the broader meaning about competence in a particular field. **Disciplinary literacy** involves the specialized ways of knowing and doing that characterizes a particular field of study (Shanahan & Shanahan, 2012).

We will dive deeper into this shift in Chapter 3. For now, we want to stress the importance of viewing the ways each discipline makes meaning of our complex world as an essential means to teach our students how to transfer their learning to new situations. A focus on disciplinary literacy provides students with the technical vocabularies and practices necessary to evaluate and produce disciplinary knowledge, instead of simply memorizing it. To accomplish this, teachers need to facilitate inquiry that allows students to explore how each discipline asks and examines questions, makes and debates claims, and draws and defends conclusions (Moje, 2015).

Teaching the ways of knowing in any given field means shifting from teaching *subjects* to cultivating academic *disciplines* in students. The word "subjects" implies content coverage. "Disciplines" implies training, order, self-control, and application of standards to thoughts and actions. Students need to understand this so they are not only the *receivers* of knowledge, but become disciplined *makers* of knowledge. They must learn to construct knowledge the way that practitioners—historians, scientists, mathematicians, rhetoricians—construct knowledge in the real world. This occurs when students' thinking in the classroom reflects the type of thinking and reasoning done in the field.

The ability to question, critique, and create new disciplinary knowledge can be viewed as a social justice issue. Without an ability to access and understand the types of texts used by experts in the field, how can we expect students to be successful in the job market or from becoming critical consumers of the increasingly complex and situated bodies of knowledge that shape public policy (Hammond & Jackson, 2015)? When students are able to read critically across various disciplines while incorporating their own ways of knowing and funds of knowledge, they develop a sharpened ability to be discerning consumers of knowledge—capable of interrogating it, challenging it, and participating in the discourse surrounding its production and communication (Moje, 2007). The more diversity that is introduced to each field's perspective, the more accessible and equitable it can become.

In order to move from teaching atomized standards to teaching for disciplinary literacy that transfers, teachers need a clear, compelling vision of the discipline—or, in the case of elementary school teachers, the several disciplines—they teach. And although there are many resources available to aid educators in articulating such a vision, it is up to each of us to do the hard work of establishing that vision for ourselves, which we will do in the next chapter.

Expansive Framing to Facilitate Transfer

We used to think that if we said something or covered it, students should have learned it. We now understand that this is not how learning works. Now we think about what we want our students to understand and apply years after they've left our classrooms. What do we want them to do in their adult lives, as a result of our teaching? And then we think about how we want students to engage with this content so that it lasts. These simple shifts have made a significant difference in how we teach.

Students—all humans—cannot pay attention to several things at once. If we treat everything with equal merit and weight, we cannot be surprised that some of it sticks and much of it is forgotten (Bruner, 1977). By contrast, when we continuously revisit the most powerful concepts of the disciplines we teach in multiple situations, students begin to grasp the organizational structure that facilitates transfer of learning to new situations (Willis, 2018).

When we focus on organizing concepts, we can also harness students' prior knowledge. Choose one of these words and, thinking broadly, imagine all of the ways that students have encountered these concepts: "energy," "survival," "equilibrium," "power," "equivalence," "proportions," "interdependence." All children have observed the ways that *energy* is enhanced or reduced by food or sleep, or a lack thereof; and all children have witnessed moments when their parents or other caregivers have used their *power* as adults over the children's lives, such as receiving consequences when a family rule was violated. Imagine if we more intentionally used these experiences when teaching students about the concepts that anchor our curriculum.

In fact, the simple act of framing students' learning in more expansive ways, encouraging them to consider how it applies to the world outside the classroom, increases their ability to retain and transfer knowledge (Engle et al., 2012; Willis, 2018). When we are too narrowly focused on the standards listed in our unit plan, we can unintentionally create a learning environment where students come to believe the role, function, and purpose of their academic learning has no relevance to the wider world. If we don't take real time to explain and frame learning in ways that encourage students to apply it to contexts outside of school, why would we expect them to do so themselves?

Consider the differences between these two classrooms in Figure 2.7.

Figure 2.7   Understanding Expansive Framing

Classroom A	Classroom B
The teacher introduces a new unit of instruction by displaying the standards for the students, explains which will be featured on the next summative assessment, and launches into instruction. The message this sends to students is clear: What you are about to learn is important because it is on the test. Even if the teacher follows up with a brilliantly executed lesson where students are completely engaged, the framing has communicated what they've learned might not be useful when the learning experience ends, even if the data suggests it was "successful."	The teacher still introduces the standards and eventual summative assessment, but the teacher also spends some time framing ways their learning can be used in a variety of other contexts outside of school. For example, an English teacher may explain how one's ability to tailor a message for a specific audience is relevant in politics, entertainment, or the professional world. Or a science teacher can break down how the scientific process can provide students with cognitive tools they can use to ask better questions, track data, and reach new conclusions in areas of their life outside the laboratory.

Linking students' learning to contexts outside of school expands the social boundaries of their learning, encouraging them to consider different times, locations, people, or texts where the understanding they gain from the lesson might be relevant. Unlike Classroom A, Classroom B illustrates **expansive framing**, which refers to the ways that teachers and students integrate everyday experiences and different contexts into the main content of the curriculum. We can convey to students that they're allowed, encouraged, and will even be responsible for transferring what they know to other contexts (Engle et al., 2012).

In addition to helping students transfer more effectively, harnessing real-life experiences helps position students as creators of knowledge too. When this framing is present, students begin to learn with the understanding they'll be expected to transfer

Expansive framing:
The ways that teachers and students integrate everyday experiences and different contexts into the main content of the curriculum.

what they learn to future situations and won't have a teacher explicitly explaining how their learning will confirm, complicate, or negate their understanding of conceptual relationships. Each of the authors of this book have repeatedly experienced moments with students who describe how this culture seeps into their daily lives. It's like pattern recognition software has been downloaded into their brains and they can't switch it off!

NEXT-DAY STRATEGY

Think about how you might use expansive framing to help your students consider ways the content you are teaching can be applied to their lives. Are there organizing concepts that, considered broadly, can be tied to students' prior knowledge and experiences? Are there ways students can apply what they've learned to situations in the real world?

Mental Organization Aided by Iterative Learning

Every teacher we know has at one point been shocked by how quickly students seem to forget what we've taught them. When we intentionally help students to grasp the organizing structure of a subject, they will both remember what they've learned better *and* transfer their learning to new situations. Mental organization allows us to effectively retrieve information when we need it again, building a schema in our brains.

A schema is a mental structure that help us understand how things work. It has to do with how we organize knowledge. As we take in new information, we connect it to other things we know, believe, or have experienced. And those connections form a sort of structure in our brains. Deep learning involves this ability to place specific pieces of knowledge into our more expansive schema of understanding (Meta & Fine, 2019).

How do we help students build schema? We do it by harnessing the power of transfer to deepen understanding and facilitate connections in the brain. Learning is an iterative and recursive process, not a linear one. Though the goal of learning is to transfer our knowledge to future contexts, the act of transfer also helps us become better, more discerning learners. By being able to better navigate new contexts, we are not only able to apply our knowledge more effectively, but also take away more as a result.

Due to the linear nature of most curriculum design, it's easy to assume that we should save transfer tasks for the end of a unit or learning experience. We often hear teachers say something along the lines of, *This is great! I teach students about the concepts for a few weeks and then I design an assessment where they must apply their understanding to a new situation. If they can transfer their learning, we've hit our goal!*

However, if we wait for the end of a unit for students to transfer their understanding, the results will likely be disappointing. Even though our brains are hardwired to seek patterns and make connections, it's often a subconscious process. Consider a child who hates eating broccoli and, without ever having tried them, decides she won't eat peas either. Chances are, she probably isn't thinking to herself, "Based on my prior experience with green food, I've decided that I will not be trying peas!" Instead, she's subconsciously drawing conceptual relationships from sets of examples. And when it comes to more abstract, academic learning, most students and adults are not adept at calling upon their prior understanding (Perkins & Salomon, 1988, 1992).

That is why the Learning Transfer Cycle (Figure 2.8) is such a simple yet powerful visual to keep in mind when planning learning experiences. When we approach unit design as an iterative process, we're constantly encouraging students to apply what they've learned to new contexts and examine how those contexts confirm, complicate, or contradict their understanding of a conceptual relationship. Based on their findings, they can add increasing depth and complexity to their understanding of the relationship. This cycle is much more reflective of the way we learn outside of school—where we're constantly encountering new information, assimilating it to our preexisting schema, and updating our perspective and understanding.

Figure 2.8   The Learning Transfer Cycle

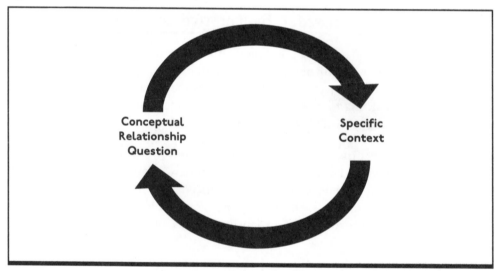

SOURCE: Stern et al., 2017.

Think about it in our own lives as adults. When we're learning about an ongoing political issue in our community, looking for ways to improve our performance at work, or working to be a better spouse, we don't simply find an answer, take a test, and move on. If we want to actually improve, we constantly try to learn more, apply our learning, and update our understanding as a result.

We want teachers to play with these ideas—before going through all of the steps of course and unit planning—to begin to experience the joy that comes from witnessing learning that transfers. The conceptual relationship question stems are easily one of the most powerful ways to observe the potential of building organizing schema that allows students to unlock new situations, and we hope you will experiment with them right away.

NEXT-DAY STRATEGY

Take two concepts that you are currently teaching and plug them into one of these question stems. Remember, fill the blanks with transferable **concepts** and not overly specific details.

- How are _____ and _____ connected?
- What is the relationship between _____ and _____?
- How does _____ impact/affect/influence _____?
- What effect do _____ and _____ have on _____?
- How do _____ and _____ interact?
- What is the role/purpose of _____ in _____?

The following question stems work well for early elementary or as scaffolding questions before reaching the ones above:

- What is the difference between _____ and _____?
- What happens when _____ interacts with _____?
- Why does _____ make _____ [do whatever it does]?
- Why does _____ need _____?

Ask your students to draw a T-chart in their notebooks or whiteboards with two columns: My current thinking and My refined thinking. Pose the question at the start of the lesson and ask your students to give their best responses under My current thinking. At the end of the lesson, ask your students to return to the same question and answer it under My refined thinking and then pair them up to discuss their responses and respond to the question, *How does monitoring our thinking influence learning and understanding?* Next, think of another context where the concepts are present and ask students to return to the question yet again at the end of that learning experience.

SHIFT #5: THE ROLE OF ASSESSMENTS

What do you notice about the differences between Classroom A and Classroom B in Figure 2.9? Jot down your thoughts in the column on the right.

The key difference here demonstrates perhaps the most tremendous shift, from treating assessment as an accountability event to treating assessment as a *system of feedback*.

When we think of assessment as an event or make it synonymous with "test" and "quiz," we cultivate an environment in which teachers create exams to hold students accountable for the learning of the unit, and students spend time guessing what will be on the exam. In this scenario, students often have no sense of how they're doing until the exam—the big event—and, even then, might not be able to accurately gauge their learning until the teacher returns the test with a score at the top.

Figure 2.9   Key Differences About the Role of Assessments

Key Differences	Classroom A	Classroom B	What Do You Notice?
Shift #5: Assessments	The teacher announces that the unit exam will take place in three weeks. As the unit goes on, students continually ask, *Is this going to be on the test?* as a way of determining the importance of the content. When students lose focus, the teacher often attempts to regain their attention by reminding them that the test is coming soon.	This teacher designs assessments that will measure transferable ideas and then plans instruction to prepare students to experience success on the assessment. As the unit goes on, both teacher and students continually monitor students' evolving understanding of the concepts and ability to transfer what they know.	

Conversely, when teachers and students perceive assessment as a *system of feedback about learning*, we create an environment where we constantly measure where we are against where we're going using a wide variety of tools—tests and quizzes, sure, but also journal entries and discussions, even personal reflection. Students stop asking, *Will this be on the test?* and teachers stop using the test as a gotcha for kids whose effort and attention throughout the unit was lacking. The fundamental purpose of assessment is to allow teachers, students, parents, and the larger community to gain an accurate picture of the quality of learning taking place—largely to inform our next steps on the learning journey, rather than a means to judge teachers and students.

> When we plan for assessment, we are developing a plan for monitoring and measuring student growth over time.

When this book discusses planning for assessment, we do not mean writing a test, but rather developing a plan for monitoring and measuring student growth over time. We want students to discuss examples of strong and weak work and share what they notice based on the success criteria. We want them to regularly set goals, evaluate their own progress, and figure out what to do next based on teacher and peer feedback and self-assessment.

Well-known thought leader Professor Yong Zhao reminds us to keep long-term goals in mind as we design schooling. For instance, how useful are reading interventions that increase test scores but decrease students' interest in reading (Zhao, 2013)? We ultimately want our students to be curious, lifelong learners, and our assessment policies should align with this important pursuit.

A key question we ask ourselves is, *How do our assessment practices impact student motivation and student ownership of learning?* For example, we have encountered many teachers who think that because their test scores are good, they are teaching well and do not need to improve their craft. We encourage all teachers to ask themselves about the long-term goals for their students. If the scores are good but students hate learning or are struggling with anxiety, we need to rethink a few things about our practice.

Let's look at this shift in a modern world history course. In a *non-transfer-focused* classroom, the class might spend a few weeks on World War I, examining its causes, course, and impacts. Then, on to the rise of totalitarian dictators and the Great Depression, followed by World War II and the start of the Cold War. Along the way there would be tests and quizzes, perhaps some papers or projects, to assess students' understanding of each development. Each unit is bookended by a summative assessment that measures students' knowledge of each particular topic. Even if each lesson plan is perfectly aligned to the test and delivered in an engaging manner, the understanding students develop has little utility once they hand in the summative assessment.

In *transfer-focused* classrooms, assessments determine how well students can transfer their understanding to novel situations, which means that assessments must present a scenario that students have not previously investigated together in class. Consider the example in Figure 2.10 for a modern world history course. The teacher would pose the two conceptual questions and students would answer them as they explore each fact-rich context. The conceptual questions focus students' attention to these broader principles, and students deepen and refine their understanding by examining the similarities and differences of each new context.

Figure 2.10 Modern World History Example

Abstract Conceptual Questions	Context for Investigation
What is the relationship between sovereignty and power? What is the purpose of congressional approval of military intervention?	Students learn about World War I, using facts from the events as evidence to support their responses to the questions. Students' inquiry would allow them to uncover enduring, transferable ideas. Students study the period leading up to World War II and come to realize that in a democracy, public opinion of wars impacts a leader's ability to intervene. Students apply their conceptual understanding to the Cold War, exploring varying degrees of military action across the globe. Students complete a research project where they identify current events related to these concepts and present them to the class.

After studying the period from World War I to the Cold War through the lens of organizing concepts like sovereignty, power, freedom, and security, students would be presented with the images in Figure 2.11 and 2.12 on the unit assessment.

Students would not have studied drones, nor would they have studied Pakistan in this course. They would be asked to analyze several short news articles both in favor of and against the United States' use of drone strikes in Pakistan and use their understanding of the deeper structures of sovereignty, power, freedom, and security to argue in favor of or against the use of drone strikes.

Figure 2.11   Image of an Unmanned Drone

IStock.com/koto_feja

Figure 2.12   Map of Pakistan

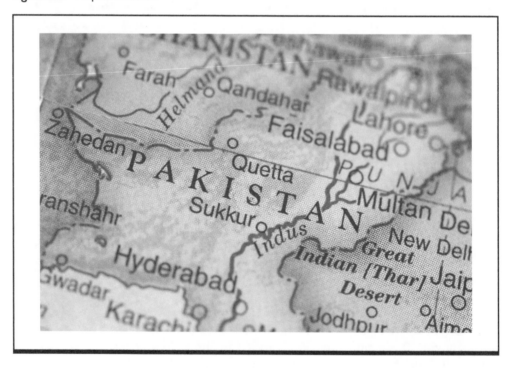

Would this assessment gauge students' knowledge of World War I or Hitler's regime? No, not directly. Teachers would need to confirm students' understanding of the key details of history through shorter quizzes or other assessments. But this assessment measures what matters most: students' ability to transfer their learning to a novel situation. Chapter 7 goes into more detail about designing assessments as a system of feedback about learning. Our final two shifts involve players generally outside of the classroom—school leaders, parents, and the community.

SHIFTS #6 & #7: THE ROLES OF LEADERS, PARENTS, AND THE COMMUNITY

What do you notice about the differences between Classroom A and Classroom B in Figure 2.13? Jot down your thoughts in the column on the right.

The sixth shift reflects the sad reality that for some teachers, much of school leadership and parental interactions revolve around grades or marks, or poor behavior of students. What if we shifted toward a true *partnership*, led by the students, focused on the long-term growth of our children? We have witnessed student-led conferences completely transform the culture of a school and advocate for these types of shifts when moving toward a transfer-focused classroom.

A critical component of a positive community is involving parents. Parents are a significant member of the classroom community and should be included in their students' learning journey. Possible methods for involving parents are exhibitions and student-led conferences. Students document their experiences and growth in learning

 Figure 2.13   Key Differences About the Role of Parents, Leaders, and Community Members

Key Differences	Classroom A	Classroom B	What Do You Notice?
Shift #6: Leaders and Parents	In this classroom, much of the interaction between teachers and leaders or between teachers and parents revolves around performance and assessment, namely, scores or grades. Usually, interactions are initiated when things are not going well such as poor scores or student misbehavior.	In this classroom, teachers partner with parents and school leaders in a collaborative relationship. They consider the long-term growth of students including their academic and overall well-being. Students often lead the interactions among them, discussing how well they are learning and what each person could do to better support learning.	
Shift #7: The Community	In this classroom, learning stays in the four walls of the room. Students often think that school learning stays at school and that everything else such as their hobbies, their hopes and fears, their relationships, pop culture, and current events are not related to what they are learning in school.	In this classroom, students' prior experiences are harnessed to provide insights into concepts. Community members offer guidance on many topics such as media literacy or entrepreneurship. Students transfer their learning to real-world situations with authentic audiences from their community.	

throughout a unit, quarter, or semester in order to best showcase their current understanding. Rather than the teacher or a progress report communicating this information to the parents, students are given the opportunity to tell their own story. Student-led conferences and exhibitions not only instill a sense of ownership and pride but also allow parents to interact on a more personal level in the classroom community.

NEXT-DAY STRATEGY

Ask your students to collect evidence of their learning among their work or assignments and explain which item they feel most proud of or where they've shown the most growth to a parent or guardian. Ask your students' parents what their long-term goals are for their children. Ask, *What do they hope for their children in the future?* And think about ways you can incorporate parents' hopes into your lessons.

The final shift features the concept of *authenticity* or real-world impact. This important feature is strongly connected to the shift toward student ownership. Today's students want to make a difference in the world around them (Senge, 2010; Wagner, 2012; Spencer & Juliani, 2017). Ideally, students transfer their learning to a novel, real-world challenge, requiring them to engage with an authentic audience and ultimately observe real change or impact. We can engage community members, and through technology, the wider world to support our students in their growth and development.

Another aspect shown in Shift #7 is a move to expand the view of the subjects we teach to include important elements that our students need to navigate the 21st century. Chapter 4 will go into more detail into these new competencies such as media literacy and entrepreneurship. When students transfer their learning to authentic contexts, they almost always need to combine the concepts and skills of the traditional subjects such as mathematics and social studies with other domains.

This book seeks to prepare students for the messy and complex situations in the real world through combining disciplinary literacy with **modern literacies**, our term for the countless initiatives and competencies that seek to bring new ways of thinking, knowing, and doing into education. We will go on our own curriculum writing journey to sequence learning experiences that take students on an interdisciplinary expedition to acquire, connect, and transfer concepts from disciplinary literacies and modern literacies.

Modern literacies: Countless programs, initiatives, philosophies, and pedagogies that all seek to bring new ways of thinking, knowing, and doing into education and unites them under one conceptual umbrella.

Take for instance the concept of interdependence. We may begin by examining different examples such as how plants and animals need each other as food sources, shelter, and reproduction. We may then explore the concept through the processes of photosynthesis and pollination. We come to understand that interdependence in nature has more magnitudes than we had previously thought.

We now want to build on our disciplinary science knowledge and layer it with modern literacies from the UN Sustainable Development Goals. We examine the concept of human environmental impact and how our use of plastics ends up as tiny particles consumed by animals such as fish, which we then consume. This is a facet of interdependence among living things and material goods that has more weight and complexity, especially once we realize the plastic has ended up in our food supply.

Finally, we move to an even more complex context and examine what happened in Yellowstone National Park when wolves were reintroduced for the first time in decades. A cascading effect occurred: The wolves reduced the deer population, which allowed more grass and other plants to grow, which changed the way rivers flowed, due to increased root systems of the grass, plants, and trees. This presents an amplified and dramatic aspect of interdependence and human environmental impact that we had not previously understood. As you proceed through the following chapters, consider how your students' understanding of concepts expands and deepens as they connect and transfer them to new contexts.

The Learning Transfer Spectrum

We can gradually increase the real-world impact of students' learning. In the previous chapter, we introduced the vertical axis of the Learning Transfer Spectrum, from similar to dissimilar transfer. In Figure 2.14, we've added a second dimension to Perkins and Salomon's (1988) similar and dissimilar transfer spectrum: transferring learning from the academic world to the real world.

Students may practice transferring their learning to very dissimilar situations, but if those situations are all school tasks instead of real-world challenges, we will end up with students who can write an essay on imagery and repetition but never apply what they've learned to the political ads on TV or social media. However, if we provide opportunities for students to transfer their learning to real-world situations, we will empower them to do more than ace tests.

Not only does teaching for transfer help us set students up to be innovators, but it enables us to personalize students' classroom experience to ensure a greater degree of relevance and choice within the curriculum. We can honor their prior knowledge

Figure 2.14   The Learning Transfer Spectrum

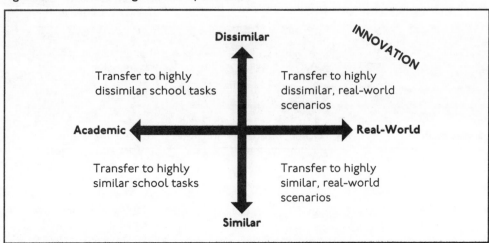

SOURCE: Adapted from Stern et al., 2017.

and experiences by comparing new learning situations to their conceptual experiences. Students can also explore whatever context they want to study, as long as the concepts are present in the new situation. This opens up a range of possibilities for co-constructed learning experiences that pair educators' expertise with students' personal areas of interest. This aligns with what Yong Zhao calls personalizable education (2018). **Personalizable education** differs from personalized learning in that it allows students to become creators of their learning experiences as opposed to choosing from a list curated by the teacher.

Personalizable education: Students become creators of their learning experiences as opposed to choosing from a list curated by the teacher (Zhao, 2018).

Figure 2.15 provides examples of the typical types of contexts teachers and students can use to promote transfer within different disciplines. Of course, options aren't limited to this list, but hopefully it provides a good frame of reference for the types of learning experiences to consider when planning learning that transfers.

Notice, too, that personalizable transfer tasks are natural places to incorporate research and digital literacy skills into the curriculum. Students can use their understanding of conceptual relationships from class to better make sense of

Figure 2.15   Using Transfer for Personalizable Learning

Content	Typical Type of Transfer	Personalizable Experience Sample
English Language Arts	Other texts or media	Students read *The Lord of the Flies* as a class and compare and contrast the author's use of concepts like symbolism and characterization with books they choose for literature circles.
Mathematics	Other ways of depicting concepts or solving problems	Students learn about measures of center and how to display data and choose the best display based on the data they collect and the message they want to deliver.
Science	Other living things, ecosystems, examples of energy, chemical reactions, etc.	Students learn about flow of energy in an ecosystem and then apply this by exploring a different ecosystem that is of interest to them.
Social Studies	Other cultures, countries, or time periods	Students learn about conflict and change in the context of the causes of the American Civil War. They then explore a different civil war to see what role conflict and change played in the start of the war.

information they find on their own through tools like internet search engines and academic databases. Each of these shifts captures a different dimension of how classrooms, schools, and communities might evolve to keep pace with our rapidly changing world.

THE ACT MODEL IN ACTION

Before we dive into how to design more detailed curriculum and instruction for learning that transfers, we want to zoom in on a learning design that captures how all these shifts might look across a unit. The ACT model is listed again in Figure 2.16 for review.

Figure 2.16   The ACT Model

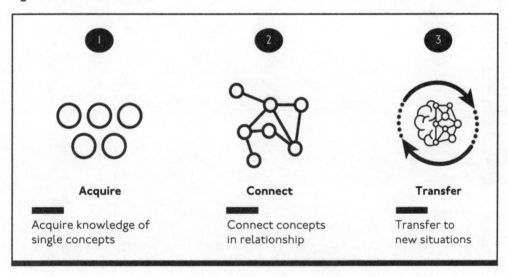

Acquire

Acquire knowledge of single concepts

Connect

Connect concepts in relationship

Transfer

Transfer to new situations

To help anchor our exploration of the ACT model, we will walk through one of our planning tools—the Unit Storyboard. It will provide a concrete look at how the ACT model can help you plan and facilitate for learning that transfers. Let's consider an example our social studies specialist Nichelle Pinkney created.

To ensure student learning was anchored in authentic contexts, Nichelle began by considering topical, real-world issues, and current events. Considering their relevance and importance to our current moment, she decided to explore the United Nations' Sustainable Development Goals to find points of intersection with her curriculum. By focusing on the broader concepts found within her standards, it took no time at all to compile a list of shared concepts spanning both documents—*institutions*, *equality*, *sustainability*, and *development*. She titled her unit Stability and Agility: Development in the 21st Century.

As she continued through the planning process, her vision took shape. She realized the subtle ways metrics like the Human Development Index account for death rate, per-capita income, and life expectancy but ignore the role that institutions play in shaping those realities. How might excluding discussion of those institutions frame developing countries in a negative light? How might students evaluate where haves and have-nots *come from* instead of simply acknowledging they exist? Each question motivated Nichelle to dig deeper and made her more excited to share with her students.

Next, Nichelle planned learning experiences that would help students to acquire understanding of institutions, equality, sustainability, and development so that they could eventually answer some of the meatier questions she previously pondered herself. These concepts were not the only ones that would play a role in helping students make sense of the contexts she'll curate, but they will anchor each context and facilitate learning that transfers.

Scan to see this example storyboard and resources

The storyboard would serve as her blueprint and her students' journey map, both of which revolve around the anchoring concepts pulled from her standards and authentic contexts. See Figure 2.17 for the acquire phase of her storyboard.

Figure 2.I7   Acquire Phase of the Storyboard

SOURCE: Nichelle Pinkney, 2020.

Next, Nichelle looked for contexts that would help students understand the relationship between those concepts. One of her goals for the unit was to have students unpack the somewhat biased framing of *developed* and *developing* countries. She'd accomplish that task by having students analyze the relationship between the anchoring concepts across several contexts to deepen and refine their understanding of each.

To construct her conceptual question, Nichelle consulted the conceptual relationship question stems and inserted the relevant concepts, asking, *What is the relationship between institutions, equality, sustainability, and development?* She chose several articles on education as her first context for scaffolded student inquiry. By selecting a topic that students are comfortable with and knowledgeable about, they would be better equipped to manage the cognitive load required to answer the context's respective conceptual question.

To better focus student attention on relevant information within the context, Nichelle added the additional guiding question, *How do institutions impact development?* As they went through each context, they used the CLICK thinking tool, listed in Chapter 8, to track how their thinking evolved over the course of the learning experience. See Figure 2.18 for the connect phase of the storyboard.

Figure 2.18   **Connect Phase of the Storyboard**

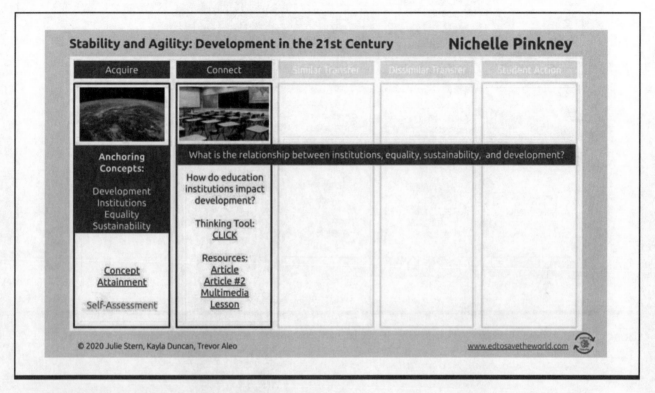

SOURCE: Nichelle Pinkney, 2020.

Building on the conceptual understanding students developed during the connect phase, Nichelle provided students with several new resources and a new guiding question: *How do government institutions influence developing societies?* This context, question, and resources encouraged students to explore how the rule makers and lawmakers of a country determine what a society looks like by transferring the conceptual understanding they developed in the last phase.

It's a topic that requires students to have rich, important discussions like *What is the role and function of a government? How can it transform society for the better? What might that look like?* As students move through each resource, they add more information to their CLICK thinking tool, refining their understanding and gleaning deeper and more complex insight into the unit's central conceptual question: *What's the relationship between equality, sustainability, and development?* See Figure 2.19 for the similar transfer phase of her storyboard.

Nichelle was most excited to share her Dissimilar Transfer example with her students. While planning the unit she had a conversation with her niece about the 2018 film *Crazy Rich Asians*, which showed some of the most opulent parts of Singapore. While watching, her niece mentioned how shocked she was that it appeared to be such a wealthy country. Her surprise made Nichelle realize that region of the world is rarely presented as being developed in most American curriculum, despite its modern features.

Figure 2.19   Similar Transfer Phase of the Storyboard

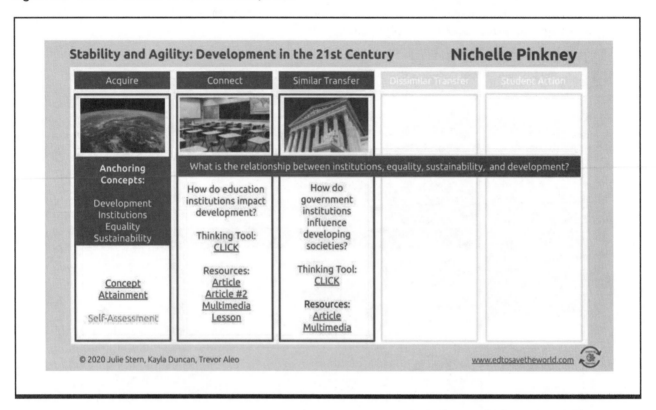

SOURCE: Nichelle Pinkney, 2020.

This incongruity inspired her to pick an article that asked students to question the very notion of developed versus developing countries. It poses the question, *Are we all developing countries now?* After moving students through several contexts that allowed them to understand the relationship between institutions, equality, sustainability, and development, Nichelle was really pushing students' thinking. Students used the BOLT thinking tool described later in Chapter 8 as a way to design a concept map that visually captured the relationship between all the concepts. This was accompanied by a paragraph explanation.

Nichelle asked students to consider what new criteria might emerge that would more accurately determine whether or not a country is developed. This helps move students to a position where they aren't just making sense of content, but are thinking like disciplinarians, creating and hypothesizing about knowledge like social scientists. See Figure 2.20 for the dissimilar transfer phase of the storyboard.

Finally, Nichelle designed an open-ended assignment in which students created a multimedia product exploring the ways institutions must work in balance with one another to meet sustainability and development goals for a country of their choice. Students were afforded the freedom to choose their country, the modality of their presentation, their framing of the content, and a bunch more besides. More importantly, they were afforded an opportunity to present their final product to a team of local nonprofit organizations to generate interest and awareness in the community about ways to pass local policy that supports and promotes community institutions in a *healthy* way. See Figure 2.21 for the student action phase of the storyboard.

Figure 2.20   Dissimilar Transfer Phase of the Storyboard

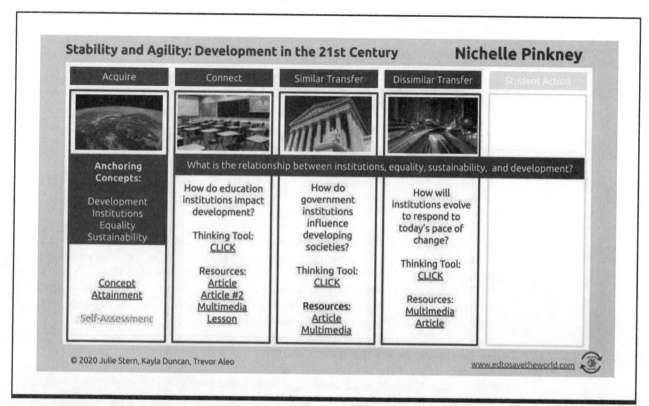

Figure 2.21   Student Action Phase of the Storyboard

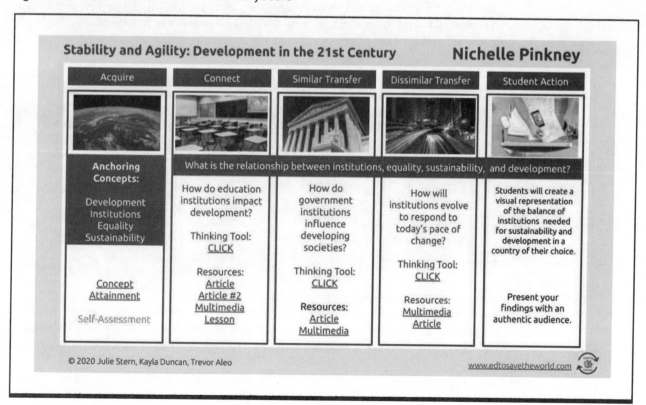

We hope this brief overview of the ACT model in action provided inspiration for how we can facilitate learning transfer to real-world situations, and we hope you are ready to dive in to the planning process.

CONCLUSION

The seven shifts outlined in this chapter are necessary to truly realize the power of learning that transfers and necessary to transform teaching and learning to meet the demands of our rapidly changing and unpredictable world. We know that many schools and individual teachers are well on their way to embracing these shifts, while others may feel like this is quite a lot to absorb.

Occasionally, we meet teachers who are overly critical of themselves and how they taught before they learned about how learning and transfer work. We have had similar thoughts ourselves sometimes. As Maya Angelou said, "Do the best you can until you know better. Then when you know better, do better." We used to teach in a linear way. We used to try to think of ways to engage our students that could easily be called entertaining them. We sometimes even used grades or marks as a way to motivate our students to pay attention. Now we know better.

It is our job to design the type of learning that will *empower* our students. We want them to be *more* than engaged. We want them to be invested—to become engrossed in intellectual pursuits and, above all, to become their own teachers. These shifts in our practices have had profound impacts on the ways in which students and teachers interact in the classroom. Additionally, we found that student motivation naturally increases when we shift to learning that transfers. Their preoccupation with grades and marks decreases when they see the value of applying their learning to multiple situations. Another way we like to explain the ways our thinking has evolved is shown in Figure 2.22. And the rest of this book will detail exactly how to answer the questions on the right side of the figure.

Figure 2.22 Ways Our Thinking Has Shifted About Curriculum and Instruction

We used to think	Now we think

What topics do I need to teach?
 	
How do I break the topic down to my students?
	What are the transferable organizing concepts and skills that my students need for the 21st century?
	
	What do, and which of, my students . . .
	
	    already understand?
	
	    partially understand?
	
	    misunderstand?

Before we move to the next chapter, take a moment to reflect on your current practices for each of these shifts as you read through the essential shifts in Figure 2.23. Notice areas that may need some reframing in order to reap the full benefits of learning that transfers.

Figure 2.23   Essential Shifts for Learning That Transfers

	In a Non-Transfer-Focused Classroom	In a Transfer-Focused Classroom
Student role	Receiver of knowledge Collector of disconnected bits of information	Director of their own learning Cognitive apprenticeship
Teacher role	Instructor of knowledge Director of learning	Designer of empowering lessons Modeling thinking
Curriculum	Atomized bits of knowledge and skills, not necessarily connected to students' lives	Deliberately builds organizing schema, honors students' prior knowledge and experiences
Assessment	What do students know and what can they do?	How well are students building organizing schema? How well are we teaching?
Instruction	Linear; students study one topic at a time then move on, mastery signals moving on to something new	Iterative; connected to students' prior knowledge, transfer deepens learning, understanding is interrogated
Leadership	Enforcer of rules Checker of grade books	Partners with teachers for long-term student growth
Parents	Called upon for grading, reporting, or student misbehavior	Partners with teachers for long-term student growth
Community	Operates separately from the school	Collaborator and provider of valuable, practical learning for students

online resources   Available for download at www.learningthattransfers.com.

THINKING PROMPT

At the beginning of this chapter you answered three questions about the roles of several factors—teacher, students, curriculum, instruction, assessment, parents, leaders, and community—in your classroom. Let's take a moment to revisit the following questions to reflect on how your thinking has evolved:

- What do you think the primary role of the **student** should be in your classroom? The role of the **teacher**? What shifts do you need to make in your practice to establish these roles?

- What is the role of **curriculum, instruction, and assessment** in your classroom? Based on your learning in this chapter, what adjustments do you want to make in your practice so these three elements can promote learning that transfers?

- What is the ideal role of **parents, leaders**, and the **larger community** in your classroom? What steps will you take to reorient these roles in your classroom moving forward?

_____

_____

_____

_____

_____

CHAPTER THREE

Disciplinary Literacy

How Can We Unleash the Power of the Subjects We Teach?

"Here is an essential principle of education: to teach details is to bring confusion; to establish the relationship between things is to bring knowledge."

—Maria Montessori

Why does this chapter matter?	Zooming out to think about the larger purpose of our disciplines helps us to choose the most essential learning that transfers and ground lessons in authentic contexts.
What will I be able to do by the end of this chapter?	I will be able to articulate a disciplinary vision and use it to select disciplinary lenses that students apply to nearly every situation in my course.

"Why do we have to know this?" It's the age-old question students pose when they doubt the importance of the content they're asked to learn. It's hard to blame them. Most adults have little use for the quadratic formula or periodic table, not to mention the Battle of Waterloo or *Moby Dick*. When it boils down to it, any one atom of our content—any single text or algorithm, any piece of information or skill on its own—is not all that essential to the daily demands of life, or even to tackling the greatest challenges facing humankind. However, we continue to require that all students study language arts and mathematics, history and science, in some form for years upon years.

Despite the relative insignificance of any one *part* of these disciplines in isolation, we have designed school around the idea that, when taken as a *whole*, these disciplines are essential components of being educated. The question, *Why do we have to know this?* is the cry of students mired down in the parts of our disciplines, yearning for the whole. If they truly understood the beauty and utility of each discipline, they'd already have their answer. We need to design curriculum and instruction so that students understand the larger structure of the disciplines because it is the connections between and among organizing concepts that facilitate transfer to new situations, both within the discipline and beyond.

For most students, the differences among the disciplines are differences of topic. Biology is about cells and evolution. History is about wars and kings. In reality, the major differences among academic disciplines are differences in *ways of knowing*; disciplinary literacy refers to the unique ways each field constructs knowledge about the world (Pace & Middendorf, 2004). Disciplinarians in every domain think and create according to well-established patterns and rules, which they use to turn information into knowledge and knowledge into wisdom. It should come as no shock that students struggle to see this, since the way they *do* science and history at school is largely the same: read a textbook, take notes from a lecture, circle multiple choice answers.

To help students (and ourselves) notice the distinct ways of knowing that pertain to each discipline, ask them to imagine the following classroom assignment: Explain the causes and impacts of the Great Influenza of 1918. How would each discipline approach the same topic differently?

- **History:** A historian would investigate the political, social, or economic conditions that led to the spread of the flu. He may analyze evidence from the past, such as logs kept by nurses, diary entries that chronicle the impacts on a particular family, or government campaigns to discourage the spread of the disease.

- **Science:** A scientist would work differently. Her process might involve designing an experiment to determine how the flu virus operates on a cellular level or tracing the path of the disease from contagion to recovery within the body.

- **Mathematics:** A mathematician would have yet another approach. He might compile data and create a mathematical model of the disease as it spread through the population. Is the growth of the disease linear? Exponential?

- **Literature:** A literary scholar would analyze the poems written by those who watched their loved ones suffer from this deadly disease, considering carefully their use of language. Is their tone hopeful? Devastated? Disillusioned?

Each discipline offers a unique take on this topic because each discipline employs unique ways of knowing and reasoning about the world. Historians make sense of the world by making inferences from evidence about the past. Scientists develop and test hypotheses about the way the world works through controlled experiments. Mathematicians curiously seek to model real-world phenomena as closely as possible using numbers, equations, graphs. The evidence used by the historian is not necessarily valid to the scientist as she comes to argue what is *true* about the world—and vice versa.

What is history? What is science? In this chapter, we'll set out on a curriculum planning journey that starts with the whole of each discipline, because the structure or organization of a discipline is what facilitates transfer. With a compelling vision for each discipline in mind, we can then recognize the essential role played by each course that makes up the entire K–12 journey in that discipline and bring our vision to life.

When we, as individual teachers or curriculum developers, consider how each course fits within a student's journey through school, we can view our standards or outcomes of learning in a more holistic light. Similarly, a clear purpose for each course can bring

THINKING PROMPT

Before we move on, take the time to ponder the following questions:

- How do you currently think about the content that you teach?

- What drives your decision-making on what content, topics, concepts, or skills are the most important?

_____

_____

_____

_____

_____

increased clarity about the importance of individual units and lessons. When we continually move between these parts and wholes, bringing them into greater alignment with one another, we lay the optimal foundation for teaching toward expertise and teaching for transfer.

CHAPTER STRUCTURE

The thinking prompts and design steps in this chapter allow us to gain a clear vision of the purpose of the discipline(s) that we teach. Ideally, this is done collaboratively with other teachers, leaders, students, and parents, but it can also be completed by individual teachers. Consider working your way through each exercise individually or collaboratively with your department or other thought partners. In a perfect world, we recommend inviting parents and students into this process to co-create a vision based on the unique needs and interests of your students and their families.

This chapter offers several thinking prompts to guide reflection while moving from a standards-focused classroom to a transfer-focused classroom. For each step in the curriculum planning process, we offer protocols that can be completed by individuals, course teams, or departments.

Although our sequence of steps is intentional, moving from the widest possible view of the curriculum to the most narrow, we don't presume that curricular work is linear in nature. Nor do we assume that each educator or team would be best served by the same, rigid process. Feel free to select one or two of these exercises and customize them to best suit your needs.

The thinking prompts and design steps in this chapter are grouped around the following topics:

- The power of disciplinary lenses

- Establishing a vision for each discipline
  - The role of your discipline(s) in real-world challenges
  - The purpose and significance of your discipline
  - The masters of the disciplines at work

- Your course in the larger context of a student's journey through school
  - A student's journey through school: Where have they been? Where are they going?
  - De-atomize the standards

- Selecting disciplinary lenses
  - Human experience concepts

- Vertical alignment to promote disciplinary depth

The Course Overview Template in Figure 3.1 provides a space to articulate your thinking as you go through this process. We will begin with selecting a few potential *real-world challenges* as they can provide a north star toward transfer of learning in meaningful and authentic ways. Then, we will focus on the disciplinary vision, how the course contributes to the disciplinary vision and **disciplinary lenses** in this chapter. This disciplinary envisioning process provides clarity of thought about the most powerful ways to promote learning that transfers. It is a helpful tool to revisit when it comes to the myriad decision points that teachers face in designing empowering learning experiences. We will tackle modern literacies and the story of your course in the next two chapters.

The first section of this chapter contains three thinking prompts that will help you to think about the larger purpose of your discipline and how it will serve students long after they've left your classroom. By the time you finish reading the first section and responding to the thinking prompts, you should feel confident in crafting a powerful disciplinary vision and be closer to selecting two to three disciplinary lenses that will frame your entire course. The following sentence frames are optional ways to articulate your disciplinary vision, and we will return to them at the end of each section.

Disciplinary lenses: The highly transferable disciplinary ways of knowing and doing within the discipline itself that should be applied all the time, like a set of lenses that students put on when thinking like a practitioner in this field.

- This discipline is important for my students because _____ _____.

- It can inspire students by _____ _____.

- By the time my students are adults, I hope they continue to _____ _____.

Figure 3.1   Course Overview

Zooming Out: Course Overview		
Course Title		**Real-World Challenges**
		What are some real-world challenges that could use the thinking of your course in order to tackle?
Disciplinary Vision		**How this course contributes to the disciplinary vision**
Why is this discipline important to your students? How can it inspire them?		*How does this course illuminate the greater purpose of your discipline(s)? What do you hope students will do by the time they are adults as a result of this course?*
Disciplinary Lenses		**Modern Literacies**
What are the most essential disciplinary practices within the context of your course that students must acquire, connect, and transfer in order to be effective practitioners of the discipline(s) I teach? When students encounter a new situation, what are the two or three concepts or practices that you want them to consider, every single time?		*What new or additional concepts beyond the established disciplines will be a focus of your course to help students to navigate our complex world (one–three concepts)?*
Story of the Course		
Use the following questions to help write the story of your course: • *What is the purpose of your course?* • *What idea lies at the heart your course? What concept(s) form(s) the core?* • *If students could only internalize one thing from your class, what would it be?* • *How does this course help students become who they want to be?*		

online resources 🔖 Download at www.learningthattransfers.com.

THE POWER OF DISCIPLINARY LENSES: FOCUSING OUR ATTENTION TO MOVE STUDENTS TOWARD EXPERTISE

One of the most significant steps we can take for learning that transfers is to discern which conceptual tools will best serve students along the journey. We can ask ourselves, *What are the most essential disciplinary practices within the context of my course that students must acquire, connect, and transfer in order to be effective practitioners of the discipline(s) I teach? What are the two or three concepts or practices that I want students to consider, every single time they encounter a new situation?*

According to Dr. Gerald Nosich (2005), a pioneer in designing curriculum to promote critical thinking, all courses—even college-level courses—can be boiled down to a few fundamental and powerful concepts that facilitate students' abilities to grasp the underlying structure of the discipline. Deep understanding and skillful application of these concepts will help students to reason through nearly everything else they learn throughout the year. We call these essential concepts *disciplinary lenses* because they *are so highly transferable within the discipline itself that they should be applied all the time,* like a set of lenses that students put on when thinking and behaving like a practitioner in this field.

For instance, the disciplinary lenses of *author*, *audience*, and *purpose* in literature help young readers analyze nearly any text they are presented with. Imagine the second-grade teacher who spends considerable time developing students' understanding of just these three concepts and their relationships to one another. With every text that students read, he pauses to have them visualize the author. Who created this? What do we know about him or her? What might his influences be? The teacher takes the time to show videos of authors talking about their work and their writing process. He has students write "author's statements" to accompany the stories they compose themselves. The teacher does the same deep work with the concepts of audience and purpose. Soon, students instinctively look for these elements when they engage with a new text. They begin to ask themselves, how are the author, audience, and purpose of this text related to one another? Over the course of the year, they see over and over again that authors tailor what they write to their intended audience in order to achieve their purpose for writing.

Think of all of the other profound and useful ideas students might uncover by focusing on these three concepts:

- An *author* chooses words carefully to paint a picture of the story in the *audience*'s minds.

- The *purpose* of a persuasive text is to convince the *audience* of the *author*'s main idea.

- Two *authors* might write very different texts on the same topic because they are writing for different *audiences* or have different *purposes*.

- *Authors* of informational texts use extra features—bold words, sidebars, icons, captions, subheadings—to help the *audience* understand their ideas and achieve the author's *purpose*.

- *Authors* of literary texts use illustrations to convey meaning about characters, setting, and the plot so that the *audience* can better understand the story.

Notice that many other disciplinary concepts—word choice, topic, point of view, persuasion—can be taught in relation to the three disciplinary lens concepts selected. Notice, too, that these concepts are so fundamental that they underpin nearly every act of reading, so whether the teacher presents students with a fairy tale or an article on weather patterns, they can unlock meaning in the text through their understanding of author, audience, and purpose.

This idea may feel daunting at first, but the exercises throughout this chapter will help you to think about and select the disciplinary lenses for your course. We have built an entire podcast around the idea of disciplinary lenses, asking experts to boil their fields down to the three most important concepts or ideas. From leadership to gardening, nonviolent action to socioemotional learning, the experts from an enormous variety of areas have been able to do it, and most have commented on the usefulness of the task. We like to think of it as an efficient path from beginner to informed in any field.

ESTABLISHING A VISION FOR EACH DISCIPLINE

Before we jump to selecting disciplinary lenses, we want to think about the role of each discipline in navigating the world. The following thinking prompts help all teachers to gain a depth of understanding about the purpose and significance of disciplinary literacy in navigating our world.

The Role of Your Discipline(s) in Real-World Challenges

When we are focused on learning that transfers, a useful place to start is reflecting on the ways in which we want students to use their learning to impact the world around them. This thinking protocol helps to keep our focus on the long-term benefits of our course in helping students live meaningful lives.

Consider crafting an event or series of events for parents, students, and teachers to co-create a vision for the type of schooling that will truly prepare students to thrive in a complex world. We've compiled a list of videos that illustrate the ways in which our world is changing. Perhaps select a couple of them to frame the conversation and adapt the following steps as you see fit.

Scan this QR code to access our Complex World Playlist.

Step 1: Identify Challenges

Pick up a newspaper, magazine, or open up a few news websites and skim headlines. As you go, stop to read and build background knowledge about the topics or issues that seem to keep coming up. Push yourself to consider a variety of perspectives. What challenges seem to dominate the discourse of a more liberal audience? A conservative one? What are the main challenges faced by specific groups such as those based on race, class, gender, or sexual orientation?

Beyond the news, consider researching the initiatives underway by major universities, nonprofits, corporations, and interest groups. Keep track of some of the major issues and dilemmas you find in a chart similar to the example in Figure 3.2. You may want to personalize the categories to fit your findings.

Figure 3.2 Real-World Challenges Examples

Category	Current Challenges	Concepts From My Discipline That Might Help Students Understand These Challenges
Political	Political polarization	(Social Studies) discourse, democracy, civic responsibility, alliances, compromise
Economic	Unemployment	(Mathematics) data, representation, patterns, rate, quantitative reasoning
Social	Racial discrimination	(Language Arts) fear, control, bias, point of view, argument, evidence, perspective
Environmental	Climate change	(Science) human–environment interaction, pollution, living things, survival, adaptation
Technological	Rise of AI, hacking, fake news	(PE) decision-making, teams, collaboration, human-body systems, group dynamics
Health	Obesity	(Science) DNA, cells, organism, digestion, mental health, tissues, organs, energy
Local		
National		
International		

online resources Download blank template at www.learningthattransfers.com.

THINKING PROMPT

Jot down some real-world challenges that might require the thinking of your disciplines in order to tackle.

_____

_____

_____

_____

_____

If you're not sure where to start, the United Nations' Sustainable Development Goals are a great entry point. These seventeen goals to transform the world demonstrate the variety of challenges students will grapple with in their lifetime. A few of the goals are listed with corresponding real-world challenges in Figure 3.3. Many schools around the world are aligning their curriculum to these global goals as a way to bring relevance to teaching and learning and to harness younger generations' desire to make a difference. The conceptual connections required to tackle these challenges are significant and can provide us with a useful set of criteria for determining the most important concept and skills in our curricular aims.

Scan this QR code for links to resources on SDGs.

Figure 3.3   United Nations Sustainable Development Goals (SDGs) Examples

Sustainable Development Goal	Real-World Challenge
Zero Hunger	Millions of people are undernourished every year around the world.
Affordable and Clean Energy	Billions of people still rely primarily on inefficient and polluting cooking systems.
Peace, Justice, and Strong Institutions	Less than half of all countries worldwide have compliant national human rights institutions based on the internationally agreed standard.
Climate Action	Pollution, species lost, and global warming are creating catastrophic conditions around the world.

SOURCE: All data compiled from https://sustainabledevelopment.un.org/sdgs.

Step 2: Consider the Role of Your Discipline(s)

How might the concepts and skills in your discipline help students understand modern problems? How does the thinking of your discipline give students the tools to solve these problems? Record some thoughts in the chart (see Figure 3.2).

When we start with scanning the world for a set of complex challenges, we can work backward to determine how the conceptual structures involved in these scenarios might eventually lead students to this more complex, dissimilar transfer. Even early elementary teachers can benefit from this exercise to help focus attention on what matters most for students to lead meaningful lives.

For example, when COVID-19 and protests against racial injustice both dominated the news in the United States in June of 2020, author Julie Stern considered the many concepts embedded in these situations, and thought of ways to ensure her young children understood the issues deeply, even if they were not directly exposed to the news stories. Julie used story books to create teachable moments for her four- and six-year-old children to build conceptual connections in their habits and minds. Figure 3.4 shows some of the concepts that Julie focused on with her kids.

Figure 3.4   Concepts Embedded in COVID-19 and Racial Injustice (for young children)

Disciplines	Example Organizing Concepts
Language arts, the arts, socioemotional learning	belonging, fairness, caring for others, resilience, creativity, self-regulation, courage, speaking up, justice, community
Science, health, physical education	personal safety, decision-making, healthy eating, physical activity, energy, emotional health, physical health, teamwork

NEXT-DAY STRATEGY

Select a short video, poem, political cartoon, or news story about a real-world situation and either ask your students which concepts might be embedded in the situation or model for your students how you figure out which concepts are present in real-world situations and how what they are currently learning is connected to this real-world situation.

Middle school science teacher Julia Briggs encountered an example in an International Baccalaureate textbook about how birds of prey were decreasing in an area where ecotourism—or travel designed to support conservation efforts—was high. She also came across an example of how the traditional dyeing of fabrics known as batik dyeing could be harmful to the women making the fabric (Termaat & Talbot, 2018). She thought about how these two contexts might connect to specific science content she was currently teaching.

She identified similar concepts in both contexts such as *solubility, displacement, chemical persistence,* and *environment.* She realized that students could analyze a chemical spill in preparation for these more complex scenarios, and that looking at waste disposal in the school lab might be an even closer scenario to her lesson on displacement reaction and how chemical reactions become products. Take a look at the illustration of her thinking in Figure 3.5. She worked backward from dissimilar toward more similar transfer so that she could scaffold the transfer for her students.

Figure 3.5   Grade 8 Science Example

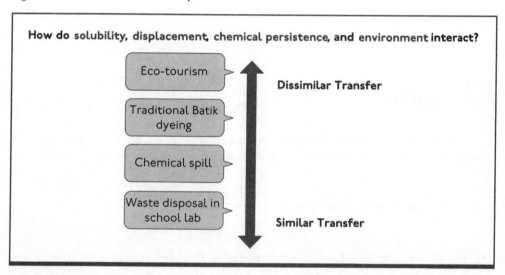

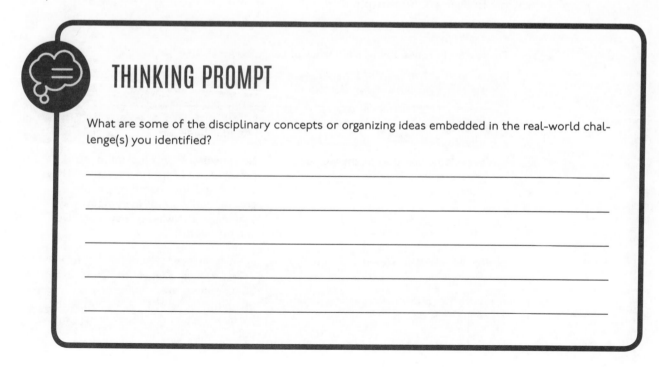

THINKING PROMPT

What are some of the disciplinary concepts or organizing ideas embedded in the real-world challenge(s) you identified?

_____

_____

_____

_____

_____

The Purpose and Significance of Your Discipline

The thinking prompt above asks us to step outside our discipline and view it from afar. Consider why the discipline might matter to students and society more broadly. This is particularly important because most students will not go on to become practitioners of the specific disciplines we teach. They may never publish a novel or launch a rocket into space. However, they can certainly appreciate the value added to the world by those who have done so, just as someone with little aptitude for dance can fall in love with the ballet.

NEXT-DAY STRATEGY

Ask your students to complete the purpose and significance thinking prompt with you. It will lead to insights into their point of view and how we might craft our disciplinary vision in student-friendly language.

Attempt to see your field from the point of view of an uninformed admirer. Stand in awe of the power this discipline has. Marvel at the problems it can solve and the meaning it can create. Sometimes the purpose of our disciplines is lost in the complexity of curriculum drafting and the endless hustle and bustle of lesson planning. However, when used as the launchpad for instructional design, they invite students into the wonder of the content we teach. Consider the secondary English language arts example in Figure 3.6 and the multiple-discipline elementary example in Figure 3.7 for inspiration.

Figure 3.6   Purpose–Role–Significance of Language Arts

What is the purpose of my discipline?	It is to help humans effectively interpret, communicate, and create texts that inform, persuade, or entertain their intended audience.
What role does it play in the world?	Narratives are our oldest and most powerful tool for understanding. They are created and shared by people, groups, and systems in complex ways that shape the way we view ourselves and our world.
Why is that role an important one?	Literacy, in its variety of forms, allows us to be participants in the creation and evaluation of texts that reflect and inform the society in which we live. Without it, we lack the tools to affect change within our society.

Figure 3.7   Purpose–Role–Significance of Grade I

What is the purpose of my discipline?	Mathematics helps us to count things so we can stay organized and fair. Science helps explore the natural world and conduct investigations. Language arts allows us to explore new worlds, express ourselves, and to communicate. Social studies helps us to understand how people interact and live together in groups.
What role does it play in the world?	All of these disciplines help us to make sense of our world, to work together, and to enjoy life.
Why is that role an important one?	If we ignore any of these, we will not be well-rounded; we need each of these disciplines to live a meaningful life.

THINKING PROMPT

Take a moment to step outside of your discipline and ask yourself the three questions in Figure 3.8.

Figure 3.8   Purpose–Role–Significance of My Discipline

What is the purpose of my discipline?	
What role does it play in the world?	
Why is that role an important one?	

The Masters of the Disciplines at Work

Working through the purpose, role, and significance of the discipline is a good way to examine its parts, but it doesn't quite capture the artistry or urgency that makes the discipline a compelling pursuit. This exercise, then, compliments an examination of the logic of the discipline with an examination of its beauty.

NEXT-DAY STRATEGY

Ask your students to complete the masters of the discipline thinking prompt with you. It will lead to insights into their point of view and how we might craft our disciplinary vision in student-friendly language.

Consider one of your students' favorite masters. For example, many young children are enamored with the children's book series *Elephant and Piggie* and *The Pigeon* series by Mo Willems. Julie's four-year-old son lies in bed giggling as he remembers lines from the stories. What is it about the series that sparks such lasting and authentic joy? Figure 3.9 shows an example of how we can learn from disciplinary masters for an early elementary classroom. Notice that the bolded words are all concepts.

Admiring Mo Willems's ability to present these concepts in a way that connects with children helps us to understand the beauty of the discipline of language arts. Once we go through this exercise, we can keep what we learn from the masters of the discipline at the forefront of our minds as we design our learning experiences. All of the thinking prompts in this chapter will help us to select the most powerful disciplinary lenses and concepts that foster student appreciation of the overall structure of these disciplines, which will facilitate learning that transfers. Figure 3.10 illustrates a master mathematician example to support teachers of mathematics to consider as you complete your own master at work thinking prompt.

Figure 3.9   Early Elementary Language Arts Master Mo Willems

Observe the master at work.	Willems uses **humor, surprise, silliness, absurdity, punctuation, gesturing, facial expressions, simplicity**, and different sized **fonts** in his stories.
• Describe the exemplar. What qualities set it apart? What do you admire about it? What gives it life? What makes it powerful and necessary?	The stories are about **friendship, courage, insecurities, misunderstandings, mistakes, learning, forgiveness, gratitude, kindness, perspective**, and more. He is masterful at **weaving universal human emotions** and **insecurities** with **silliness** and **humor**. That's what he does best and what many famous authors, artists, filmmakers, and composers do well.
• Describe the mind that created it. What abilities set this master apart? How do they think, build, discover, create? What about this mind demands our admiration?	

Figure 3.10   Mathematics Master Maryam Mirzakhani

Observe the master at work.	Mirzakhani is the only woman to win the Fields Medal for her significant contribution to the world of mathematics. Her specific topic, which **integrates** mathematics and science, is beyond the scope of K–12 education, however Mirzakhani's mindset toward mathematics is what can and should be replicated.
• Describe the exemplar. What qualities set it apart? What do you admire about it? What gives it life? What makes it powerful and necessary?	She enjoyed **collaboration** and embraced **multiple perspectives** when solving a problem. Her **perseverance** in embracing complexity shows all students can learn maths if they have patience. She would get excited about **discovery** of new ideas rather than one right solution and embraced **nonlinguistic representations** to **model** complex mathematics.
• Describe the mind that created it. What abilities set this master apart? How do they think, build, discover, create? What about this mind demands our admiration?	

Nonlinguistic representation: Ways of demonstrating knowing that does not use written words, such as drawing, charades, sculpting with modeling clay, etc.

THINKING PROMPT

Select an exemplar of masterful work within the discipline and complete the questions in Figure 3.11.

Figure 3.11   The Masters at Work

Question Prompts	Responses
Observe the master at work. • Who in this field inspires awe? • Describe the exemplar piece of work. What qualities set it apart? What do you admire about it? What gives it life? • Describe the mind that created it. How do they think, build, discover, create? What about this mind demands our admiration?	
Consider the discipline as a whole in light of the master's work. • What does this person and their work illuminate about the discipline? • What makes it inspiring, energizing, and joyful?	

ARTICULATING A DISCIPLINARY VISION

Now that we have completed three thinking prompts that look at a more holistic view of our discipline(s), we are ready to synthesize our results into a short phrase, or one to two sentences, that will serve as our disciplinary vision. This statement will guide us in planning curriculum and designing instruction that reveals the overall structure of the courses we teach.

A dynamic department head of physical education, Alan Dunstan, puts it this way, "What do we ultimately want for our students? Very few of them will go on to play professional sports—but we want *all* of them to stay physically active into their adult lives. So, we ask ourselves, *How do we design our courses to increase this likelihood?* That guides all of our planning."

DESIGN STEP

The sentence stems below could help you to articulate it into a concise vision statement. Next, place your vision in the corresponding section in the course overview template from the beginning of the chapter. We will then turn to *how your course contributes to the vision* and selecting *disciplinary lenses* in the next section.

- This discipline is important for my students because _____.

- It can inspire students by _____.

Disciplinary Vision
Why is this discipline important to my students? How can it inspire them?

VERTICAL ALIGNMENT: YOUR COURSE IN THE LARGER CONTEXT OF A STUDENT'S JOURNEY THROUGH SCHOOL

Now that we've developed a clear vision of the overall goals of our disciplines, we can turn to the standards or learning outcomes anew through this clarity of the long-term value of what it is we are teaching our students. Though there are pros and cons to standardized curriculum, it's undeniable most teachers are responsible for teaching standards laid out by departments of education, or even individual schools and departments. Even if your course is not standards based in the traditional sense, you are most likely guided by externally defined learning goals coming in the form of a textbook or even a common understanding of what English literature or chemistry courses should include.

Standards—and other externally defined curricular goals—are a great way to ensure continuity and clarity for teachers, and they guarantee a cohesive, well-sequenced learning experience for students. The problem is, when we lose sight of the overall purpose and function of our discipline outside the confines of our classroom, standards quickly turn in to checklists for completion instead of checkpoints that help to build the conceptual structure that leads to transfer. That is why we started our planning process by articulating a vision for the discipline as a whole. Our disciplinary vision helps us keep the big picture in mind while we sift through the specific details of a particular course.

The following exercises aren't meant to replace standards, but to help us view them in a different light. Instead of seeing standards or other content priorities as the *goals* of the curriculum, consider them the *means* to achieving a greater *end:* your disciplinary vision. The standards are the vehicle, while your vision is the destination. You help students experience the ways of knowing your discipline, to see its utility and beauty, to understand the logic of it *through* the standards. Both are essential components of a rich, dynamic learning experience. Without the content defined by the standards, the vision is hollow; without the vision, the standards have no higher purpose. With that in mind, make your way through the following exercises to help you design a cohesive course that uses standards in a nonstandardized way.

A Student's Journey Through School: Where Have They Been? Where Are They Going?

In this thinking prompt, we will examine the scope of learning in each discipline from kindergarten through twelfth grade. This allows us to understand where our students have been prior to our course—what they have been exposed to in previous mathematics, science, history, or language arts classes—and where they're headed next. It also serves to remind us that we are carrying the torch for but one leg of this journey. Keep in mind the key idea presented earlier in this chapter: Good curriculum views each *part*—course, unit, lesson—in relation to the *whole* of a student's experience and the larger discipline itself.

THINKING PROMPT

I. **Access the learning standards** or list of courses required by your school system for K–12. For instance, the chart in Figure 3.12 shows the highest priority Common Core math standards for Grades K–8.

II. **Look for strands and patterns across the grade levels.**

- What has my school system deemed to be the most important aspects of this discipline?
- What gets repeated?
- What are we emphasizing?

_____

_____

_____

_____

(Continued)

(Continued)

III. **Look for progressions.**

- How does each level build upon the others?

- What have we deemed as foundational?

- What experiences in the discipline are students bringing with them to my course? What am I preparing them for?

_____

_____

_____

_____

IV. **Look for omissions.**

- What has my school system deemed relatively unimportant for students to know and do within this discipline?

- What is left out?

- What is gained and lost by omitting these elements or topics?

_____

_____

_____

_____

V. **Admire the whole and your role within it.**

- What would it mean for every graduate to have truly mastered the standards in this discipline after their full K–12 journey? What would they know and be able to do?

- How would the world be a better place if every person had mastered this body of knowledge and skills? Conversely, what would happen if none of this were taught in schools?

- How does my course contribute to the larger scope of students' education?

_____

_____

_____

_____

Figure 3.12   Common Core Priority Outcomes for Math, Grades K–8

K	1	2	3	4	5	6	7	8
Know number names and the count sequence	Represent and solve problems involving addition and subtraction	Represent and solve problems involving addition and subtraction	Represent and solve problems involving multiplication and division	Use the four operations with whole numbers to solve problems	Understand the place value system	Apply and extend previous understandings of multiplication and division to divide fractions by fractions	Apply and extend previous understandings of operations with fractions to add, subtract, multiply, and divide rational numbers	Work with radical and integer exponents
Count to tell the number of objects	Understand and apply properties of operations and the relationship between addition and subtraction	Add and subtract within 20	Understand properties of multiplication and the relationship between multiplication and division	Generalize place value understanding for multi-digit whole numbers	Performs operations with multi-digit whole numbers and decimals to hundredths	Apply and extend previous understandings of numbers to the system of rational numbers	Analyze proportional relationships and use them to solve real-world and mathematical problems	Understand the connections between proportional relationships, lines, and linear equations**
Compare numbers	Add and subtract within 20	Understand place value	Multiply and divide within 100	Use place value understanding and properties of operations to perform multidigit arithmetic	Use equivalent fractions as a strategy to add and subtract fractions	Understand ratio concepts and use ratio reasoning to solve problems	Use properties of operations to generate equivalent expressions	Analyze and solve linear equations and pairs of simultaneous linear equations
Understand addition as putting together and adding to, and understand subtraction as taking apart and taking from	Work with addition and subtraction equations	Use place value understanding and properties of operations to add and subtract	Solve problems involving the four operations, and identify and explain patterns in arithmetic	Extend understanding of fraction equivalence and ordering	Apply and extend previous understandings of multiplication and division to multiply and divide fractions	Apply and extend previous understandings of arithmetic to algebraic expressions	Solve real-life and mathematical problems using numerical and algebraic expressions and equations	Define, evaluate, and compare functions
Work with numbers 11–19 to gain foundations for place value	Extend the counting sequence	Measure and estimate lengths in standard units	Develop understanding of fractions as numbers	Build fractions from unit fractions by applying and extending previous understandings of operations	Geometric measurement: understand concepts of volume and relate volume to multiplication and to addition	Reason about and solve one-variable equations and inequalities		Use functions to model relationships between quantities
	Understand place value	Relate addition and subtraction to length	Solve problems involving measurement and estimation of intervals of time, liquid volumes, and masses of objects	Understand decimal notation for fractions, and compare decimal fractions	Graph points in the coordinate plane to solve real-world and mathematical problems*	Represent and analyze quantitative relationships between dependent and independent variables		
	Use place value understanding and properties of operations to add and subtract		Geometric measurement: understand concepts of area and relate area to multiplication and to addition					
	Measure lengths indirectly and by iterating length units							

* Indicates a cluster that is well thought of as a part of a student's progress to algebra, but that is currently not designated as major by the assessment consortia in their draft materials. Apart from the one asterisked exception, the clusters listed here are a subset of those designated as major in the assessment consortia's draft documents.
** Depends on similarity ideas from geometry to show that slope can be defined and then used to show that a linear equation has a graph which is a straight line and conversely.

SOURCE: Grades K–8 Focus Documents, Achieve the Core (2020)

De-Atomize the Standards

After considering the breadth and depth of students' K–12 experience in the discipline, we narrow our attention to focus on our individual courses. Teachers are often asked to break down or *unpack* the standards they are tasked with teaching. There is nothing wrong with this. In order to truly understand the demand of a standard—all the things it is asking students to know and do—this process is necessary. But it is also runs the risk of being unintentionally reductive and, without a reciprocal process to build the standards back up, leads to an atomized view of the curriculum. Each standard is pulled apart and subdivided until the whole of the course is unrecognizable.

This thinking prompt is the counterbalance to unpacking the standards. Instead of examining each one with a microscope, let's stand back and view them with a broader lens.

I. **View all your standards together in one place.**

Gather up or create your own list of standards, written out in full rather than abbreviated by number or other shorthand. Print them out if they only exist in an electronic format. If you teach elementary school, gather the standards for each discipline you are charged with teaching. If you have multiple sources of standards—for example, specific content standards from your state in addition to the Common Core State Standards for literacy, or Advanced Placement and International Baccalaureate guidelines—be sure to include them all.

II. **Read the standards with the goal of seeing the bigger picture.**

This sounds obvious, but it's less intuitive than you might think. Resist the urge to break things down, or skim and skip. Read each word, but don't ruminate on the particulars. As you read, ask yourself, *What larger purpose does each standard, or group of standards, seem to serve?* Consider, for example, the pre-K science standards in Figure 3.13.

Figure 3.13   Sample Pre-K Standards

ESSI. Earth's Place in the Universe

PreK-ESSI-I(MA). Demonstrate awareness that the Moon can be seen in the daytime and at night, and of the different apparent shapes of the Moon over a month.

- Clarification Statement: The names of moon phases or sequencing of moon phases is not expected.

PreK-ESSI-2(MA). Observe and use evidence to describe that the Sun is in different places in the sky during the day.

SOURCE: http://www.doe.mass.edu/frameworks/scitech/2016-04.pdf

Taken alone, the two standards listed seem to indicate that preschoolers need to be taught a litany of facts about the sun and moon, including

- The moon can be seen in the daytime

- The moon can be seen at night

- The moon appears to take on different shapes over the course of a month
- The sun is in different places in the sky at different points in the day

In fact, the clarification statement under the first standard indicates that some teachers might presume the need to teach four-year-olds the names and sequencing of the phases of the moon. When we read each standard narrowly, in isolation, it transforms into an overwhelming list of *stuff* kids must know.

By contrast, if we read these standards more holistically, seeing the forest and not just the trees, we build them back up onto a coherent portion of learning that feels much more doable. For instance, if we focus on the overarching structure of these standards, we realize that learning about the sun and moon is really just a way of coming to understand something about Earth's place in the universe. Do we need kids to identify all the phases of the moon? Of course not. We need them to understand that the Earth is part of a larger universe, which also contains the moon and sun. In fact, teaching all the phases of the moon would likely *obscure* the actual goal of the standards since it would lead teaching and learning away from an understanding of *Earth's Place in the Universe,* bogging students down in unnecessary details.

As you read your standards, ask yourself the following questions to focus on the bigger picture:

- How does each standard relate to the larger category or heading that contains it?
- What does each section add up to? What is the sum of the parts?
- When we put the pieces together, what are we building?
- What story do these standards tell?

DESIGN STEP

CONNECT TO YOUR VISION OF THE DISCIPLINE

Finally, once you have a holistic view of your course, consider the ways in which your course contributes to students' overall understanding of the discipline you teach. Return to the vision you established in exercises one through three of this chapter and complete the section of the course overview that articulates how your specific course contributes to the overall disciplinary vision, shown again in Figure 3.14. Ask yourself the following:

- How does this course help students come to know what my discipline(s) is or are about?
- What do I hope students will do by the time they are adults as a result of this course?

Figure 3.14 **Course Overview**

How does this course contribute to the disciplinary vision?
How does this course illuminate the greater purpose of my discipline(s)? What do I hope students will do by the time they are adults as a result of this course?

DETERMINING DISCIPLINARY LENSES FOR YOUR COURSE

After completing the previous thinking prompts, we are in a great position to select two or three disciplinary lenses for our entire course. In Thinking Prompts 1 through 3, you worked toward a compelling vision of your discipline. In Prompts 4 and 5, you considered ways that the K–12 curriculum, and your course in particular, could be used for students to achieve that vision. Now we are ready to select the disciplinary lenses that will help students to grasp the disciplinary vision.

Disciplinary lenses are so highly transferable within the discipline itself that they should be applied all the time, like a set of lenses that students put on when thinking like a practitioner in this field.

We can ask ourselves, *What are the most essential disciplinary practices that students must acquire, connect, and transfer within the context of my course in order to be effective practitioners of the discipline(s) I teach? What are the two or three concepts or practices that I want students to consider every single time they encounter a new situation?*

Before we jump into selecting the lenses, we want to note that some of the examples listed may sound more like skills while others do not. Some disciplines are more naturally procedural oriented, such as the arts, physical education, world language, and language arts. Some disciplines are more content oriented such as social studies and science. Mathematics is content heavy, but one goes about demonstrating knowledge mostly through procedures. The important point here is that all disciplines have ways of knowing and ways of doing, and although some are more tilted in one direction, we need both knowledge and skills to become competent in any field.

Let's reflect upon one of the most skilled basketball players of all time, LeBron James. His procedural skills as a player—such as passing, shooting, dribbling—are undeniable. But watch him speak in an interview and you quickly realize his knowledge of the game is also unmatched—such as his ability to perceive the positions of players on offense and defense in his mind's eye and anticipate the potential plays and corresponding consequences of his moves.

What's most important is that knowing, doing, and thinking have an intertwined relationship and are all essential for transfer. Skills can also be considered concepts or organizing ideas that help us to categorize our world. For instance, empathy, inference, and proportional are all regarded as important skills as well as concepts that help us to organize our world.

In pre-algebra, for example, the disciplinary lenses of *representation, knowns,* and *unknowns* can help students approach any problem they encounter. In an eighth-grade math class, the teacher might return to these core ideas every time a student is struggling to understand new procedures or persevere through challenging problems. When a student is stumped on a word problem, she might simply say, *Hmmm. Let's try thinking this through by naming what we know and what we don't know.* or *Hmmm. I see that you're having difficulty working with this equation. I wonder if it would help to represent the problem as a graph or table of values.* Soon, students' inner dialogue takes on this form as well. Instead of asking for help, they check with themselves first: *What do I know or not know? How can I represent this information another way?* No matter the topic, these concepts give students a way in that transfers throughout the course.

In a high school government class, the teacher may select *individual rights* and *common good* as the disciplinary lens concepts, teaching them as competing values that form the roots of nearly every political debate that students might come across. Should marijuana be legalized? Some argue for the individual right to consume the drug, while others believe that it is in the common good to protect citizens from the harms of drug use. Should the government be able to use our cell phones to track our movement? Some might argue "no" because they value the individual right to privacy, while others would answer "yes" because they see the potential for increased safety, which is in the common good. Whatever the political question entails, at least one of these concepts would provide a framework to help students think it through in order to understand others' opinions and to formulate their own.

In elementary school, disciplinary lenses do not have to be specific to one content area. Caroline Lepps, teacher for Edmonton Catholic Schools and Learning Transfer Endorsed Educator, identified the disciplinary lenses of *same, different,* and *sort* for her primary students. She explains, "These can be applied across multiple disciplines. I wanted to keep the concepts [lenses] simple, accessible, but also to be able to bring depth to their understanding through the contexts that evolve. I see these transferring both within the discipline of mathematics and across other disciplines as well."

Notice that there is a difference between disciplinary lens concepts and other important concepts in your course. Disciplinary lenses form the foundation for reasoning within the discipline. They are meant to be so universally applicable within the discipline that they would help a student approach nearly any topic, lesson, or exercise throughout the year and beyond. They are concepts that, when understood deeply, create the habits of mind required to deal with novel situations flexibly, systematically, and confidently. We will select additional concepts to focus on when we begin unit planning, but these lenses are the concepts that establish a firm disciplinary focus for our entire course.

Elementary or primary teachers are often responsible for teaching more than one discipline. In some cases, the courses are taught separately, and in other cases there is a cross-disciplinary approach to teaching the academic disciplines. We will tackle cross-disciplinary learning in more detail in Chapter 4. For now, we believe there is value in selecting at least one disciplinary lens for each of the core academic areas. This ensures that students begin to build flexible yet disciplined habits of mind as they move through school.

Figure 3.15 offers examples of concepts that fit these criteria. Remember these are simply examples to jumpstart your thinking, and we listed more than two or three simply to provide more fodder, but two to three disciplinary lenses per course is substantial.

DESIGN STEP

Determine two or three disciplinary lenses to guide your course planning. Consider the following questions:

- If I randomly selected any standard, opened up to any page in my textbook, or pulled out any difficult assignment, which two or three ideas would I want students to activate in their minds to think things through?

- If students could only remember two or three key ideas from my course, which ideas would most equip them to approach new phenomena?

- What ideas do we come back to again and again in my course?

- Whenever we begin a new unit or topic, what do I want my students to look for? When they approach a new text or problem, what should they pay attention to?

- Which concepts unlock all the others?

_____

_____

_____

_____

_____

The lenses you choose can be recorded in the corresponding section of the course overview template. Fill them out below, and be sure to transfer them to your larger Course Overview table at the beginning of the chapter.

Disciplinary Lenses
What are the most essential disciplinary practices within the context of my course that students must acquire, connect, and transfer in order to be effective practitioners of the discipline(s) I teach? When students encounter a new situation, what are the two to four concepts or practices that I want them to consider, every single time?

Scan the QR code for more examples of disciplinary lenses.

Of course, this list is meant to be illustrative, not exhaustive. Experts draw upon hundreds of important concepts like these as they maneuver within their disciplines. For the purposes of the K–12 classroom, though, we can narrow our focus in order to give students time to acquire, connect, and transfer a manageable set of conceptual tools. Remember, even though we are striving to help our students think like experts in the field, they are still novices. So, resist the urge to teach all of these (or more). Two or three disciplinary lens concepts per year are plenty!

Figure 3.15   **Sample Disciplinary Lenses**

Discipline	Sample Disciplinary Lenses
Mathematics	pattern, precision, generalization, representation, properties, sensemaking, critique, estimation
Science	questions, problems, models, investigations, data, solutions, evidence, living things, interdependence, energy, force, motion
Social studies	source, reliability, point of view, empathy, time, context, period, causation, comparison, evidence, argument, power, authority, resources
English language arts	purpose, author, audience, mode, message, meaning, structure, discourse, interpretation, time, context, period, design
Physical education	balance, control, decision-making, strategy, teamwork, vitality, discipline, stamina, willpower, endurance
Art, Music, Drama	audience, design, purpose, message, texture, mood, balance, body, time, energy, dynamics, harmony, rhythm, melody, composition
World language	patterns, symbols, conventions, communication, history, identity, sense of time, sense of possibility, precision, culture, values, worldview, situations

We also urge you to resist the urge to turn these concepts into checklists, acronyms, or token posters to adorn the walls of your classroom. For instance, many students have been asked to fill out SOAPSTone graphic organizers to identify the speaker, occasion, audience, purpose, summary, and tone of a text without understanding what any of these things really means. While protocols like this are well-meaning and theoretically *could* help students develop useful habits of mind, they usually end up as hollow paint-by-numbers tasks because they lack a conceptual underpinning. They skip over learning and go straight to doing.

Instead, we suggest that teaching these concepts through the ACT model—guiding students to acquire a rich understanding of each concept, uncover the relationships among the concepts and mentally organize them into connected networks of meaning, and to continually transfer them to new situations within the discipline—will pay dividends over the course of the year.

Human Experience Concepts

Teachers may want to consider human-centric concepts either as disciplinary lenses or as anchoring concepts when we arrive there in unit planning, especially teachers of the arts, English language arts, elementary, social studies, or even modern languages. **Human Experience Concepts** are the organizing ideas that help us to better understand who we are as individuals and as a collective species, and are inherently complex and interesting, especially to young people as they navigate and seek to understand who they are in the world.

In an attempt to respond to our modern world of disruptive technology and obsessive consumerism, education has begun placing more and more emphasis on job-ready

Human Experience Concepts: The concepts that explore and acknowledge the enduring ideas that shape and inform our humanity.

skills and computing than abstractions like *truth, courage,* and *beauty.* Though we believe skills and technology play an important role in education, we also think it's vital our classrooms and curriculum take time to explore and acknowledge the enduring concepts that shape and inform our humanity—Socrates style. Disciplinary work doesn't occur in a contextual or relational vacuum, after all. Scientists, historians, and mathematicians aren't robots whose existence is defined by their profession. They are humans with emotions, beliefs, values, and ideologies that affect their work in both obvious and subtle ways. The knowledge, inventions, policies, and theories they produce can drastically impact our lives for better or worse, so we can't over-value the importance of fostering understanding of ourselves and each other alongside developing disciplinary literacy.

If we only see school as a place to prepare students for the workforce, we are selling the role, purpose, and significance of education short. At its best, education has the potential to help us transform ourselves and our world, but it requires intentional planning and prioritizing. It's with that spirit that we encourage you to consider the role of Human Experience Concepts in your discipline. The good thing about these concepts is many of them already exist in your curriculum, lurking just beneath the surface—hidden by initiatives, testing schedules, and atomized unit design. Figure 3.16 lists a few common examples of these concepts.

In some disciplines, like social studies, they are easy to spot. Concepts like *sovereignty, ideology, control,* and *resources* are the heart of a social studies curriculum anchored and organized by concepts. However, these are often broad, examining history from a structural and systemic level. What if we were to zoom in on individual figures and moments throughout history to examine how more intimately human concepts impacted people throughout history? How has *ego* led to military blunders and political miscalculations? How does *belief* impact people's ability to outlast bigger, stronger, and more well-resourced groups? What's the role of *bias* in determining the effectiveness of a queen, president, or emperor?

Figure 3.16   Sample Human Experience Concepts

Humanities and the Arts		Science	Mathematics
Friendship	Power	Survival	Question asking
Insecurities	Control	Equilibrium	Pattern seeking
Belonging	Chaos	Balance	Meaning-making
Truth	Ignorance	Interdependence	Communication
Courage	Identity	Force	Equality, equal
Fear	Bias	Attraction	Simplicity, simplified
Dreams	Beauty	Symbiotic	Precision
Experiences	Injustice	Interaction	Symmetry
Family dynamics	Hate	Adaptation	Deviation
Redemption	Justice	Diversity	Balance
Authenticity	Systems	Systems	Flexibility
Storytelling	Freedom	Variation	Order
Ego	Belief	Cooperation	Solution

With some reframing, they are readily apparent in English language arts. Though we support the shift toward regarding English language arts is a process and skills-based discipline, we can't help but wonder whether or not students are inspired by lists of decontextualized reading, writing, and speaking skills. After all, isn't the point of reading, writing, and speaking to better understand and connect with the human experience? To be clear, we aren't advocating for a return to traditional text-centric instruction, but rather to the spirit of treating stories as a context to collaboratively develop wisdom about the world. For example, Shana Sabourin, a high school English teacher in Prince William County, weaves learning experiences exploring the relationship between *identity, freedom, dreams,* and *experiences* alongside her traditional composition and genre-based units.

What if we explored the stories of famous scientists alongside their discoveries and hypotheses in our science courses? How might one integrate concepts like *cooperation, success, skills, variation,* and *diversity* into curricula that seek to teach students how to protect and sustain habitats and environments in addition to learning about them? The science about climate change is clear. What is more murky, however, is understanding how people can be convinced to make the necessary changes to slow its effects on our environment before it is too late to reverse the damage. Though scientific phenomena may occur independent of humans, understanding our relationship with the world on a personal and interpersonal level will help ensure we don't just understand science in the abstract, but in more authentic, anchored, and embodied ways as well.

THINKING PROMPT

How might you incorporate Human Experience Concepts in your course?

_____

_____

_____

_____

_____

Vertical Alignment to Promote Disciplinary Depth

Disciplinary lenses ensure that students notice and become adept at applying the more important disciplinary concepts to new situations. Teaching students to transfer disciplinary lens concepts can be even more transformative when we vertically align our lenses across several grade levels and courses.

Consider a student moving through a thoughtfully aligned sequence of social studies courses from sixth through twelfth grade, as depicted in Figure 3.17. Each year, students investigate the relationships among the same set of disciplinary lenses: evidence, accounts, and theories, with some relevant subconcepts coming into play as makes sense for each course. However, rather than simply repeating the learning of prior years, each course is designed to help students grapple with the concepts in a new way, leading to deeper understanding and a more complex web of relationships in students' minds.

Figure 3.17   Vertical Alignment of Social Studies Through Concepts: Evidence, Accounts, and Theories

Grade/Course	Conceptual Questions
6th-grade Geography	What is the role of **evidence** in constructing **theories** in geography?
7th-grade Ancient History	How does **lack of evidence** impact **accounts** of the ancient past?
8th-grade US History I	How do **accounts**, **reliability**, and **truth** interact in creating **historical accounts**?
9th-grade World History I	How do **omissions** affect **reliability** of historical **accounts**?
10th-grade World History II	How are **selectivity** and **bias** related when it comes to constructing theories of the past?
11th-grade US History II	How do the historian's **ideals and values** impact the **accounts** they construct?
12th-grade US Government and DC history	How do **questions** shape the **evidence** I select and the **theories** I propose?

online resources   Download a blank vertical alignment template at www.learningthattransfers.com.

Of course, not all educators are in a position to organize this type of alignment within the discipline. But, to the extent possible, we recommend those with the resources and influence to coordinate disciplinary lens concepts beyond your own classroom do so. At a minimum, consider working with teachers one grade level above and one grade level below the course you teach to ensure there is strong disciplinary cohesion from one grade level to the next. Is it more work? Certainly. But the potential for developing student expertise and promoting learning transfer is well worth it!

The conceptual relationship question stems serve as a solid starting point in relating two or more disciplinary lenses to craft a vertical conceptual framework that increases in sophistication as students move from one grade level to the next.

Remember, fill the blanks with concepts and not details.

- How are _____ and _____ connected?
- What is the relationship between _____ and _____?
- How does _____ impact/affect/influence _____?
- What effect do _____ and _____ have on _____?
- How do _____ and _____ interact?
- What is the role/purpose of _____ in _____?

The following question stems work well for early elementary or as scaffolding questions before reaching the ones above:

- What is the difference between _____ and _____?
- What happens when _____ interacts with _____?
- Why does _____ make _____ [do whatever it does]?
- Why does _____ need _____?

DESIGN STEP

Articulate vertical alignment and progression. The following questions can aid in planning. Scan the QR code to see more templates and examples for Vertical Alignment.

- Which additional concepts best align with the content of the grade level or course?
- Does the progression ensure increasing sophistication from one level to the next?
- Do the questions lead students toward the disciplinary vision?
- What concepts will help students tackle messy real-world problems if we intentionally deepen their understanding year after year?

_____

_____

_____

_____

_____

CONCLUSION

As this chapter draws to a close, let us return to a key idea mentioned at the outset: our aim is to transform the standards-focused classroom—the one so attentive to each tiny parcel of content or isolated skill that it has forgotten the higher purpose of learning—into a transfer-focused classroom where teachers use the content of their course as a means for cultivating disciplined ways of thinking in their students. Imagine how school would change for the better if educators made this one, simple shift. Instead of mastering a body of knowledge created by others, students would become adaptive experts capable of using the thinking of each discipline to solve real-world problems. Although we cannot predict the exact challenges that future generations will face—manifestations of the climate crisis, intractable global conflicts, economic disruptions, injustice in its myriad forms, or even the wide variety of personal dilemmas that plague each of us from time to time—we certainly know that they will be better off if they can draw on the logic of a scientist, precision of a mathematician, the empathy of a literary scholar, and the skepticism of a historian, for instance, to navigate these situations.

Now that you have crafted a disciplinary vision, articulated how the standards or learning outcomes fit into the larger disciplinary whole, and selected essential course concepts, you are ready to apply the ACT model to your course. But before we turn to unit planning—which will happen in Chapter 5—we will reflect upon the additional tools our students need to navigate our complex world. The next chapter pushes us beyond the long-established disciplines to emerging areas that are crucial to meet the demands of our changing times. The course overview that was presented at the beginning of this chapter is repeated in Figure 3.18 in case you want to synthesize your work into this document. We will continue with the modern literacies in the next chapter.

Figure 3.18 Course Overview

Zooming Out: Course Overview	
Course Title	**Real-World Challenges**
	What are some real-world challenges that could use the thinking of your course in order to tackle?
Disciplinary Vision	**How does this course contribute to the disciplinary vision?**
Why is this discipline important to my students? How can it inspire them?	How does this course illuminate the greater purpose of my discipline(s)? What do I hope students will do by the time they are adults as a result of this course?
Disciplinary Lenses	**Modern Literacies**
What are the most essential disciplinary practices within the context of my course that students must acquire, connect, and transfer in order to be effective practitioners of the discipline(s) I teach? When students encounter a new situation, what are the two to four concepts or practices that I want them to consider, every single time?	

online
resources   Download at www.learningthattransfers.com.

THINKING PROMPT

Take a moment to reflect on how your thinking has evolved over the course of the chapter.

- How does **each discipline** impact the **ways we think about our world**?

- What is the role of **disciplinary literacy** in a classroom focused on learning that **transfers**?

_____

_____

_____

_____

_____

CHAPTER FOUR

Modern Literacies
What Do Our Students Need to Navigate Today's World?

"Our Age of Anxiety is, in great part, the result of trying to do today's job with yesterday's tools and yesterday's concepts."

—Marshall McLuhan

Why does this chapter matter?	Students need more than academic conceptual understanding to be successful in their future. Modern literacy concepts help ensure students understand and are able to transfer concepts and skills not explicitly taught in the standards.
What will I be able to do by the end of this chapter?	I will be able to choose modern literacy concepts that support my course and age group of students.

Of all the phrases floating in education's buzzword soup, "21st century learning" has become one of the soggiest. It's not that there's anything inherently wrong with it. On the contrary, its popularity speaks to its relevance. It's used by everyone everywhere. We've used it ourselves! Chances are, you have too.

But what do we actually mean when we talk about 21st century learning? Is it related to students' proficiency with technology and familiarity with STEM? Or more human-oriented skills like collaboration and communication? Or maybe it's about individual habits of mind and socioemotional learning? Systems thinking? Entrepreneurship? Something new entirely? Depending on whom you ask, you'll probably get a lot of different answers.

That's the thing about language—it's slippery. Even more so when we're trying to nail down something as complex as the future of education in an age of exponential growth and change.

In addition to helping us communicate, language experts claim that we use language to signal to others that we're members of a community (Gee, 2014). By talking about 21st century skills, educators show each other, our students, and even society that we're aware that the world is changing, and we know education must change with it. Our use of sleek, modern phrases like "Future-Ready" and "21st Century Skills" is how we push back against the cognitive dissonance caused by wanting to change the world through education while working in a field often associated with the monotony, uniformity, and misery of industrial era factories.

Whether you're passionate about ethical reasoning or digital citizenship, whether you've implemented socioemotional learning or learning competencies, we're united by our belief that traditional curriculum isn't enough to prepare the students of today for the problems of tomorrow. This chapter takes the countless programs, initiatives, philosophies, and pedagogies that all seek to bring new ways of thinking, knowing, and doing into education and unites them under one conceptual umbrella that we are calling modern literacies.

Much the same way disciplinary literacies equip students with the confluence of knowledge, skills, and habits of minds that comprise each academic discipline (these are important too!), we believe the myriad of skills, initiatives, and programs listed above are all working to help students become meaningful participants in modern social, political, and economic life (Gee, 2010). For the last century, traditional print-based literacy (also still important!) has been vital in helping citizens engage and navigate those domains. Soon, though, modern literacies will become just as vital. Increasingly, students need to learn to communicate their ideas using **multimodalities**, which includes more than one mode of communication, such as print, video, images, audio, and tactile.

Consider all of the different competencies that students need to navigate today's complex world. Figure 4.1 contains a list of a few common examples. This is certainly not an exhaustive list, but simply a way to demonstrate examples of additional skill sets students need to live meaningful lives.

Figure 4.1 Examples of Modern Literacies

Responsibility	Creativity	Digital citizenship
Self-regulation	Design thinking	Multimodal communication
Character education	Cross-cultural communication	Collaboration
Empathy	Ethical decision-making	Media literacy
Adaptability	Financial literacy	Entrepreneurship

Competencies like these will require us to incorporate new bodies of knowledge into school's curriculum. They force us to look beyond the current opposing binaries of content knowledge versus generic thinking skills and start considering how disciplinary ways of knowing, thinking, and doing are converging in ways that create new transdisciplinary hubs like the Digital Humanities or Evolutionary Anthropology.

Multimodalities:
More than one mode of communication, such as print, video, images, audio, and tactile.

Regardless of whether we're teaching students to infer like a historian or code like a programmer (or something in between), we can ensure they can transfer their understanding to new situations. One of the most powerful aspects of the ACT model is that it can be used to break down traditional learning standards *and* bodies of knowledge like modern literacies, because it is designed to focus student attention on the deeper structures of each of these domains.

THINKING PROMPT

Before we begin, take a moment to reflect on your current thinking about these questions:

- What does your school currently do to prepare students for a rapidly changing world?

- How do you currently plan for cross-disciplinary integration among the different subject areas?

_____

_____

_____

_____

_____

CHAPTER STRUCTURE

This chapter outlines several thinking prompts and course design steps to help you consider the modern literacies that might be most appropriate for your context. Just as we suggested in Chapter 2, consider involving parents, students, board members, and the larger community in these conversations.

This chapter has a series of Thinking Prompts to facilitate thinking and inform planning, followed by Design Steps that will be used directly in planning empowering learning experiences that facilitate learning transfer. The prompts and steps in this chapter are organized around the following sections:

Determining Modern Literacy Concepts
- Returning to real-world challenges
- Narrowing our focus for each course
- From competencies to concepts
- From concepts to conceptual connections
- Building a bridge between disciplinary literacy and modern literacy

Horizontal alignment to promote cross-disciplinary breadth
- Multidisciplinary alignment
- Interdisciplinary alignment
- Transdisciplinary alignment
- The importance of metacognition

DETERMINING MODERN LITERACY CONCEPTS

Broadening the scope of our curriculum in intentional ways will help us center ways of knowing, doing, and thinking that are more representative of our increasingly multicultural and multimodal society. These modern literacies are the types of competencies that help students design a better future (Kalantzis et al., 2016). It is the type of learning that will eventually take students beyond our curriculum, pushing them to ask deeper questions and seek more profound answers.

Importantly, the term "modern" is evergreen—able to bend and flex with the unseen changes that will occur after our world adjusts to new technologies, possibilities, and events like COVID-19. Some of these skills are actually quite old. For instance, collaboration was just as vital in penning the US Constitution in 1787 as it will be embarking on an entrepreneurial venture decades from now. Others are incredibly new, like being able to discern if the video you're watching is a "deep fake" or being able to design.

We want to capture the fact that, with the sun setting on the first quarter of the 21st century, we must start looking forward, but also do better acknowledging how our past continues to shape our present and future. And, in that same spirit, consider how tomorrow might look different. What if we devoted time to studying ethics in schools today? Or anti-racism? Or systems thinking? Or ways all three bodies of knowledge can be used in conjunction with each other to create a more equitable society?

The possibilities both excite and exhaust us. The purpose of this chapter, then, is to acknowledge that no single teacher or classroom can incorporate *all* of these modern literacies in an effective way. And yet, every single teacher and classroom must incorporate *some* of them in order to make school learning relevant to today's complex world. Just as Chapter 2 helped us to distill a manageable set of disciplinary lenses as year-long mental tools to be applied to each new situation for our entire course, this chapter will help us distill a powerful, yet doable set of modern literacy concepts to help bridge the gap between disciplinary expertise and innovation in the 21st century. We will explore where you can leverage the thinking of your course to achieve modern literacy goals. We can't do it all, so do what fits best into your constellation of concepts.

Returning to Real-World Challenges

Again, in order to transition to a transfer-focused classroom, we consider the long-term view of our students' learning journey. Before we consider the various modern literacy competencies and initiatives that are currently exerting their force on schools, it's essential to understand for ourselves *why* these particular programs are making their way into our classrooms. What are they good for? Where are they leading us?

Of course, we all understand to some degree that these skills—collaboration, cultural competency, design thinking—are tools that students will need to be successful in life beyond school. Employers want new hires to have these capabilities. Our communities need citizens with these skill sets. We have a vague notion of their usefulness. But before we can incorporate these things into our curriculum in a compelling, urgent way, we have to spend considerable time understanding the nature of the challenges our kids (collectively and individually) will need to navigate in the future.

Step #1: Identify Challenges

Let's continue with the same real-world challenges we selected at the start of Chapter 2. You can either continue with the ones already selected or add additional ones—it's up to you. This time, we will think about what concepts and skills students might need that are *not* typically taught in schools in order to address these challenges. The same chart from Chapter 2 is repeated again in Figure 4.2 as an aid to tracking your thinking. You may want to personalize the categories to fit your findings.

Figure 4.2   Real-World Challenges

Category	Current Challenges	Concepts From My Discipline That Might Help Students Understand These Challenges
Political		
Economic		
Social		
Environmental		
Technological		
Health		
Local		
National		
International		

Scan the QR code to see examples of real-world challenges and resources for all content areas

 Download blank template at www.learningthattransfers.com.

Step #2: Review the Role of Your Discipline(s)

Think back to the vision you established for your discipline in Chapter 2. Perhaps elaborate on or recall your responses to these questions: How does the thinking of your discipline help students understand modern problems? How does the thinking of your discipline give students the tools to solve these problems? Record some thoughts in your chart (see Figure 4.2).

Step #3: What's Missing?

THINKING PROMPT

Select one of the challenges you've identified and consider the knowledge, skills, and attitudes outside of the traditional academic disciplines that students will need to navigate it. Consider the following:

- What would it take for students to be **well-informed** about this issue? What will they need in order to avoid the trappings of misinformation?

- What will it take for students to **imagine solutions and act for change**? What do students need to believe about the world and about themselves to be part of the solution?

- What will it take for students to **collaborate with others and be leaders** in this space? What communication tools and skills must they have? What skills will they need to create diverse coalitions? What competencies will they need to unite stakeholders and persuade powerholders?

_____

_____

_____

_____

_____

Step #4: Reflect

Take a moment to step back and think about (or discuss with others) the relationships between the following:

- Your discipline and 21st century challenges

- Your discipline and modern literacies

- Modern literacies and 21st century challenges

These steps allow us to move toward the real-world impact end of the Learning Transfer Spectrum. Do you remember the middle school science example in the last chapter? As teacher Julia Briggs tracked local stories in the news, she thought about the concepts outside of her discipline that were important to the dissimilar contexts she wanted her students to explore. She realized that concepts of responsible consumption, production, and fairness or justice emerged with each new situation. See Figure 4.3 for a visual of how her contexts brought additional concepts and conceptual questions.

Figure 4.3   Modern Literacies Example Across the Learning Transfer Spectrum

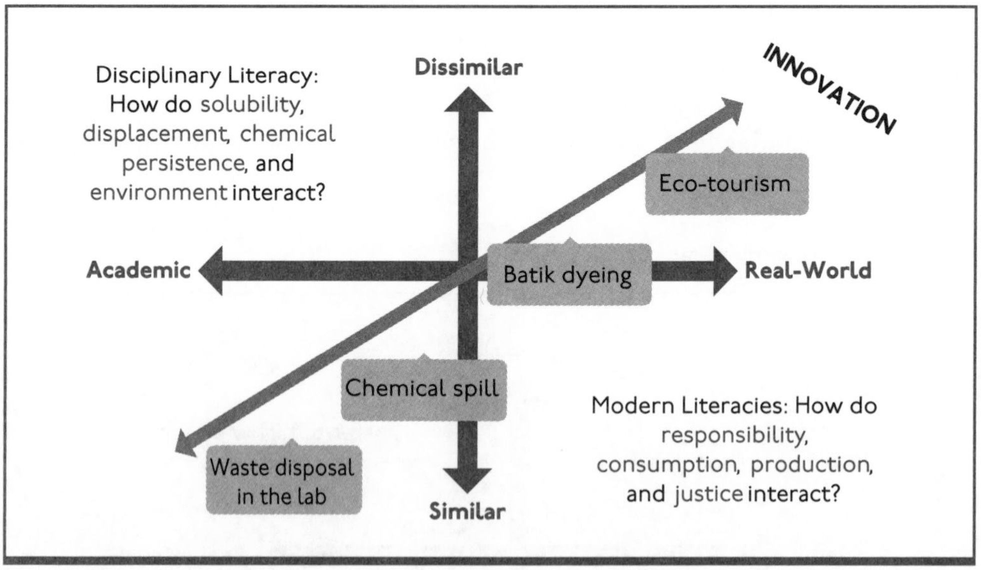

Narrowing Our Focus for Each Course

Once we acknowledge that no teacher is capable of incorporating all the various modern literacies into their curriculum in a meaningful way, the next question to grapple with is, *Which* modern literacies should we teach? There is no simple answer to this question. But, once we have narrowed our focus to a small subset, these concepts have the power to enrich and amplify the disciplinary core of our course.

Take, for example, the visual arts classroom centered around the disciplinary literacy concepts of *perspective, emphasis,* and *movement.* As students study works of art, they examine the artist's perspective, determine which aspects of the piece are being emphasized, and consider the various ways in which an artist creates a sense of movement in a piece that remains still. They consider the ways in which these three concepts are interrelated. They transfer their understanding of these concepts to their own art projects.

There is plenty here to make learning coherent and meaningful for students, but an art course that concerns itself solely with art is still somewhat flat, as is the science classroom that concerns itself only with science, or the history classroom that teaches history for its own sake. Including a complementary set of modern literacy concepts is necessary to round out the curriculum into something more multidimensional.

Consider that same visual arts class once the modern literacy concepts of *advocacy* and *empathy* are added to the mix. Suddenly, students are asking and answering questions such as, *How can I use art to advocate for myself and others? How can art enable me to walk in someone else's shoes? How can I use my knowledge of perspective, emphasis, and movement to create art that elicits empathy and urges change?* Students in this classroom might paint portraits of homeless veterans and design a public exhibition to advocate for increased mental health funding for those who have served in the military. Or they might craft a mural in the cafeteria that inspires their peers to be "upstanders" instead of "bystanders" when they witness an act of bullying.

Just as disciplinary lenses help students unlock new situations *within* an academic discipline, modern literacy concepts help students transfer their disciplinary understandings *beyond* the discipline.

Notice that the addition of modern literacy concepts helps build a bridge between the academic components of the curriculum and the real-world applications we want students to engage in. Just as disciplinary lenses help students unlock new situations *within* an academic discipline, modern literacy concepts help students transfer their disciplinary understandings *beyond* the discipline. In other words, modern literacies help us move learning from left to right on the Learning Transfer Spectrum depicted in Figure 4.4.

Figure 4.4   The Learning Transfer Spectrum

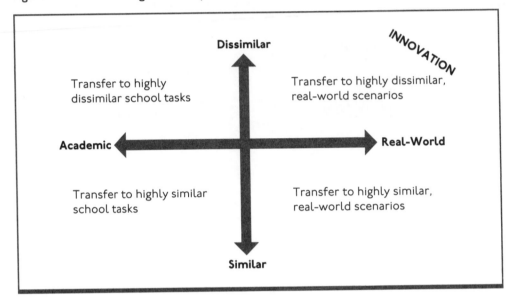

The following steps can help you narrow down the seemingly infinite list of modern literacy targets to a manageable set of competencies that fit naturally with your particular course.

Step 1: Start With School-Based Guidance, if Possible

Many schools and education departments have already adopted specific competencies or skills for 21st century learning or socioemotional learning. If this is the case for you, start with the frameworks you're already using rather than adding extra layers of complication. Have you been asked to participate in the Great Kindness Challenge or to teach mindfulness practices? Is *grit* the concept that dominates conversation? Or is your school pushing for cultural competency or working hard to improve diversity, equity, and inclusion practices? Or is "design thinking" the buzzword of the day? Even more simply, is there a *learner profile* or *portrait of a graduate* that outlines competencies your school hopes to develop in all students? A school mission statement? If so, start there.

Just as you gathered up all the standards or other content guides for your course in Chapter 2, gather up and print out, if at all possible, all the various initiatives you've been asked to incorporate into your instruction.

Keep in mind that these initiatives often lack a paper trail, so to speak. They live in the articles administrators ask you to read, or in the themes present in professional development workshops. They float in the air of department meetings. Try to nail down those intangible modern literacy initiatives as well. Write them down so you can see them all in one place.

Step 2: Consult Other Frameworks

If your school or local context does not yet have specific skills or competencies identified, the lists in Figures 4.5 through 4.8 offer several potential resources that you can consult for determining which competencies might make most sense for your students. Or, even if your school has adopted a set of modern literacy goals, consider what value the frameworks presented in Figures 4.5 through 4.8 could add.

The Partnership for 21st Century Learning, a network of organizations, names the 4 Cs necessary to success in the modern world.

The International Society for Technology in Education, or ISTE, has a set of seven standards that paint a portrait of digital literacy.

Common Sense Education, in collaboration with Harvard's Project Zero, has put together a set of five essential dispositions for digital citizenship.

Figure 4.5   The Four Cs

- Communication
- Creativity
- Collaboration
- Critical thinking

Figure 4.6   ISTE Student Standards

Standard	Explanation
Empowered learner	Students leverage technology to take an active role in choosing, achieving, and demonstrating competency in their learning goals, informed by the learning sciences.
Digital citizen	Students recognize the rights, responsibilities, and opportunities of living, learning, and working in an interconnected digital world, and they act and model in ways that are safe, legal, and ethical.
Knowledge constructor	Students critically curate a variety of resources using digital tools to construct knowledge, produce creative artifacts, and make meaningful learning experiences for themselves and others.
Innovative designer	Students use a variety of technologies within a design process to identify and solve problems by creating new, useful, or imaginative solutions.
Computational thinker	Students develop and employ strategies for understanding and solving problems in ways that leverage the power of technological methods to develop and test solutions.
Creative communicator	Students communicate clearly and express themselves creatively for a variety of purposes using the platforms, tools, styles, formats, and digital media appropriate to their goals.
Global collaborator	Students use digital tools to broaden their perspectives and enrich their learning by collaborating with others and working effectively in teams locally and globally.

SOURCE: https://www.iste.org/standards/for-students

Figure 4.7   Common Sense Education's Core Dispositions for Digital Citizenship

Disposition	Steps You Can Take
Slow down and self-reflect	Notice your gut reaction. Push beyond your first impression. Recognize that situations can be complex. Routinely take stock of your habits. Pay attention to "red flag feelings."
Explore perspectives	Be curious and open minded. Think about other people's points of view. Care for other people's feelings. Weigh different people's values and priorities as well as your own. Consider moral, ethical, and civic responsibilities (the Rings of Responsibility).
Seek facts and evidence	Investigate and uncover relevant facts. Seek and evaluate information from multiple credible sources. Weigh evidence from different sources.
Envision options and possible impacts	Envision possible courses of action. Consider how different choices reflect your values and goals. Stay alert to responsibilities to yourself and others. Evaluate possible impacts.
Take action	Decide on a course of action that feels positive and productive. Make changes in digital habits to support well-being. Ask for help when you need it. Be an ally and upstander for others.

SOURCE: Common Sense Education.

The Collaborative for Academic, Social, and Emotional Learning, also known as CASEL, offers a framework of socioemotional targets to guide the teaching of essential intrapersonal and interpersonal skills, shown in Figure 4.8. Similarly, the International Baccalaureate has a learner profile, filled with complex concepts and processes such as open-mindedness, risk-taking, caring, and more that fit well within this modern literacies framework.

Step 3: Consider Your Students

Think about which modern literacy competencies your students need most.

- **What are they getting elsewhere at school?** For instance, if mindfulness is part of the PE curriculum and students rotate through a technology special once per week, a third-grade teacher might choose to focus on cultural competency to guarantee a well-rounded experience for students.

Figure 4.8 CASEL Socioemotional Learning Competencies

Competency	Included Components
Self-awareness	• Identifying emotions • Accurate self-perception • Recognizing strengths • Self-confidence • Self-efficacy
Self-management	• Impulse control • Stress management • Self-discipline • Self-motivation • Goal-setting • Organizational skills
Social awareness	• Perspective-taking • Empathy • Appreciating diversity • Respect for others
Relationship skills	• Communication • Social engagement • Relationship-building • Teamwork
Responsible decision-making	• Identifying problems • Analyzing situations • Solving problems • Evaluating • Reflecting • Ethical responsibility

SOURCE: https://casel.org/core-competencies/

- **What are they getting at home or through extracurricular activities?** We don't recommend making assumptions or over generalizing about what students are experiencing outside of school, but understanding the social and cultural context of your students' families may help you prioritize some modern literacies over others.

- **What do your particular students need most to lead meaningful and impactful lives?** Do students have unhealthy relationships with social media, or are they stressed and overwhelmed by the demands of school? Would developing a growth mindset help unleash their potential? Consider the whole student.

Based on your answers to these questions, narrow the many possible modern literacy focus areas down to five or six.

Step 4: Look for Concepts That Naturally Augment Your Discipline and Course

Ask yourself which modern literacy concepts fit most naturally with the disciplinary literacy concepts you've already selected for your course. For instance, a biology class grounded in the concepts of interdependence and homeostasis might become more well-rounded by adding *ethical responsibility* to the mix. The history classroom focused on bias and evidence would be a natural place to incorporate media literacy, teaching students to navigate internet sources and detect fake news. The elementary school physical education class taught through the concepts of fitness and teamwork seems the perfect place to incorporate nearly any other socio-emotional goal, but it might be more difficult to incorporate "global collaboration" into the course.

As you work through the possibilities, consider the following approaches:

- **Look for harmony:** Which modern literacy goals are most similar to the disciplinary concepts I've already selected? Which modern literacy goals connect easily to the content of my course?

- **Look for balance:** Which modern literacy goals fill a gap in my curriculum? Which modern literacy goals might serve as the missing piece? For instance, if students often think of mathematics as a solitary pursuit, you might select *collaboration* as a modern literacy focus to shift their expectations.

- **Look from the student perspective:** Which modern literacy goals might encourage reluctant students to buy in to my course? Which modern literacies will my students most value? What do they need? For instance, adding a focus on empathy or allyship might empower sixth graders to better navigate the social complexities of middle school. Adding a focus on social justice might turn apathetic English language arts students into avid readers and writers.

Narrow your options down to two or three key ideas.

Step 5: Envision and Use Your Gut

So many modern literacy initiatives are adopted and scrapped two weeks into the school year because they start to feel like burdensome add-ons to an already cluttered curriculum. A good way to check your narrowed list is to envision your curriculum through each possible lens and gauge your own level of enthusiasm for each option. If you are excited and passionate about the modern literacy concepts you choose, and the resulting orientation of your course, you will be more likely to teach them well (and not just turn them into a bulletin board display in the back of the room).

> ## THINKING PROMPT
>
> Which modern literacies seem most suited to your context?
>
> _____
>
> _____
>
> _____
>
> _____
>
> _____

Dividing Modern Literacies Among Disciplines

The previous exercises were meant for individual teachers to consider on designing a single course. Another approach to consider, especially if you are working as a multigrade-level and course curricular team, is to divide up important modern literacy goals among the disciplines according to their most natural homes. For instance, if students are learning how to assess the reliability of information found online in their English language arts course, and focusing on leadership and teamwork in PE, teachers in other disciplines can lead the way with other important competencies, which results in a well-rounded experience for kids when taken as a whole.

The key here, though, is to not allow the skills to become isolated in disciplinary silos, lest students leave with the impression that teamwork is only for sports and thinking critically before consuming online media is restricted to English class. Knowing that students are focused on leadership and teamwork in PE, teachers in other disciplines must deliberately ask students to transfer the understandings and skills honed in PE to their math, history, English, art, foreign language, and science tasks. Although the competency might take center stage in one realm—PE—students still need to practice transferring across other realms in order to benefit from this approach.

Whichever approach you choose, they key is to encourage transfer of learning from one subject area to another, a kind of conceptual cross-training. The beauty of the ACT model is that it facilitates this type of learning. Students who have *acquired* an understanding of modern literacy concepts and created mental *connections* among them in one course can then *transfer* this understanding to contexts across the curriculum, always returning to refine and strengthen their original understanding.

From Competencies to Concepts

Just as we can teach the most important concepts of mathematics, science, language arts, for example, through the ACT model, we can use this model to teach the concepts embedded in these modern literacies. Practically everything in life can be viewed through this mental model. Remember the three basic steps for learning transfer? See Figure 4.9 for a review.

Let's take, for instance, the important realm of digital literacy. We can break this down into concepts such as safety and privacy. Students must *acquire* and consolidate surface level learning with each of these important concepts. Next, they can start to see patterns emerge about the relationships between them as they explore situations in digital literacy, such as *How does privacy impact safety online?* These *connections* will better allow them to *transfer* their understanding to new situations in their academic and personal lives.

Once you've identified the specific competencies or areas of focus, we want to identify corresponding concepts and draft conceptual questions that will help students build organizational understanding of these competencies, and then use the ACT model to help students acquire, connect, and transfer understanding of those conceptual relationships. Take a look at Figures 4.10 and 4.11 for an idea for how you can apply the ACT model to these important competencies. Look for nouns or organizing ideas that students can explore in multiple contexts or situations.

Figure 4.9   The ACT Model

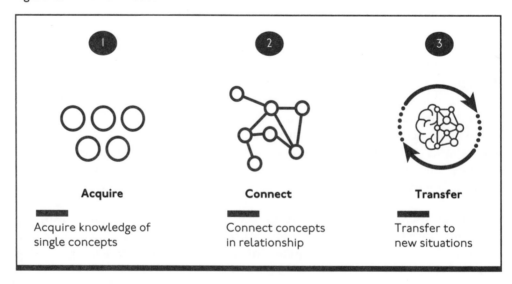

Figure 4.10   Example for ISTE Standards for Digital Literacy

ISTE Standard	Concepts
1. Creativity and innovation Students demonstrate **creative thinking**, construct knowledge, and develop **innovative products** and **processes** using **technology**. a. Apply **existing knowledge** to generate **new ideas, products, or processes.** b. Create *original works* as a means of **personal** or **group expression.** c. Use **models** and **simulations** to explore complex systems and issues. d. Identify **trends** and **forecast possibilities.**	• Creativity • Innovation • Creative thinking • Knowledge construction • Innovative products • Innovative processes • Technology • Existing knowledge • Idea generation • Product generation • Process generation • Original works/originality • Personal expression • Group expression • Models • Simulations • Complex systems • Complex issues • Trends • Possibility forecasts

Figure 4.11   Example for CASEL Competencies for Socioemotional Learning

CASEL Competency	Concepts
Responsible decision-making The ability to make **constructive choices** about **personal behavior** and **social interactions** based on **ethical standards, safety** concerns, **social norms**, the realistic evaluation of **consequences** of various **actions**, and a consideration of the **well-being** of oneself and others. • Identify problems • Analyzing situations • Solving problems • Evaluating • Reflecting • Ethical responsibility	• Constructive choices • Personal behavior • Social interaction • Ethical standards • Safety • Social norms • Consequences • Actions • Well-being

DESIGN STEP

COMPETENCIES TO CONCEPTS

Take one competency you have identified as critical to teach explicitly to your students. Practice identifying the concepts (nouns or short phrases) that underpin the competency. Start with a narrative explanation of the competency by writing your own description or pulling one from an outside resource. Then break it down into its component parts. What are the building blocks or basic elements of this competency?

Figure 4.12   Competencies to Concepts

Competency	Concepts

DESIGN STEP

Record the two or three modern literacy concepts you have chosen in Figure 4.13 below. Then, make sure to flip back to Figure 3.1 and record the modern literacies you chose in your course overview document.

Figure 4.13   Modern Literacies in the Course Overview

Modern Literacies
What new or additional concepts beyond the established disciplines will be a focus of your course to help students to navigate our complex world (one to three concepts)?

From Concepts to Conceptual Connections

For some of us, narrowing our focus to a few manageable and well-fitting ideas is freeing. Now we can block out the noise of all the other modern literacies in order to pursue those that matter most. For others of us, narrowing the list induces a bit of panic. *But what about all the other important modern literacies that don't make the cut?*

Just because you've narrowed your *focus* to two or three modern literacy goals doesn't mean that all the other important 21st century competencies no longer matter. It simply means that now you have a nucleus around which the other modern literacy goals can orbit.

For instance, consider the fifth-grade teacher who selects *kindness* and *resilience* as their modern literacy focus concepts. Does this mean that it's unimportant to teach digital collaboration skills or mindfulness practices? Is this teacher doing a disservice to his colleagues by ignoring the schoolwide focus on multicultural education? Not at all. It means that those things can be touched upon through their relationships to the selected concepts.

The fifth-grade teacher focusing on kindness and resilience can begin to ask questions like these:

- How does kindness translate to *digital spaces*?

- What is the relationship between resilience and *mindfulness*? Can mindfulness practices make us more resilient?

- In what way might learning about *other cultures* help us become kinder and more resilient?

The beauty of the ACT model is that it helps teachers work through the concepts that underpin their craft the same way it helps students work through concepts in the curriculum. Once we establish a few individual concepts to work with, we can reintroduce the other concepts in relationship to our chosen areas of focus.

Building webs of meaning among concepts for ourselves can help us see that just because we've prioritized a few concepts in order to make manageable the plethora of modern literacy goals we have for our students, we aren't casting aside everything that didn't make our cut. Paradoxically, by moving some concepts to the core and others to the periphery we are actually able to incorporate *more* modern literacies into our classrooms because we've given ourselves a more coherent structure in which to apply them.

THINKING PROMPT

STEP 1: IDENTIFY

Write each of the major modern literacy initiatives or concepts you've identified as important—both the two or three focus concepts you selected in Exercise #1 and the others that you consider important but did not choose—on its own index card or sticky note.

STEP 2: ORGANIZE AND CONNECT

Physically place your focus concepts in the center and arrange the other cards in relation to your focus concepts and to each other. Ask yourself the following:

- How do these fit together?

- Which concepts serve as gateways to others?

- Which concepts can be grouped together?

(Continued)

(Continued)

- What happens when I rearrange or reorder these ideas?

- How is everything related?

Keep arranging until your web of concepts mirrors the infrastructure you hope to build in students' brains as they investigate modern literacies throughout the year.

STEP 3: PUT IT INTO WORDS

Now, taking on the perspective of a student in your class, translate your web of concepts into prose. What do you hope students will say they have learned after investigating these concepts in your course? Use first person language. The following sentence frames might help you get started:

- Before taking this class, I had never really thought about _____ and _____ before, but after doing _____, _____, and _____, I now realize that _____.

- I used to think/believe _____, but now I think/believe _____ because _____.

- I am so grateful that my teacher pushed me to consider how _____ relates to _____, because now I understand that _____.

- Although I may forget much of what I learned this year, I will always remember that _____.

- I wish everyone could take this class so they would also come to understand that _____ and _____ impact _____ by _____.

- I am now more prepared to _____ because I understand that _____.

Once we've identified the modern literacy concepts, we can craft questions of conceptual relationship. These questions frame the learning experiences or specific contexts students will explore to deepen their understanding of the connections among concepts. Recall the Learning Transfer Cycle in Figure 4.14.

Figure 4.14   The Learning Transfer Cycle

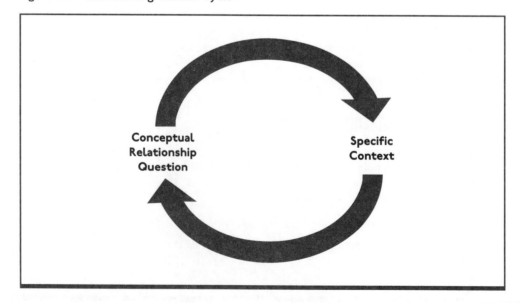

DESIGN STEP

Take a minute to plug your modern literacy concepts into the question stems below. You will continue with this step in the unit planning process, but for now, it's helpful to get a sense of how the modern literacy concepts work in the ACT model and to begin to think of contexts or situations that illustrate the conceptual connections.

Remember, fill the blanks with *concepts* and not details.

- How are _____ and _____ connected?
- What is the relationship between _____ and _____?
- How does _____ impact/affect/influence _____?
- What effect do _____ and _____ have on _____?
- How do _____ and _____ interact?
- What is the role/purpose of _____ in _____?

The following question stems work well for early elementary or as scaffolding questions before reaching the ones above:

- What is the difference between _____ and _____?
- What happens when _____ interacts with _____?
- Why does _____ make _____ [do whatever it does]?
- Why does _____ need _____?

Building a Bridge Between Disciplinary Literacy and Modern Literacy

Each time that we explore a specific context and return to answer the conceptual question, our understanding of the deeper structure of our world is refined and deepened. A corresponding visual in Figure 4.15 illustrates how exploring increasingly dissimilar contexts deepens learning.

We have overlaid these concentric circles on the Learning Transfer Spectrum to illustrate how the conceptual questions can frame a set of increasingly dissimilar, real-world learning experiences where students transfer their understanding multiple times in the learning journey. See Figure 4.16 for an illustration of what we mean.

As transfer shifts from academic to real-world, the demand on students increases substantially. While academic exercises can be designed to minimize distractions and extraneous variables, real-world issues are full of noise and complicating factors. For instance, a math teacher can write a simple story problem asking students how much wire is required for a farmer to build a fence around his corn field to get kids to apply their understanding of perimeter. But an actual farmer solving the same problem must account for much more than just the measured border of his property. The contours of

Learning That Transfers

Figure 4.15   Learning Transfer Cycle Deepens Learning

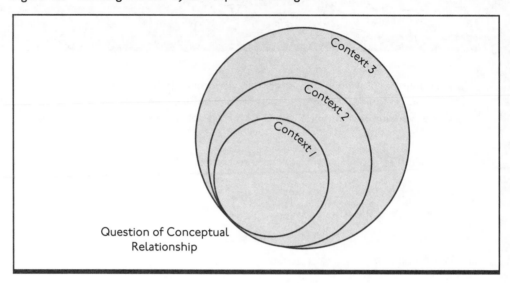

Figure 4.16   Overlay of the Learning Transfer Cycle on the Learning Transfer Spectrum

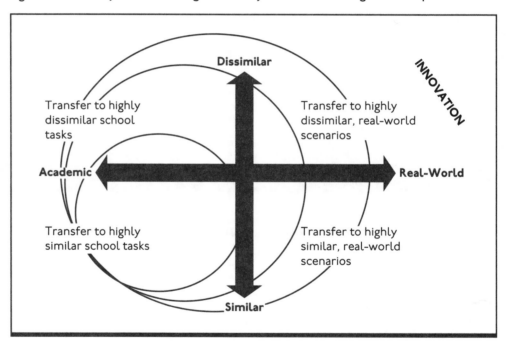

the ground, placement of irrigation channels, and anticipated waste of materials due to the nature of building an actual fence, all impact the amount of wire that is *actually* required to construct such a structure. Similarly, when attempting to solve a problem like the climate crisis, classroom exercises can focus on the scientific or technological aspects alone, while a real-world solution requires attention to economic costs, political feasibility, the nature of diplomacy and cross-cultural collaboration, and the complexities of changing public perceptions and habits.

We move toward the real-world side of the spectrum when students use their conceptual understanding to

- Solve complex, *real* challenges
- Utilize concepts from multiple disciplines

- Present their findings to authentic audiences

- Impact the world around them

Essentially, as we ask students to transfer their understandings derived in an academic context to increasingly "real" phenomena, they will require tools beyond the discipline, including those found in modern literacies. Consider the following examples from a third-grade interdisciplinary class, a seventh-grade world history class, and a ninth-grade Algebra I class and contemplate the following questions:

- How do the *disciplinary literacy concepts* (italicized) interact with the **modern literacy concepts** (bolded)?

- How does the sequence of learning experiences build a bridge between the disciplinary literacy concepts and modern literacy concepts?

How Do Healthy Choices, Active Lifestyles, Culture, and Resilience Interact?

Grade 3—*healthy choices* (health), *active lifestyle* (PE), *other cultures* (social studies), **resilience**

- Students examine stories from other cultures about how those cultures make healthy choices and maintain an active lifestyle. They look at difficulties some of these cultures may face and how they develop resilience in the face of obstacles; they reflect on the role of resilience in living healthy lives.

- Students investigate their own communities to compare healthy choices and active lifestyles to the cultures from other communities. They also compare common obstacles and the ways that people show resilience to overcome those obstacles (e.g., where they live is very cold for much of the year, and people figure out ways to maintain physical activity such as indoor water parks or winter sports).

- Students make action plans for how they will demonstrate resilience to potential obstacles in their lives, how they will make healthy choices, and maintain active lifestyles. They share two things they learned from other cultures that they would like to try in their own lives. They ask their families to sign healthy lifestyle plans.

See Figure 4.17 for an illustration of what these contexts look like on the Learning Transfer Spectrum.

How Does the Author's Point of View and Bias Impact His or Her Account of What Happened?

World History—*point of view, bias*, **digital literacy**

- Students read teacher-provided primary source accounts of factory work in 18th century Britain. As they analyze the sources, they consider the question, *How does the author's point of view and bias impact his or her account of what happened?*

- Students read teacher-provided primary source accounts of working conditions in modern sweatshops, still asking themselves how *point of view* and *bias* impact the accounts.

- Students investigate various companies' labor practices by finding their own sources online. They keep asking themselves how point of view and bias shape the messages they are finding and teaches them ways to identify bias in internet sources. They create awareness posters to place around the school about the labor practices of common products used among the students in the school.

Figure 4.17   Grade 3 Progression Example

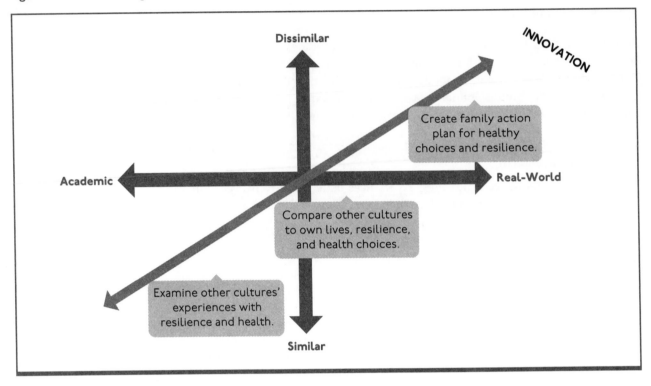

See Figure 4.18 for an illustration of what these contexts look like on the Learning Transfer Spectrum.

Figure 4.18   World History Progression Example

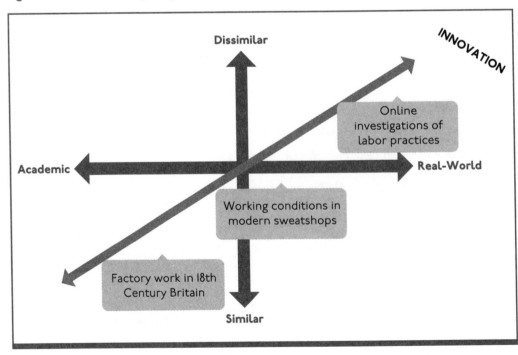

How Does Our Ability to Critique Representations Help Us Better Communicate Information?

Algebra I—*representations, critique,* **multimodal communication**

- Students create different representations of linear and nonlinear relationships—equation, table of values, and graph—and then critique each other's work based on how clear and accurate it is.

- Students consider different representations of data related to climate change, including equations, table of values, and graphs that show both linear and non-linear relationships between carbon emissions and global warming. They critique each representation and debate which one communicates the relationship between these two elements most compellingly.

- Student groups research the proposed carbon emission standards set forth by the Paris Climate Agreement, create table of values and graphs to depict the data, and forecast the impact of the plan. Then they critique the plan and design a social media campaign consisting of a variety of communication modes, from visual memes to audio clips, videos, and plain old text, to communicate their analysis to an audience of their peers.

See Figure 4.19 for an illustration of what these contexts look like on the Learning Transfer Spectrum.

Figure 4.19   Algebra I Progression Example

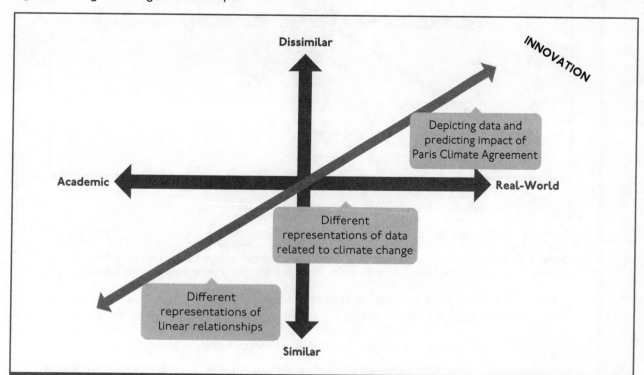

Step 1: Brainstorm

Imagine the series of experiences that might build a bridge between the disciplinary literacy concepts you've selected (from Chapter 2) and the modern literacy priorities you've identified in this chapter. Use the template in Figure 4.20 or 4.21 to help you.

Keep in mind that this is just an exercise, not a unit plan set in stone! The primary goal here is to understand the relationship between the disciplinary literacy and modern literacy components of your course.

THINKING PROMPT

This prompt will come in handy in Chapters 6 through 8 when we get to unit planning. For now, we simply want you to play with how disciplinary literacy and modern literacy concepts are linked in your context.

Figure 4.20   Bridging Disciplinary and Modern Literacy Template

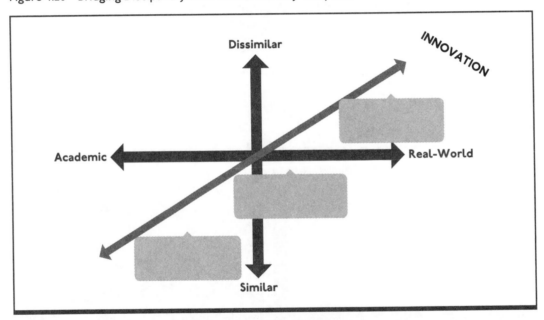

If you prefer more space or an easier visual to navigate, you can use Figure 4.21 to brainstorm three contexts that could bridge the disciplinary literacy and modern literacy concepts.

Figure 4.21   Bridging Disciplinary Literacy and Modern Literacy Template 2

Steps	Learning Experiences
Start with disciplinary lenses in a discipline-specific (academic) context.	

Steps	Learning Experiences
Bridge	
Incorporate modern literacy concepts in a more complex, real-world context.	

online resources ⌕ Available for download at www.learningthattransfers.com.

Step 2: Reflect

- How might modern literacies help students transfer their understanding of disciplinary literacy concepts to real-world scenarios?

- In what ways do your modern literacy concepts reinforce and extend disciplinary literacy concepts?

HORIZONTAL ALIGNMENT TO PROMOTE CROSS-DISCIPLINARY BREADTH

Whether students are looking to raise awareness about pollution in a local pond, or attempting to address unemployment, the nature of these problems involves the concepts and thinking of more than one discipline. Considering the complexity of modern life, institutions, and systems, very few real-world problems are limited to a single discipline. This isn't new, life has always been interdisciplinary, but the complexity and number of overlapping fields will only continue to increase as we learn more about ourselves and our world. An interdisciplinary approach to learning not only illustrates the relevance and interconnected relationships of different domains, it also allows students to view issues or problems from multiple perspectives, increases the strength of their mental model, integrate ideas from multiple disciplines, and be innovative problem solvers (Repko, 2008).

Most problems that we encounter are what author David Epstein calls wicked contexts—domains where there's a lack of discipline-specific models, repetitive patterns, or clear feedback that can be consistently relied upon to solve problems. Epstein (2019) makes the claim that "breadth of training predicts breadth of transfer. That is, the more contexts in which something is learned, the more the learner creates abstract models, and the less they rely on any particular example. Learners become better at applying their knowledge to a situation they've never seen before, which is the essence of creativity" (p. 76).

Many mathematics teachers have seen examples of this in the classroom. If students are asked to understand and solve problems across multiple representations and formats, they are much better at transferring their understanding to problems that are structured differently. Conversely, if students only practice problems that are very similar, it is hard for them to later transfer and solve a different problem that isn't structured the same way or in a very familiar context.

Conceptual connections provide an important link between and among the disciplines, and as a means to access new and complex situations. Consider this example from neuroscience: Students learning about magnets can relate information of other areas about the concepts of positive and negative. For instance, they can read a story about how opposites attract, a familiar concept found in many fables such as the *Frog and Toad* stories (Lobel, 1970). Each context, no matter how different in surface features, builds neural pathways that create patterns in the brain when accessed through organizing concepts and their connections, enabling easier retrieval (McTighe & Willis, 2019). Conceptual connections provide both disciplinary depth and cross-disciplinary breadth.

The goal is to point students to the deeper structures of how the world is organized, and that is achieved through concepts and their connections. If we want to move education away from its current emphasis on isolated standards and siloed subject areas and toward transferable concepts and skills, we can work to balance the deep and narrow disciplinary work of individual subjects with a broader interdisciplinary perspective. This balance will allow students to apply the *conceptual structures* of the disciplines in meaningful ways (Kalantzis & Cope, 2013). Domain-specific expertise and interdisciplinary thinking are not a set of competing perspectives but are a complementary set of tools.

> Innovations that make a sizable impact only happen in what Johansson (2017) calls the "intersection"—where the concepts from one field intersect with the concepts from another.

In fact, Frans Johansson (2017), author of the breakthrough book, *The Medici Effect*, believes that the type of innovations that make a sizable impact only happen in what he calls the "intersection"—where the concepts from one field intersect with the concepts from another. These points of intersection lead to a cascade of new ideas and insights that fuel meaningful problem-solving and might even open whole new domains of study.

The examples detailed in *The Medici Effect* are proof of the power of intersectional thinking and learning transfer—architectural design inspired by nature, investment bankers gleaning insight from grain traders, and Disney's Pixar Studio's design process where computer-based animators take acting lessons in order to breathe life into the characters. These examples demonstrate the innovation that is possible when we explore the intersection between different disciplines and remove the barriers that trap us in one mode of thinking.

If we want curriculum to align with the goal of creating innovators, we should consider ways to encourage students to integrate different bodies of knowledge and give them opportunities to apply that learning to the real world. Much like we encourage schools to articulate a conceptual framework across grade levels to build disciplinary depth, we propose creating a cross-disciplinary conceptual framework for modern literacies. This process aids teachers in coordinating their efforts to build these important skills in an intentional and concerted way.

The trickiest thing about proposing cross-disciplinary instruction for secondary schools is that everything is set up to be siloed: departmental structure, curriculum, planning times, even teacher training. These factors create structural hurdles and mental barriers that make it more difficult. Although the structural issues will have to be tackled at the school or district level, we've developed some tools based on a few different approaches that will provide choice in helping educators create some more organic points of intersection and overlap with their curriculum.

First, let's establish a concrete term and definition for different approaches to cross-disciplinary learning design: **multidisciplinary**, **interdisciplinary**, and **transdisciplinary** (Refsum Jensenius, 2012).

- **Multidisciplinary:** Learning experiences requiring knowledge from several disciplines, but each stay within their boundaries

- **Interdisciplinary:** Learning experiences requiring analysis, synthesis, and harmonizing links between disciplines to create a new, coherent whole

- **Transdisciplinary:** Learning experiences that transcend the traditional boundaries of several disciplines

Though we believe these definitions are helpful, it's important to not get too caught up in the minutiae of each. We don't supply them as a means to impose rigid requirements, but to provide a language that helps you conceptualize the different types of cross-disciplinary teaching and learning that's possible. Each approach is illustrated in Figure 4.22 and defined in Figure 4.23; the circles represent the different disciplines, with increasingly more cross-disciplinary alignment from left to right.

Multidisciplinary: Learning experiences requiring knowledge from several disciplines, but each stay within their boundaries.

Interdisciplinary: Learning experiences requiring analysis, synthesis, and harmonizing links between disciplines to create a new, coherent whole.

Transdisciplinary: Learning experiences that transcend the traditional boundaries of several disciplines.

Figure 4.22   Common Approaches to Cross-Disciplinary Integration

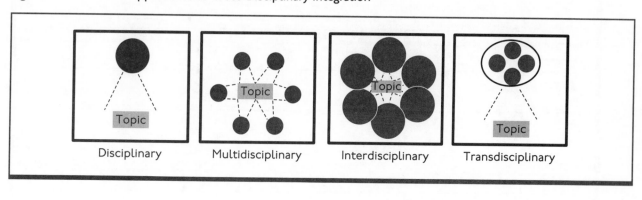

Disciplinary   Multidisciplinary   Interdisciplinary   Transdisciplinary

Figure 4.23   Defining Common Approaches to Cross-Disciplinary Integration

Cross-Disciplinary Approach	Description	Ways to Create Organic Alignment and Intersection
Multidisciplinary	Learning experiences requiring knowledge from several disciplines, but each stay within their boundaries	Find a real-world issue and consider the different ways each discipline might approach solving it. This can be done simply by combining a single discipline with a modern literacy.
Interdisciplinary	Learning experiences requiring analysis, synthesis, and harmonizing links between disciplines to create a new, coherent whole	Look at standards, curriculum documents, disciplinary lenses, etc., and find concepts and skills that overlap or intersect with each discipline.
Transdisciplinary	Learning experiences that transcend the traditional boundaries of several disciplines	Create a list of concepts that transcend the traditional disciplinary boundaries and can be an anchoring and organizing force in each grade level or department's curriculum.

SOURCE: Descriptions adapted from Refsum Jensenius (2012).

THINKING PROMPT

At this point, which of the approaches seems like the most logical place to start based on your current context? It's important to note that all of these approaches can be accomplished by an individual teacher—it's all about which modern literacies and, potentially, additional disciplines you feel comfortable incorporating into your own course. Of course, it helps if multiple teachers of the same group of students coordinate their efforts, but that is not essential. We can integrate a modern literacy into a single course to promote cross-disciplinary breadth.

_____

_____

_____

_____

_____

Multidisciplinary Alignment: Staying Within Disciplinary Boundaries

Perhaps the simplest approach to cross-disciplinary teaching, especially at the secondary level, is to pick a real-world challenge and have each discipline draw up their own list of concepts and skills that would be necessary to solve this problem. Students won't be blending concepts and skills from several disciplines as much as they'll be focusing on how experts from each unique discipline might approach solving a particular problem. It's reflective of the type of real-world problem solving that occurs when experts from different fields work separately from one another on solving a problem.

Consider a schoolwide project where each class is thinking about the different ways that they can help raise awareness about pollution happening in a local river. Each department draws up separate concepts based on how their uniquely positioned discipline might approach the problem, and then use the ACT model to gradually build to this real-world transfer task. Once students have acquired, connected, and transferred their understanding of discipline-specific concepts, they are ready to apply them to the pollution in the local river.

During science classes, students may conduct a project where they take samples from the river and conduct a lab to evaluate and record the level of contamination in their samples. To better understand why the pollution problem started in the first place, during mathematics classes students might form data collection committees where they go into the community to create and compile a data set providing insight into local perspectives and attitudes on things like recycling, sustainability, and waste. Meanwhile, during English language arts classes, students could focus on persuasive writing or speaking so they can change the hearts and minds of their friends and neighbors. After several rounds of revision, each student will submit a short video to the town public comments website about why the town should start giving more time and attention to local conservation efforts.

In this example, each discipline is operating relatively independent of one another. They all might be working toward the same goal, but there is little overlap of content or concepts. Each discipline's learning experience is focused on developing its own unique ways of knowing, doing, and thinking. We don't see that as necessarily a good or bad thing! It's all about what works best for the educators, students, and situation.

THINKING PROMPT

How would this approach work in your current situation?

_____

_____

_____

_____

_____

Interdisciplinary Alignment:
Overlap and Harmonize Two or More Disciplines

Another way to approach cross-disciplinary teaching and learning is to look for common overlapping and intersecting concepts that already exist within your existing curriculum. This is most easily accomplished by focusing on more similar disciplines—English language arts pairing with history or mathematics pairing with science, for example. Students still approach learning experiences from a distinct disciplinary perspective, but unlike multidisciplinary, the edges of each will eventually start to overlap into one another and strengthen the thinking and resulting learning due to their harmony.

For instance, an English class might be exploring Macbeth's journey from honorable nobleman to disgraced king at the same time an American history class is learning about the wiretapping conducted by Nixon during the Watergate scandal. Even though these events occurred in radically different historical contexts, they are both excellent contexts to explore ways power, greed, and ambition impact one's morality and leadership. Students might still be studying these events separately in each class, but they're able to leverage the conceptual understanding they've gained in one discipline to interpret a situation from a different discipline. The knowledge gained from each class remains anchored by their disciplinary frame but overlap. These intersections create an interesting grey area where students can gain insight that will help them transfer understanding across disciplines.

> In an interdisciplinary approach, students might study events or content separately in each class, but they're able to leverage the conceptual understanding they've gained in one discipline to interpret a situation from a different discipline.

Or consider a project where students are attempting to raise awareness about the United Nations' Sustainable Development Goal, "Clean Water and Sanitation." Typically, teachers might explore issues of sustainability in science class where they learn about how plastic pollution harms coastal ecosystems. Students might make a poster, deliver a speech, or design a video demonstrating their understanding of concepts related to the field of science based on several contexts. When taking an interdisciplinary approach, however, students are able to examine the issue from a variety of perspectives that help them understand the depth and complexity required to solve these problems. Because the thoughts and actions of human beings are so often at the center of sustainability challenges, one central transfer point across these diverse issues is our understanding of our own species.

Building on the conceptual connections across disciplines can provide a more integrated understanding of the complex topics embedded in the UN Sustainable Development Goals, such as reducing poverty, pollution, and hunger across the globe. Instead of only focusing on helping students understand problems like climate change from a scientific perspective, they can explore the underlying cultural and cognitive mechanisms that shape our beliefs and perspectives about those topics, or that motivate humans to engage in unsustainable behaviors in the first place. This perspective is currently being leveraged to great effect by our collaborators, Susan Hanisch and Dustin Eirdosh, at *Global Education for Sustainable Development* (www.globalesd.org), whose curriculum is centered on understanding the human condition as an interdisciplinary theme. Their growing collection of open-access resources is anchored by cross-cutting concepts and principles from anthropology, behavioral science, and sustainability science.

As important as it is for students to understand the dangers of climate change and risks of plastic pollution, it's equally important they understand how human behaviors brought us to the current situation in the first place, and why people develop certain beliefs about those topics. Understanding the origins and effects of the values that inform people's perspective will help them understand how to change the minds and hearts of those who might otherwise oppose their work. In this way, the idea behind Global ESD is to provide an interdisciplinary scientific basis that can harness several disciplines to achieve understanding around the giant issues that our current generation of children will have to solve.

Consider how much more potent students' ability for real change might be if they used interdisciplinary concepts like development, culture, cooperation, heritage, interdependence, and sustainability to supplement and connect across their disciplinary understandings. With this frame in mind, students might study different cultures through analyzing their traditional stories that are passed down through the generations in English language arts, research current and historical examples of effective social cooperation in social studies, and learn about the ways computer simulations of sustainable resources use dilemmas to reveal meaningful and transferable insights through mathematics.

For instance, kindergarten teachers could infuse responsibility and ethical decision-making into a unit on human–environmental interaction. The key difference here is that the students move fluidly between concepts and skills within mathematics, science, and language arts, without interrupting the flow of their learning for "science class time" or "language arts class time." See Figure 4.24 for an example unit on caring

Figure 4.24   Kindergarten Interdisciplinary Example

Unit Title: Caring for Nature		
Real-World Contexts: school playground, local park, plastic pollution in water systems	**Modern Literacies**: responsibility, ethical decision-making	
Disciplinary Lenses: interdependence, communication, quantity	**Compelling Question**: What are the best ways for us to interact with other living things and our environment?	
Science Conceptual Questions What makes something living? What makes something part of nature or the environment? What is the relationship between people and nature? How do our senses impact our learning? How do my classmates impact my learning?	**English Conceptual Questions** How can I develop oral communication skills? What is the role of body language in communication? What makes active listening different from passive listening?	**Mathematics Conceptual Questions** Why do we count? What effect does the order of objects have on counting? What is the purpose of the last number when we count? What is the role of counting in our everyday lives? How can we represent quantities in everyday life with numbers?

Students will examine many common habits of the school community and determine a plan, which they will present orally to the principal, for ways to increase responsibility and ethical decision-making within the school.

for nature. The science content drives the unit, while the practices of language arts and mathematics are infused into the topic of nature. We will walk through unit planning steps in Chapter 6; this is simply to show one way in which all of the elements can come together for an interdisciplinary unit.

THINKING PROMPT

How would this approach work in your current situation?

_____

_____

_____

_____

_____

Transdisciplinary Alignment: Blur the Lines Separating the Different Disciplines

Another way to approach cross-disciplinary instruction is to have students interpret and analyze a shared set of broad concepts through different contexts, moving even more fluidly among the long-standing academic disciplines. We might apply various disciplinary lenses to the context at hand, but there is much less conscious effort to label the concepts and skills as "mathematics" and so on. We find the Human Experience Concepts introduced in Chapter 3 are a great entry point for transdisciplinary alignment, as students consider the ways in which each discipline approaches these concepts. Figure 4.25 includes examples of these concepts again as a reminder.

In this approach, the concepts and their relationship provide a sense of coherence across each discipline, blurring the lines between the disciplines, even if still technically using the tools and ways of thinking of the specific disciplines. It's a great way to encourage staff and students both to engage in fruitful dialogue about concepts that play a vital role in shaping the human experience.

For instance, students could pursue a transdisciplinary unit exploring the concept of _authenticity,_ exploring questions such as, _How do we determine what is real, valid, and true? What does it mean to be authentic?_ They could investigate authenticity in relationships, song lyrics, social media posts, news stories, famous sports' players, politicians, consumer goods, data representations, and food products. The concept of authenticity drives the exploration, and they would indeed draw upon specific concepts and skills within all of the long-standing academic disciplines, but the boundaries are certainly less firm than in the multi- or interdisciplinary approaches.

Figure 4.25   Sample Human-Experience Concepts

Humanities and the Arts		Science	Mathematics
Friendship	Power	Survival	Question asking
Insecurities	Control	Equilibrium	Pattern seeking
Belonging	Chaos	Balance	Meaning-making
Truth	Ignorance	Interdependence	Communication
Courage	Identity	Force	Equality, equal
Fear	Bias	Attraction	Simplicity, simplified
Dreams	Beauty	Symbiotic	Precision
Experiences	Injustice	Interaction	Symmetry
Family dynamics	Hate	Adaptation	Deviation
Redemption	Justice	Diversity	Balance
Authenticity	Systems	Systems	Flexibility
Storytelling	Freedom	Variation	Order
Ego	Belief	Cooperation	Solution

Many broad concepts such as *system*, *patterns*, *interdependence*, and *change* can also foster transdisciplinary exploration. The International Baccalaureate's Primary Years Program (PYP) uses this approach to harness the innate curiosity of young children as they explore the world around them. Rather than dividing instructional time around the established disciplinary boundaries such as mathematics and language arts, students typically explore transdisciplinary themes such as "How we express ourselves" and "Sharing the planet." Students learn numeracy, literacy, social studies, and more via these themes and broad concepts. We find this to be an excellent approach especially for younger students, especially when the broad concepts are rounded out with discipline-specific concepts (called related concepts in the PYP) such as quantity, word choice, tone, or authority.

At the secondary level, one can imagine the type of rich conversation that would emerge from students examining these powerful, enduring concepts from a variety of angles and perspectives. Instead of simply stating, *Systems are made of interconnected and coordinated parts* after a unit on the United States' three bodies of government, students could apply the ways of thinking, knowing, and doing of other disciplines to inquire more deeply into the conceptual relationship. Perhaps one student might suggest systems require energy to function correctly, recalling a lesson from their chemistry class. Then another could offer their understanding that, when systems collapse, those relying on them are placed in jeopardy, citing their recent analysis of overfishing in the Mediterranean. Perhaps another student might suggest that even a single errant part of a system creates undesirable results, relating it to their knowledge of mathematical proofs. Each of these perspectives would generate more discussion and a more in-depth analysis of the initial context, as well as providing a more comprehensive understanding of "systems" in the abstract.

What new insights might be gained if students were constantly switching disciplinary lenses when evaluating concepts and conceptual relationships? How might their understanding shift or evolve when a universal concept enters into a new relationship with more specific disciplinary concepts? This ability to compare and contrast disciplinary perspectives on transdisciplinary concepts leads to more profound inquiry and insight than simply crafting a single conceptual connection.

For some secondary teachers, the thought of planning horizontally with different disciplines might seem intimidating or not realistic at first. We again encourage you to think about your current situation and how you can take a step toward making this a reality. Do you have consistent writing expectations across all content areas, not just in language arts classrooms? Do you know topics in other disciplines that connect to your course? Thinking of simple connections at first can lead to much more creative and integrated planning in the future. The key is to just take the first step.

Figure 4.26 shows an example of horizontal alignment by grade level from a school in Washington, DC. Curriculum leaders worked with teachers to determine the type of reading and writing focus that all Grade 6 teachers would cultivate with their students per quarter. They also coordinated concepts related to the human experience and modern literacies of critical thinking and socioemotional learning. They also assigned the specific course that would take the lead on a research project each quarter.

Figure 4.26   Example Horizontal Alignment Across Grade 6

	Quarter 1	Quarter 2	Quarter 3	Quarter 4
Reading/Writing Focus	Literary text Argumentative writing	Informational text Explanatory writing	Literary text Explanatory writing	Informational text Argumentative writing
Human Experience Concepts	Culture and identity	Freedom	Relationships and interdependence	Power and justice
Modern Literacy: Social-Emotional Concepts	Recognizing strengths	Self-discipline	Teamwork	Empathy
Modern Literacy: Critical Thinking Concepts	Clarity	Accuracy	Precision	Clarity, accuracy, precision
Research Project per Quarter	Geography	English language arts	Earth science	Health

Scan the QR code for cross-curricular alignment planning templates.

Notice that this team of teachers decided to share several areas of focus to bring coherence to the student experience. For instance, in the first quarter of the year, students investigated the concepts of culture and identity in every class, providing a sense of continuity across disciplines. Not only did this help tie the disciplines together, it helped set them apart. As students traveled from class to class, considering these concepts in different discipline-specific contexts, they came to understand how geographers, scientists, literary scholars, and health advocates approach the concepts differently.

When it came to research, though, they decided to coordinate across disciplines to ensure that students were learning research skills throughout the year without being overburdened with several research tasks all at once. The geography teacher introduced a set of research skills that the English and earth science teachers could then build upon and extend. The health teacher could then ask students to transfer the skills gained in the first three quarters to a much more complex research task at the end of the year.

Now that we have explored a variety of approaches, let's take a moment to think about your context and what might make the most sense for you. You may want to explore the horizontal alignment tables in the companion website for further discussion and examples of how you might align your curriculum across disciplines.

THINKING PROMPT

How would this approach work in your current situation?

_____

_____

_____

_____

_____

DESIGN STEP

How might you plan for cross-disciplinary integration based on your context? What factors do you need to consider?

_____

_____

_____

_____

_____

The Importance of Metacognition

No matter how we incorporate modern literacies and other cross-disciplinary approaches, the key is to remember that the ACT model is *cyclical*, not *linear*. By this we mean that we never arrive at an end point where our understanding or skill level is complete and, thus, ready to transfer to every situation that may arise. Students cannot study leadership in one class and then apply their learning indiscriminately across the curriculum without stopping to think, unlearn, and relearn.

While we want students to recognize patterns, we must acknowledge that each situation brings unique differences that must be accounted for while applying what we know. Deciphering these differences and considering the ways in which a prior understanding is *not* transferable to a new situation is just as important as noticing the patterns.

In this way, learning for transfer is much more akin to being a jazz musician than a member of the orchestra. In an orchestral group, the goal of practice is to play the same piece of music flawlessly in concert with others in order to replicate that performance for an audience. Each note has its place and will not move. Sure, the conductor's cues may lead to slightly different outcomes each time the group plays a piece, but the group is mainly working to arrive at one preferred version of the song. With enough practice, the group can play the piece with near automaticity. Jazz musicians, on the other hand, draw upon their knowledge of music—notes, chords, harmonies, rhythms—to improvise. The goal is not to play the same song in a predictable way each time, but rather to use the principles of music to experiment with sound and play off of the decisions of other members of the ensemble. Instead of refining a performance by making it more predictable, jazz musicians practice to invent new and surprising musical experiences.

If we teach kids to approach learning like a member of the orchestra, they'll be sorely disappointed when the conceptual understanding they've developed is not the "right answer" to any real-world problem or when they realize the world is not a cookie-cutter replica of their classroom experiences. Instead, we need our kids to be students of jazz, internalizing the basic building blocks while embracing the idea that those elements should be used in new and surprising ways.

This is where metacognition—the process of monitoring one's own thinking—comes in. As students approach a messy, complex real-world situation, they will need to draw upon disciplinary expertise and modern literacies in flexible ways, always attentive to the limitations of their prior knowledge and experience. So, rather than encountering a new task with brazen confidence—*Aha! I've seen this before and know just what to do!*—students must maintain a sense of skepticism about the extent to which their current thinking applies to the context at hand.

The ACT model, when treated as a cycle with no end point, encourages students to internalize this posture. Every time they begin to transfer their understanding, they must intentionally seek out the unique features of the situation before them. Once they've worked through this new scenario, the cycle demands that they return to their prior understanding to weave in new concepts acquired in the new context and to reimagine the connections among concepts in light of their experience. In other words, the ACT model demands that students develop metacognitive awareness and constantly monitor their own thinking.

The habit of monitoring one's thinking and consciously examining the limits of one's knowledge is essential for innovation. In order to recognize creative solutions to complex problems, we have to think anew rather than rotely apply our previous thoughts. As Figure 4.27 suggests, we believe that innovation lies at the intersection of disciplinary expertise, modern literacies, and metacognition. In other words, students are best equipped to tackle the challenges of the 21st century when they can flexibly harness the power of both specialized and generalized ways of knowing.

Figure 4.27 Weaving Essential Elements to Innovation

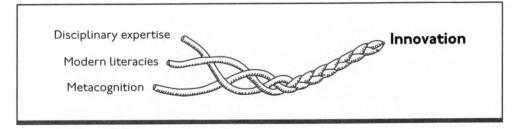

CONCLUSION

At the outset of this chapter, we acknowledged that in order to prepare students to meet the demands of the 21st century, we need to teach beyond the traditional academic disciplines. The various initiatives—new competencies, new pedagogical tools, new conceptualizations of what it means to teach and learn—aimed at preparing students for the complexities of modern life can be united under the umbrella of modern literacies. Traditionally, schools and teachers have approached these initiatives as burdensome—and stress inducing!—add-ons to an already crowded curriculum, forcing teachers to juggle too many priorities and, in the end, execute all of them rather poorly.

However, we think there's another way. By more fully envisioning the role that modern literacies play in solving real-world problems, and how they relate to the core of our disciplines, we can narrow our focus and anchor our courses in these important elements without having them feel extraneous. In fact, as long as we are teaching for transfer and guiding kids along the path from academic to real-world transfer, we will automatically be pulling in modern literacy goals, because that is what real-world transfer demands.

Coordinating this work across disciplines not only makes it more manageable for teachers and coherent for students, but also pushes students to transfer modern literacy concepts across a broader range of scenarios. Of course, they'll need to employ metacognitive practices in order to transfer their learning thoughtfully and flexibly, rather than rotely or automatically. But in doing so, they will be "practicing" like they'll be asked to "play," so to speak, since metacognition is an essential component of innovation.

THINKING PROMPT

Take a moment to reflect on how your thinking has expanded over the course of this chapter:

- How does teaching for **transfer** interact with **modern literacies** and **real-world challenges**?

- How can I build a conceptual **bridge** between **disciplinary literacy** and **modern literacy** in my course?

- How and why might we use the **ACT model** to align modern literacy instruction **across disciplines**?

- What role does **metacognition** play in all of this?

_____

_____

_____

_____

_____

CHAPTER FIVE

The Story of Your Course
How Do We Craft a Compelling Narrative to Guide Learning?

"The teacher is of course an artist but being an artist does not mean that he or she can make the profile, can shape the students. What the educator does in teaching is to make it possible for the students to become themselves."

—Paulo Freire

Why does this chapter matter?	It helps to think about the intellectual journey of our students so that they can come to appreciate the beauty of our course and how it applies to their lives.
What will I be able to do by the end of this chapter?	I will be able to sequence all of my content into a cohesive narrative and articulate the year-long journey that will engage the intellect of my students.

In this chapter, we synthesize the big picture goals of transferable learning that you established in Chapters 3 and 4—the disciplinary lenses and modern literacies that help our students apply their learning within and beyond our disciplines—into a compelling narrative that ties each unit and lesson into a cohesive whole. In other words, this chapter is devoted to big picture planning with the scope of the entire course in mind. The following chapters will dive into specific unit planning, assessment, and instruction.

> This chapter is devoted to big picture planning with the scope of the entire course in mind.

Let's review what we have discussed thus far. Today's fast-paced, complex world requires us to prepare students to navigate their world, to make sense of complexity, and construct meaningful lives and communities. In the previous chapters, we came to understand the basics of the ACT model and what might be possible with a focus on learning that transfers. We drafted a vision for our discipline that conceives of the interconnected whole instead of atomized standards or learning outcomes and considered additional modern literacies that our students need in order to be successful in a rapidly changing world.

Now comes time to design the overall story of your course so that we take students on an intellectual journey in our classrooms, instead of marching them through a pacing guide. This slight shift in mindset is the tipping point for dramatic differences in instruction. We will begin by articulating this journey in the form of a story, a narrative that describes the arc of learning from the start of the year to its end. Then, in the next chapter, we will create unit plans that align to that journey.

THINKING PROMPT

Before we move on, let's pause and reflect on your current thinking on the following questions:

- How do you currently think about sequencing your units over the course of the school year?

- How might articulating a narrative or story of your course impact student learning?

_____

_____

_____

_____

_____

CHAPTER STRUCTURE

This chapter is organized around the following sections:

- Critical steps for arranging content in a transfer-focused course
  - Prioritize thoughtfully
  - Arrange effectively
  - Supplement strategically
  - Flow cohesively
  - Create a course at-a-glance
- Articulating an overall story of your course
  - Story of your course
  - Going visual and crafting the moral of the story

THE CRITICAL STEPS IN A TRANSFER-FOCUSED COURSE

A transfer-focused course must place attention on deeper structures of both disciplinary literacy and modern literacies. You have spent the past two chapters zeroing in on the components of these literacies and now it's time to think specifically about your course.

We have pored over research, curriculum documents, and resources to identify the steps needed to use standards of learning to design a course that is both intellectually rigorous and meaningful for students. The synthesis of our findings are four important attributes listed in Figure 5.1—*prioritized* thoughtfully, *arranged* effectively, *supplemented* strategically, and *flows* cohesively. These attributes can be used whether you are working on a curriculum team or in your own classroom.

Figure 5.1 **Critical Steps for Designing a Transfer-Focused Course**

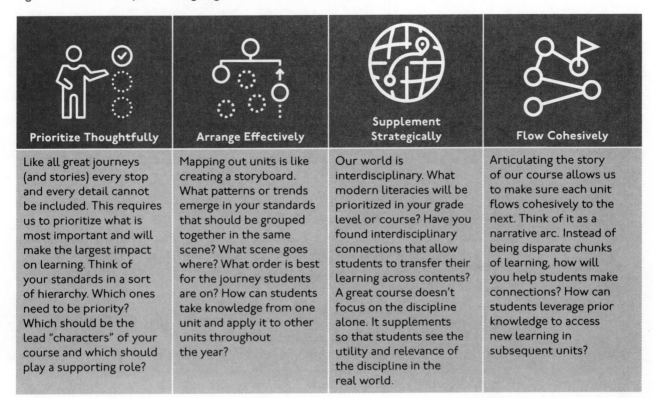

Prioritize Thoughtfully	Arrange Effectively	Supplement Strategically	Flow Cohesively
Like all great journeys (and stories) every stop and every detail cannot be included. This requires us to prioritize what is most important and will make the largest impact on learning. Think of your standards in a sort of hierarchy. Which ones need to be priority? Which should be the lead "characters" of your course and which should play a supporting role?	Mapping out units is like creating a storyboard. What patterns or trends emerge in your standards that should be grouped together in the same scene? What scene goes where? What order is best for the journey students are on? How can students take knowledge from one unit and apply it to other units throughout the year?	Our world is interdisciplinary. What modern literacies will be prioritized in your grade level or course? Have you found interdisciplinary connections that allow students to transfer their learning across contents? A great course doesn't focus on the discipline alone. It supplements so that students see the utility and relevance of the discipline in the real world.	Articulating the story of our course allows us to make sure each unit flows cohesively to the next. Think of it as a narrative arc. Instead of being disparate chunks of learning, how will you help students make connections? How can students leverage prior knowledge to access new learning in subsequent units?

The following exercises will walk you through the process of designing a course journey for your students.

Prioritize Thoughtfully

In Chapter 3, we looked at standards as a means of understanding the larger patterns and structures within the discipline, adding them up in to a coherent whole instead of breaking them down into an atomized maze. However, we are still left with an overwhelming number of standards to teach in a given school year. In fact, the problem of too many outcomes required across North American states and provinces is well documented (Ainsworth, 2019). And not just by a little—often by a lot. One analysis found that we would have to add TEN years to schooling in order to teach all that is included in many state standards in the United States (Marzano & Kendall, 1998). Exercise #1 will help you prioritize and organize standards in order to best use the content of your course to achieve your disciplinary vision.

Think about this process as analogous to building a barbed-wire fence. We need some standards, ideas, or pieces of content to serve as posts. The posts of the fence need to be sturdy, intentional features designed to support the wire and give it shape. They are planted deeply and expected to stand the test of time; a strong storm might shake the wire loose, but the posts must hold their ground. Similarly, some pieces of content must form an enduring structure upon which the rest of our content can be "strung." Five, ten, or twenty years from now, when students are attempting to assimilate a new piece of knowledge with their prior learning—when they click on an article about biodiversity, stumble upon a new romantic poem, pick up a book about Thomas Jefferson, or examine the latest report on fossil fuel emissions—they should be able to situate the new information within the posts of their mental fence.

Of course, most of the fence is not made up of posts. The majority of our content becomes, in service of this metaphor, the wire that connects one post to the next. This does not mean that the majority of our content is unimportant; the fence cannot serve its purpose without the wire. But, it does mean that the majority of our content is not built to last. Students will soon forget the particulars of *The Outsiders* or the Krebs cycle. Should they need this knowledge later in life, they will likely need to brush up on the details.

In order to prioritize and organize the standards of your course, you need to distinguish the posts from the wire. Unfortunately, curriculum documents are not always set up to make this an easy process.

Take the standards in Figure 5.2, for example. If a teacher were to attempt to march through them in order, giving each relatively equal weight, the content becomes almost incomprehensible. Day 1 is spent debating the effectiveness of isolationism while Day 2 jumps to the rise of fascism in Europe; Day 3 asks students to trace events leading to American involvement in World War II, which is followed up by locating key alliance members on a map.

However, if we step back to build a framework of meaning from these standards, three key ideas stand out as posts amid the wire: *isolationism* (Standard 1) and *involvement* (Standard 3) as methods of defending *democracy* (the overarching topic). A *framework of meaning* is the connection between organizing concepts that transfer across situations. See Figure 5.3 for a visual of this metaphor.

Figure 5.2   Sample US History Standards (emphasis added)

United States History II Content Standards, Massachusetts
Topic 3: **Defending democracy**: responses to fascism and communism
1.   Develop an argument which analyzes the effectiveness of American isolationism and analyzes the impact of isolationism on U.S. foreign policy.
2.   Explain the rise of fascism and the forms it took in Germany and Italy, including ideas and policies that led to the Holocaust.
3.   Explain the reasons for American involvement in World War II and the key actions and events leading up to declarations of war against Japan and Germany.
4.   On a map of the world, locate the Allied powers at the time of World War II (Britain, France, the Soviet Union, and the United States) and Axis powers (Germany, Italy, and Japan).

SOURCE: Standards sourced from Massachusetts Department of Education's History and Social Science Framework (2018).

Figure 5.3   Conceptual Fence Posts Provide a Framework of Meaning

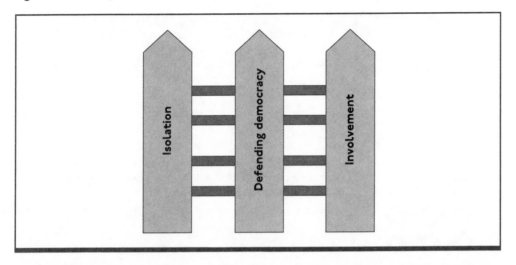

Notice that these posts are conceptual in nature and, thus, once students investigate the connections among them, can be transferred to new situations. By selecting conceptual posts, rather than factual ones, we ensure that the enduring structure of the unit is transferable rather than recallable. I'm sure we all remember that "In 1492, Columbus sailed the ocean blue," but the endurance of this fact cannot help us understand new phenomena or solve new problems. Had our teachers planned around conceptual posts rather than this factual one, we'd probably be better off.

If you take the time to consider your standards, though, you'll realize that the same set of learning goals can build many different fences. In other words, the same content can be organized into more than one framework of meaning. Which concepts are most worthy of our time? Which frameworks of meaning should we prioritize?

Many curriculum outcomes already list general or priority standards that will help guide you in this process. Reading the priority standards like a story might help you glean the shape of your "fence" and help you select conceptual posts to anchor the narrative. If you do not yet have a clear set of priority or power standards, however, this section should help you.

Consider the criteria for prioritizing standards summarized in Figure 5.4. Using the guiding questions, try to narrow your entire body of standards down to only the most essential components. If you've printed out your standards, physically highlight the priorities as you go. If you are working with an electronic copy, bold your selections or manipulate the font size so they immediately draw your eye.

The chief metric is whether or not the standards point students toward the deep, underlying conceptual structure of the discipline. Return to the *disciplinary vision* you established for your discipline in Chapter 2. Do some standards lend themselves to students doing the work of practitioners in the field? Will some standards better focus student attention on the most enduring, transferable concepts within the discipline? Which standards will best help students uncover the beauty and power of the discipline?

The second criterion is *cohesive transfer* between grade levels. Which concepts and skills reveal the underlying structure of the discipline so that students' journey from

Figure 5.4   Criteria for Prioritizing Standards

Criteria	Guiding Questions
Disciplinary Vision	Do the concepts and skills within the standard serve as powerful vessels for conveying my disciplinary vision to students?
Cohesive	Do the concepts and skills within the standard reveal the underlying structure that will transfer between grade levels creating a cohesive curriculum?
Real-World	Do the concepts and skills within the standard transfer to real-world application?
Interdisciplinary	Do the concepts and skills within the standard transfer between domains of the discipline or across disciplines creating interdisciplinary connections?
High Stakes	Do the concepts and skills within the standard have greater weight on high stakes tests?

online resources   Download at www.learningthattransfers.com.

one grade level to the next promotes the consolidation of disciplinary understanding? Are there core disciplinary ideas that only happen in one grade level and therefore need to be emphasized?

This is where working with a vertical team, K–12 or within your school, is critical. As educators, we want students to leave our classes prepared for the next level of learning. When starting this task independently, after you have narrowed down the possibilities of standards you think are essential, contact other educators who teach the grade levels above and below you and share your list. Ask them for feedback about your list and how these standards connect to their course or would leave students with holes in their knowledge.

Real-world applies to real-world transfer. Do these standards allow student to see the relevance of the discipline to their lives? Will the concepts and skills in this standard help students to live meaningful lives? Are the ideas in this standard necessary to solve complex, real-world problems?

Next, focus on standards that have *interdisciplinary uses* or the ability to be transferred across disciplines. Do the concepts and skills within the standard transfer between domains of the discipline or across disciplines? Interdisciplinary connections allow students to see the utility of their learning and will dispel the myth that academic disciplines are silos unto themselves.

Finally, it is wise to consider *high-stakes assessments* (Ainsworth, 2010). As a final consideration of what should be priority, look to your end of year exam and see what standards are weighted most heavily. Look back at your list of standards or outcomes. Are there some weighted heavily on the exam you haven't included? We do not believe this should be a chief factor for determining what to teach. However, we are aware many decisions involving funding, staffing, and even pay are based on test scores and therefore, this should be a final consideration on prioritizing standards or outcomes.

As you work through the content of your course, strive to deem no more than one-third of your standards as "priority." After all, no fence is made up entirely of posts. This is hard work and often times it is difficult to discern between two similar standards which should be priority—but less is nearly always more. Depth of understanding will ensure students both retain and transfer learning (Bransford et al., 2005). A march across a huge list of disconnected standards will lead to students forgetting what it is we've taught them (Bruner, 1977).

Prioritizing helps us identify where to focus the majority of our instructional time, not all of our instructional time. Achieve the Core recommends mathematics teachers

Real-world transfer: Situations that are new to the students (not previously studied in class) and require students to solve complex, real challenges, utilize concepts from multiple disciplines, present their findings to authentic audiences, and impact the world around them.

DESIGN STEP

PRIORITIZE THOUGHTFULLY

Read through your standards and mark them based on the criteria listed in Figure 5.4 and determine the most important learning outcomes for the year. Take notes during the process on the lines below.

_____

_____

_____

_____

_____

spend at least 65 percent of instructional time on priorities or areas of focus to ensure students have a deep conceptual understanding. Some teachers find it useful to look back at the way they've taught units in the past to notice what they naturally emphasized or prioritized. Once they make note of these priorities, they can step back from their list to examine the arc it forms and make tweaks from there.

Arrange Effectively

Of course, just because we've deemed some standards to be more powerful than others doesn't mean the other standards should necessarily be ignored. In fact, the other standards, like the barbed wire in the fence, can support the priority standards we've identified.

Now that you have identified priority standards or priority concepts as your "posts," arrange the other standards of your course around those priorities. This arrangement should build or spiral progressively so that students are able to apply their understanding to units throughout the year.

Take the standards in Figure 5.2 as an example. Once we anchor this topic in the concepts of isolationism, involvement, and defending democracy, all the other learning components fall into place. Students will explore the policy of isolationism *in the context of* the rise of fascism in Germany and Italy (Standard 2), and they will be able to locate the Allies and Axis powers on a map (Standard 4) *in order to* explain America's move from isolation to involvement in World War II. Once we can explain the standards of the unit *in relation to* the priorities, or "posts," we've established, we're on the path toward a unit that is arranged effectively. And, once this unit is over, students will be able to return to these concepts during their study of the Korean and Vietnam Wars, or the wars in Iraq and Afghanistan. Taking the time to dig deep when establishing the posts in the World War II unit will save time in the long run, since students will be able to apply this framework to all subsequent foreign policy contexts.

Arrange your standards based on their connection to the priorities you've identified for your course. As you go along, it may help to cut and paste or otherwise manipulate the text of the standards, like bolding or highlighting, so it is easy to distinguish your priorities and see how the other standards relate to them.

Keep in mind that standards might not remain in a linear sequence like they are listed on the curriculum documents. This process might require us to rethink how we arrange or structure our units to best form a comprehensive journey for students. For instance, a US history teacher charged with teaching the standards in Figure 5.2 might create a Foreign Policy unit centered on the concepts of isolationism, intervention, and defending democracy. Instead of teaching topics chronologically, he might instead group World War I, World War II, the Korean War, and the Vietnam War together as a series of contexts in which students can explore these concepts. Finally, students might transfer their learning to the Iraq War or another foreign policy scenario.

Another example of this can be seen in Figure 5.5, the Georgia Standards of Excellence for Science (2017). When new curriculum maps were released in 2017, the units did not group standards by common domain, but instead integrated the standards into units that tell a story and promote conceptual understanding.

Figure 5.5   Georgia Standards of Excellence for Physical Science

GSE High School Physical Science Curriculum Map

These are bundles of core ideas from the Georgia Standards of Excellence related to an anchoring phenomenon.

This document is part of a framework that includes lessons and resources.

Instructional Segment	Introduction	Properties of Matter	Reactions	Energy	Force and Motion	Waves	Energy Capstone
Estimated Time	1 week	7 weeks	8 weeks	8 weeks	6 weeks	4 weeks	2 weeks
Crosscutting Concepts	All	• Structure and function • Patterns • Scale, proportion, and change • Energy and matter	• Energy and matter • Stability and change	• Energy and matter • Systems and system models • Stability and change	• Cause and effect • Systems and system models • Stability and change • Energy and matter	• Patterns • Energy and matter	• Systems and system models • Cause and effect • Energy and matter
				Year-Long Phenomena: Operation of a Car or Rocket.			
Anchoring Phenomenon	Operation of a car or rocket	Elements and compounds to make a car or rocket operate https://goo.gl/LODHSo	Changes in altitude affect gases, resulting in surprising effects https://goo.gl/mbgKv8	Turning on your classroom lights requires many transformations of energy https://goo.gl/9IlwL0	Car stop—seatbelts and airbags https://goo.gl/aiFnyY	Doppler Effect https://goo.gl/Gv6Mw7	Model and explain the operation of a car or rocket
Core Ideas	All	• Structure of atoms and elements • Trends in the Periodic Table • Compounds, properties, bonds, and naming	• Atomic and molecular motion • Conservation of matter • Solutions • Acids and bases	• Heat energy • Electricity and magnetism • Nuclear energy • Fission and fusion • Radioactive decay • Energy transformations	• Forces and motion • Newton's laws • Simple machines • Gravitational force • Energy	• Electromagnetic and mechanical waves • Reflection, refraction, interference, and diffraction • Doppler effect • Energy	All

(Continued)

(Continued)

Instructional Segment	Introduction	Properties of Matter	Reactions	Energy	Force and Motion	Waves	Energy Capstone
Science and Engineering Practices			**Obtaining, Evaluating, and Communicating Information**				
	• Plan and carry out investigations • Ask questions • Develop and use models	• Develop and use models • Analyze and interpret data • Construct explanations	• Plan and carry out investigations • Develop and use models • Ask questions and design problems • Analyze and interpret data • Construct explanations	• Develop and use models • Use mathematical and computational thinking • Engage in argument from evidence • Construct explanations • Analyze and interpret data • Plan and carry out investigations	• Plan and carry out investigations • Construct explanations • Analyze and interpret data • Use mathematical and computational thinking	• Analyze and interpret data • Ask questions • Develop and use models • Construct explanations	All
GSE	All	**SPS1**a,b,c; **SPS2**a,b,c; **SPS7**a	**SPS5**a,b; **SPS3**a,b; **SPS6**a,b,c,d,e; **SPS7**a	**SPS4**a,b,c; **SPS10**a,b,c; **SPS7**a,b,c,d	**SPS7**a; **SPS8**a,b,c,d	**SPS7**a; **SPS9**a,b,c,d,e	All

SOURCE: Georgia Standards for Excellence, High School Physical Science Curriculum (2017).

The goal of this process is to make the standards more manageable to work with and meaningful for the student journey. In the physical science course outlined by the state of Georgia, standards are grouped so that each unit connects back to the operation of a car or rocket, allowing the teacher to establish a line of inquiry early in the year and pull this common thread through until the final day of the course. The content is grouped accordingly; forces and motion, Newton's laws, and simple mechanics are arranged together through the contexts of seatbelts and airbags so that students can study the concepts in real-world situations.

DESIGN STEP

ARRANGE EFFECTIVELY

Sequence your priority and supporting standards over the course of the year. Take notes during the process on the lines below.

_____

_____

_____

_____

_____

Supplement Strategically

As indicated in Chapter 4, students need more than disciplinary knowledge to be successful in modern society. As course designers, we have to determine which concepts and competencies from our modern literacies will best supplement our content to add relevance and authenticity to our units. Now is the time to determine where and how the modern literacy foci you selected in Chapter 4 will manifest themselves within your course.

Here are some considerations to keep in mind as you plot out your plan:

- **The natural arc of a school year:** At what point in the year are students most ready for these concepts? What do they need most and when?

  For instance, you may consider frontloading concepts like *kindness* and *teamwork* as the foundation of your classroom culture. You may introduce the concepts of *racism* and *discrimination* once you have established trust and credibility with your students. You might bring in the concept of *resilience* when students are working through the most challenging content of the course.

- **Content connections:** Where does the content of your course best support your modern literacy goals?

  For instance, math teachers may find it easier to bring in *ethics* or *social justice* ideas when examining data and statistics than during a geometry unit. One text in an English language arts classroom may provide a better vehicle for *socioemotional* learning than another.

- **All at once or one at a time?** Will it work best to establish a baseline understanding of your modern literacy concepts upfront, or does it make more sense to introduce each idea more gradually?

- **From simple to complex:** How should student understanding of these concepts and competencies evolve over the course of the year?

  For instance, students may begin the year by exploring a variety of *leadership* styles before finding one that best suits them. As the year progresses, they might investigate the connection between leadership and empathy or compare and contrast the idea of leadership with the idea of a role model. They might move from a more concrete to more abstract understanding as they consider formal vs. informal leadership and the idea of "servant leadership."

DESIGN STEP

SUPPLEMENT STRATEGICALLY

Sketch out a rough plan for incorporating the modern literacy goals you've set for your course. Leave room for flexibility and responsiveness to student needs, interests, and readiness. Take notes on your process below.

_____

_____

_____

_____

_____

Flow Cohesively

Now that we have prioritized, arranged, and supplemented our standards and learning expectations, it is time to think about creating a cohesive flow for our students' journey. We drafted conceptual questions in Chapters 3 and 4, and now we turn our attention to the sequence or flow of our course. For some disciplines and educators, units organized by conceptual relationships, as opposed to topics, might challenge or complicate the way they currently sequence their curriculum. For instance, how might a social studies course organize its units in order to zoom in and out of situations across time periods and regions rather than proceed chronologically or focus on one region at a time? How might more process-oriented disciplines like language arts or mathematics sequence units if discrete skills are no longer the driving force? These are challenging questions, but they're worth asking and answering.

Situating learning in authentic contexts and weaving a common conceptual thread between each unit is a powerful way to provide momentum and meaning to a course. We want our curriculum to be a tapestry of interwoven concepts that create a cohesive narrative, not a patchwork quilt of isolated units and ideas. It transforms curriculum from a slog to cover content into a quest to uncover meaning.

Reconceptualizing the order of our curriculum requires educators to step back and consider their course from a zoomed-out view, as we did in the previous chapters. Hopefully, by this point you have reconnected with those big "why" questions that motivated you to become a teacher in your field. Later in the chapter you will begin to put those compelling and conceptual questions in order and start to discern a distinct story that will help to articulate the vision for your students from day one in your class.

As we move away from the era of stringent and linear standardized testing and toward an unknown future, this vision will become the focal point of curriculum, not one-off tests. This paradigm shift might feel disorienting at first, but we believe it will ultimately be liberating for teachers. After all, we got into the profession because we wanted to help students explore the complexities of the human condition, the wonders of nature, and the organizing logic of the universe—not to pass a test! Though assessment has its place, we think teachers will be revitalized by reconnecting with their "why" and sharing that passion with their students. The questions below are a suggestion of practical questions to consider when creating your course sequence or flow.

DESIGN STEP

FLOW COHESIVELY

The following questions will help to determine the flow of your units.

- Which priority standards and arrangements are prerequisites or foundational knowledge for future units?

- How many days will you need per arrangement to ensure students can make sense of the concepts and skills? How many instructional days do you have?

- Did you leave yourself wiggle room or flexibility to adjust instruction as needed?

_____

_____

_____

_____

_____

What separates this step from the traditional pacing guide is again a simple shift in mindset. We are indeed still mapping out the order of units based on the school calendar; however, instead of moving from one disparate chunk to the next, we are intentionally planning a journey that is aligned and flows cohesively so that students see how their learning is connected and has grown throughout the year.

DESIGN STEP

CREATE A COURSE AT A GLANCE

Using the template in Figure 5.6 as a guide, fill in the basic overview of each unit in your intended sequence for the year. Modify as necessary to fit your school calendar and the number of units for your course. You'll notice that the template also has space to articulate the "story of your course." This is the focus of the next design step.

Figure 5.6 **Course at a Glance**

Course Title										
And the story of this course—big picture										
Semester 1				Semester 2						
Quarter 1		Quarter 2		Quarter 3			Quarter 4			
September	October	November	December	January	February	March	April	May	June	
Unit 1	Unit 2	Unit 3	Unit 4	Unit 5	Unit 6		Unit 7	Unit 8		

How these units connect to the story of the course

 Download template at www.learningthattransfers.com.

STORY OF YOUR COURSE

Once we have created a logical flow to our course by placing units into an intentional sequence where they build from one another, we can frame this flow in terms of a story or narrative. This helps us communicate the big picture of the course to students in a way that is accessible and meaningful. In Chapter 3, we developed a disciplinary vision and articulated how our course contributes to the overall disciplinary vision. These two pieces will aid in crafting the story of our course.

Cognitive scientist Daniel Willingham (2009) provides four compelling reasons why stories are a motivating structure for students.

1. Stories are easy to comprehend because they're a structure familiar to everyone.

2. Stories are engaging because they demand frequent medium-difficulty inferencing that encourage us to constantly think about their meaning.

3. Stories are easy to remember because they have a causal structure, and constantly thinking about the logic of that structure helps us retain information.

4. Stories have emotional resonance because they humanize abstract ideas. (pp. 66–75)

The story of our course allows us to show students that learning is not linear; it occurs through a complex set of experiences that require us to question what we understand, persevere as we experience confusion or cognitive dissonance, and ultimately gain new understandings that inevitably raise new questions and uncertainties. We want them to experience what we likely experienced as we gained insight into the content that we teach. Consider how the following structures might help you to write the story of your course.

Potential Structures for the Story of Your Course

Chronology: The most familiar and straightforward way to structure your course is to arrange it in chronological order. However, just because it's familiar doesn't mean it has to be boring! Since we've already searched for themes and patterns that emerge within our course, we won't simply be delivering units in the order that they happen, we'll be building storylines that develop a cohesive sense of national identity, literary movements, or eras of mathematical and scientific discovery.

By exploring how the events of one period or movement evolve and flow in to the next, you'll also be challenging students' ability to understand how cause and effect relationships shape history, paradigms, and scientific eras. When students have the ability to place a particular method or discovery within a broader timeline, they can think more deeply and abstractly about its context. Whether we're inferring like a historian, hypothesizing like a scientist, or composing like a journalist, the ability to trace our thinking back to a particular moment in history is a useful one.

Thesis/Antithesis/Synthesis: Although we believe the world is becoming increasingly complex, it's never been a simple place. History and science are filled with competing theories and belief systems that rose to prominence, were challenged, and were either replaced or synthesized into new theories that drove humanity forward. Famous historian Georg Hegel had an entire theory of history and philosophy based on such a pattern. What we're suggesting is certainly an over-simplification, but it can provide some inspiration for creating a narrative for your course.

For example, each quarter your students could explore a conceptual relationship that seems to make a concrete claim—for example, *systems require order and cohesion to flourish sufficiently*. Your students could read books that create that theme, study empires or nation-states at the height of their powers, or evaluate healthy biomes and ecosystems. Your next unit would then challenge that principle, showing students that *when systems become stagnant or inflexible, they can become oppressive or break down*, for example. Then your students could read texts with a similar theme, learn about the breakdown of empires, or study how human pollution is damaging various ecosystems.

The overall idea is to lead students toward a clear conclusion, then challenge them by complicating their understanding with each new unit. In addition to providing an organizing logic and sequence to your course, this will help push students to always challenge their assumptions.

Hero's Journey: Joseph Campbell was an anthropologist who studied and spent time with cultures all over the world. Though each culture was different in many ways, much of their stories followed a similar arc, a structure Campbell called the mono-myth, and we've come to know as the hero's journey. In fact, countless of our favorite movies today, from *Star Wars* to *Moana*, follow a similar structure. Due to its ubiquity, it'll be quickly recognizable to students. Below is a quick overview and example of how it can be used to help provide you with a structure for your course.

The Call to Adventure: What kind of adventure or quest will your students be embarking on in your course? How can you invite them to join in and leave their comfort zone?

Trials and Tribulations: What kind of challenges will they encounter in your course? What skills will they need to succeed? What knowledge? How can your course build these competencies in such a way that students know they'll need them to succeed on their journey?

The Abyss: Consider having students launch into a massive project or self-directed unit of study once they've acquired all the skills necessary. How can they use the knowledge they've gained thus far in your course to conquer a problem facing their classroom, school, or community?

The Return: How can you close your year in a way that promotes student reflection and spreads the word about their work over the course of the year? The end of the year is a time for students to internalize what they've learned and share it with their classroom community.

DESIGN STEP

ARTICULATING THE STORY OF YOUR COURSE

The stems below can help jumpstart your brainstorming for the story of your course. Don't worry, this is a first draft. Course planning is iterative in nature. Having an idea or two in mind as you organize and sequence your course will help inform the units you design, but the units you design will also help shape the larger story you tell. After we have thought explicitly about our units we can return to this draft and revise.

This course is about _____.

This year we will _____.

We will begin by _____, then we'll _____, and finally we'll _____ all in order to understand that _____.

_____

_____

_____

_____

_____

Going Visual and Crafting the Moral of Your Story

If you have a clear story in mind, consider two powerful ways to convey this story to students: going visual and stating the "moral" of your story. And if your story is still rather fuzzy, these steps can help you sharpen your vision.

Creating a simple, clear way of depicting the learning plan for the year can go a long way toward helping both teachers and students orient their learning as they navigate the course. Consider constructing a diagram, image, or visual metaphor to articulate how your units build upon one another. Figure 5.7 provides a visual option of inter-related gears working together as a system.

Scan the QR code to see more examples and templates for visual course stories.

Figure 5.7 **Gears as a System of Interrelated Parts Example**

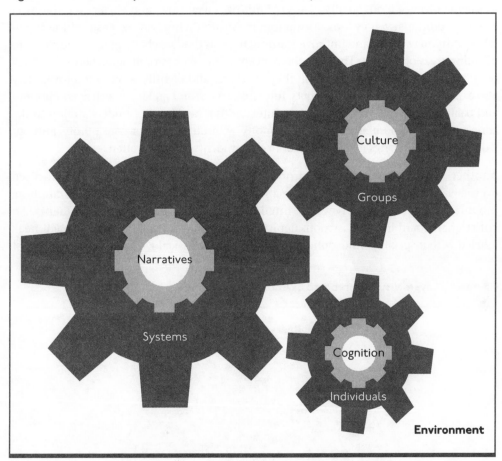

This example comes from Trevor's English language arts classroom but could just as easily fit in to a social studies course. Each major work that the class read had a particular thematic and conceptual focus that helped students develop a loose framework for analyzing the human experience. The year started by evaluating the psychology and cognition of individual characters in a work, providing students with new ways to think about how motivation drives the plot in stories and in their own lives.

Then the focus shifted to fostering an awareness of how culture interacts with our psychology to help students be better interpreters and creators of persuasive texts. To close, students learned about how systems create and perpetuate thoughts, feelings, and behaviors that cause conflict and even oppression of different groups and cultures. This was a springboard to a student lead inquiry project around a self-selected social issue. Weaved between each unit, students also considered the role that power plays in each text.

This visual metaphor provided a frame for students' inquiry and analysis throughout the year. It was presented to students in the form of a question the first day of school as a call to adventure: What's the relationship between individuals, groups, and systems and what role does power play? Each time students encountered new concepts, they were able to connect it to their prior learning and use their new learning to refine their understanding.

A second-grade teacher might, for instance, focus on the concept of equilibrium as a transdisciplinary lens for the year. She uses the "layers visual" in Figure 5.8 to show her students the layers of equilibrium—balance within ourselves, our classroom, our community, and our planet. They explore the concept of equilibrium to explore healthy decision making in their choices of food, quality of sleep, limiting screen time, and engaging in physical activity. Additionally, they look at equilibrium within themselves such as pushing themselves to try new things and improve learning in areas that are challenging, in addition to pursuing areas of interest. They use the concept to build classroom agreements that they revisit every week to gauge how well they are doing and identify ways to improve. They also explore the concept with magnets, fulcrums, levers, and pullies, as well as equilibrium and balance in ecosystems. Each new context adds a new layer of understanding to the concept of equilibrium and living in harmony with ourselves, our community, and our world. The visual hangs in their classroom and students refer to it often.

Another powerful example comes from a seventh-grade ancient history class focused on the classical civilizations of Greece and Rome. Through the metaphor of climbing mountains, the teacher conveys the intellectual journey of his course to students. An entire chalkboard in his classroom depicts a hand-drawn mountain range, each peak labeled with a specific philosopher or text from the classical world that students must

Figure 5.8   Layers Visual Storyboard Example, Second Grade

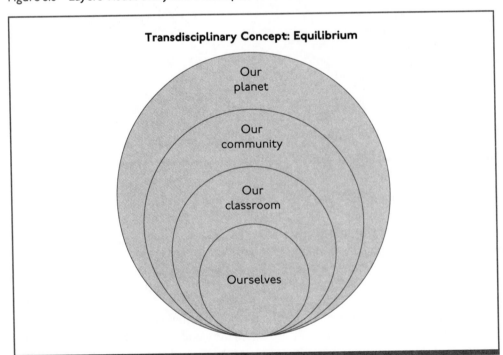

Transdisciplinary Concept: Equilibrium

Our planet

Our community

Our classroom

Ourselves

DESIGN STEP

CONVEYING YOUR "STORY" TO STUDENTS

Use the questions in Figure 5.9 to help you brainstorm visual metaphors or diagrams and ways of articulating the "moral" of your story to students. The process doesn't have to be linear. Begin with whichever component feels more natural to you. Consider how each step informs the other. Also, this is a good time to go back to fill in the last row of the course at a glance document.

Figure 5.9   **Brainstorming Ways to Share the Story of Your Course With Students**

Going Visual	Articulating the "Moral" of Your Story
• What would this course look like if I put it into a diagram or flow chart? • How do the individual units of my course interact? Is there a hierarchy, cycle, or process that I can capture? • What metaphors might provide insight into the structure of this course? • *This course is like _____.*	• What is the purpose of your course? • What is this class about? • If you had to sum up this course in one line, what would it be? • What idea lies at the heart your course? What concept(s) form(s) the core? • If students could only internalize one thing from your class, what would it be? • How does this course help students become who they want to be?

Fill out the story of your course in Figure 5.10, taken from the Course Overview graphic in Chapter 3. When completed, you can add the story of your course to the Course Overview in Figure 3.1.

Figure 5.10   **Story of the Course**

Story of the Course

Access the Course Overview Template at www.learningthattransfers.com.

_____

_____

_____

_____

_____

work hard to understand. Through grit and determination, students "summit" each peak and are rewarded with an inspiring "view" from the top.

Along with a visual depiction of your course, distilling your story into a single line, or perhaps two, can serve as a powerful compass for the course. Just like the moral of a story, the moral of your course is the articulation of the key idea you hope students take away from their year with you. Use the following questions to help you distill your vision into a compelling, memorable sentence that can be used to sum up the course. For seventh-grade ancient history, that sentence might be, *By walking the path of ancient philosophers, we can discipline our minds and achieve wisdom.*

Consider the following examples as illustrations of how teachers found the "moral" of their stories. How might these examples inspire and provide direction for discovering the "moral" of your own story?

A third-grade teacher has chosen *collaboration, resilience,* and *empathy* as the conceptual underpinning of his course. He teaches these modern literacy concepts in the context of every discipline. In social studies, students research historical figures who overcame enormous challenges to achieve great outcomes. In science, students work in teams to develop hypotheses and collect evidence. In English language arts, students step into the shoes of a variety of characters to see through different eyes. In mathematics, students cheer for each other as they take risks to solve difficult problems on the board. The teacher keeps coming back to these questions: Why is working together better than doing it by ourselves? How can empathy make me a better teammate and friend? How can we use the tools of collaboration and empathy to overcome challenges individually and as a class? These concepts and questions even guide students as they manage peer relationships and work through interpersonal conflicts. The moral of his course is this: **We can do hard things by working hard together.**

For an eighth-grade math teacher, pre-algebra is about using systems of rules to find unknowns. These three concepts—*systems, rules,* and *unknowns*—are explored over and over again through each unit. More than understanding pre-algebra, though, she wants her students to learn to think logically and methodically. When posed with a challenge, be it as small as an unfamiliar math problem or as large as saving an endangered species, she wants students to have the confidence to leverage what they know to figure out what they don't know, and to use logic to arrive at valid conclusions. So, rather than simply telling students what she wants them to know, she uses a problem-based approach to help students uncover and prove rules on their own. She doesn't ask students to take notes on and then memorize the associative property of multiplication; she asks them to investigate whether $(x * y) * z = x * (y * z)$ is true or not. Students use trial and error to develop theories about the answer, calling on what they already know about numbers and multiplication and arguing over the most eloquent ways to prove their conclusions to be true. In this way, moral of her course— **We can leverage what we know to find and prove what we don't know**—rings true in every lesson.

One high school English language arts teacher organized his course around the idea that expressing one's thoughts through writing was an essential human act that empowered students to control their own destinies. Using the disciplinary lens concept of *word choice*, he asked them time and again to examine the exact phrasing other authors used to convey their ideas. What, exactly, does Dr. Martin Luther King Jr. mean when he says that the United States had issued African Americans a "bad check"? Why did King use that phrase? What are all the other ideas implied by those words? How would his audience feel, what would they think, when they heard that metaphor? Using the anchoring concepts of destiny, freedom, and power, he guided students to consider the ways in which authors had rewritten destiny through effective rhetoric. What does freedom mean to King? What does it mean to you? How does King convince his audience to take action in order to secure his vision of freedom? What would have happened if King had never given this speech? Students spent time writing their own poems, stories, essays, and papers, in which they explored these concepts and analyzed other authors' use of them. They also discussed all the ways in which writing could empower them to achieve their goals. A well-written college admissions essay might ensure acceptance at the university of their dreams. The right cover letter might land them their dream job. Even the perfect meme or Tweet could help them influence others or stand up for what they believe in. The "moral" of this course? ***Finding the right words can set you free.***

CONCLUSION

Although there are plenty of tools out there to support teachers in unit planning, we've found that fewer resources exist for the big picture planning that we're talking about in this chapter. However, if we never stop to question why certain topics or standards are bundled together, or to reconsider the order in which we teach them, we may be missing key opportunities to improve the structure of our courses.

If we begin at the unit level, sure, there are some impactful changes we can make to reorient our classrooms toward learning transfer, but there are also quite a few limitations. It often takes a full renovation—knocking down walls, building an addition, moving and enlarging rooms—not just a fresh coat of paint or new window treatments, to change the function of a home. Similarly, we often need to redraw the entire blueprint of a course in order to maximize our ability to teach for transfer.

With transfer in mind, we can ensure that our course content is prioritized thoughtfully, arranged effectively, supplemented strategically, and flows logically and cohesively from the start of the year to the end, creating a meaningful journey for students and teachers alike. And encapsulating this journey in stories, visuals, and "morals" can help us convey the journey simply and powerfully to a wide range of stakeholders.

THINKING PROMPT

As we close out the chapter, reflect on how your thinking has expanded:

- What makes a **great course**?
- How do **essential attributes of a great course** relate to **teacher autonomy**?
- What is the impact of **storytelling** on **course design**?

_____

_____

_____

_____

_____

CHAPTER SIX

Unit Planning

How Do We Intentionally Design for Learning That Transfers?

"And education, too, is where we decide whether we love our children enough not to expel them from our world and leave them to their own devices, nor to strike from their hands their chance of undertaking something new, something unforeseen by us, but to prepare them in advance for the task of renewing the common world."

—Hannah Arendt

Why does this chapter matter?	Unit planning is what turns the story of our course into actionable steps, effectively guiding students through learning that transfers.
What will I be able to do by the end of this chapter?	I will be able to plan units that prioritize transfer and are grounded in anchoring concepts, conceptual questions, and meaningful contexts.

For many educators, the unit is the most familiar and comfortable level of curriculum design. Broad enough to account for planning meaningful chunks of learning, but concise enough that it has a clear shape and direction, units are the first thing many of us think of when we consider how we organize our course content. There are also a variety of different philosophies and frameworks for planning units. Some prefer to have meticulously mapped out documents, with every possible nook and cranny of knowledge accounted for. Others prefer adaptability and flexibility over granularity. Though we advocate for a balance of the two, we passionately believe that educators should take ownership of this process and design units that suit their particular context, content, learners, and planning style. As long as there is a shared language and understanding among a district, department, school, or team, we believe customization is excellent.

One of the most commonly used methods for unit planning is the idea of backward design, popularized by *Understanding by Design* (Wiggins & McTighe, 2005). We build upon the powerful notion that the specific learning goals should be crafted before the aligned learning experiences. In addition to aligning instruction with our assessments, what if we were to also consider real-world contexts and connections? What if we could design learning experiences that not only prepared students for summative assessments, but for authentic situations they may encounter outside the classroom as well? This extends backward planning a step beyond desired

THINKING PROMPT

Before we begin, reflect on the following questions:

- How do you currently go about the **unit planning process**?
- What is the role of **questions** in the **unit planning process**?
- What is the role of student **choice** and **voice** in unit planning?

My current thinking:

_____

_____

_____

_____

_____

academic outcomes—stretching one more layer outward and into the world outside the walls of our school.

This chapter does not require us to throw away our current units or curriculum. It simply asks us to look at them from a new perspective and consider how they can connect to real-world issues and contexts. The steps, frameworks, and tools detailed in this chapter will help create dynamic, impactful new units and breathe new life into favorite ones too. Planning at the unit level is where the rubber meets the road for most classroom teachers and Chapter 6 will serve as an excellent map to help you start planning students' learning journey.

> When too much emphasis is placed on replicating rigid forms and structures of curriculum design, practitioners can quickly become overwhelmed and disempowered. We encourage educators to adapt our templates and structures to the needs of their context.

CHAPTER STRUCTURE

Building off of the work we've done with Disciplinary Literacies, Modern Literacies, and the Story of Our Course, this chapter details a flexible framework that ensures units are cohesive and connected to our wider vision as well. The Zoom In unit planner and Storyboard tool help us to articulate the key questions, contexts, and concepts necessary to move students through a unit of learning. Equally important, it also explores ways to integrate meaningful voice and choice for students. This chapter is organized around the following sections:

- Flexible options for Unit Planning Steps
- Zooming In: The Unit Planner
  - Selecting anchoring concepts
  - Specifying with subconcepts

- o Listing facts and skills
- o Drafting conceptual relationship questions to build schema
- o Writing compelling questions to invite learning
- o Assessing for transfer
- The Unit Storyboard: planning for similar to dissimilar to real-world transfer
  - o Acquire: making meaning of anchoring concepts
  - o Connect: exploring the relationship between concepts
  - o Similar and dissimilar Transfer: unlocking new contexts
  - o Student action
- Preserving space for student voice, choice, and passions
  - o Moving students to meaningful action

FLEXIBLE OPTIONS FOR UNIT PLANNING STEPS

Curriculum development does not happen in exact, prescribed steps and we hope teachers tailor our suggestions to meet their own style and preferences. Regardless of whether you use one of our provided templates or design a custom one, these are the three essential elements of unit creation for learning that transfers.

- **Anchoring and subconcepts** are the individual concepts of the unit. Students will need to acquire and consolidate their understanding of each conceptual "building block" before they can answer the conceptual questions you pose and navigate the contexts you provide.

- **Conceptual relationship questions** direct students' attention to connecting concepts in relationship with one another. These connections reveal the structure of how the world is organized and are, therefore, critical to facilitating learning that transfers.

- **Contexts** or situations that illustrate how concepts and their connections work in different situations allow students to explore these questions of conceptual relationship. Each new situation pushes us to reconsider our understanding, to examine concepts and their connections from all sides, and deepen our grasp of how the world works.

We want to make it clear that, although we think our templates are useful, they are a means to an end. When too much emphasis is placed on replicating rigid forms and structures of curriculum design, practitioners can quickly become overwhelmed and disempowered. We encourage educators to adapt our work to the needs of their context. The goal of this chapter is to provide the tools necessary to build powerful units for learning that transfers, not follow a prescriptive formula.

For educators who design a custom unit plan template, be sure to keep the following components in mind:

- Disciplinary literacy (from Chapter 3): Articulate an age-level appropriate vision for the subjects you teach so that students see the bigger purpose of learning to think, know, and do. Connect this vision to specific disciplinary literacy concepts so that

Anchoring and subconcepts: Very discipline-specific concepts that allow students to navigate more specific contexts and examples and usually bring a sharper focus to the anchoring concepts and the disciplinary lenses.

Conceptual relationship questions: Questions that direct students' attention to connecting concepts in relationship with one another. These connections reveal the structure of how the world is organized and are, therefore, critical to facilitating learning that transfers.

Contexts: Situations that illustrate how concepts and their connections work; they allow students to explore questions of conceptual relationship. Each new situation pushes us to reconsider our understanding, to examine concepts and their connections from all sides, and deepen our grasp of how the world works.

students see how what they're learning this year connects to the overall structure of the discipline.

- Modern literacies (from Chapter 4 and below): Consider and select essential skills that students need to navigate a complex world. Weave both disciplinary literacy and modern literacy into compelling questions that invite students to solve multi-faced problems, situations, or projects in authentic contexts.

- Choose the anchoring concepts and skills (detailed below) and frame them as questions of conceptual relationship that facilitate students uncovering those connections and ways in which those concepts and skills interact.

- Assessment (next chapter): What does success look like? How will we, along with students, determine that we have been successful?

ZOOMING IN: THE UNIT PLANNER

We've designed a template that allows for systematic planning while still affording room for flexibility and student agency. Figure 6.1 provides an overview of each key component and a brief description of the type of content that could be added to adequately flesh out the ideas therein. As we move through each section of this chapter, we'll offer thinking prompts and questions to consider that will aid in completing each section.

Figure 6.1 **Zooming In: Unit Overview**

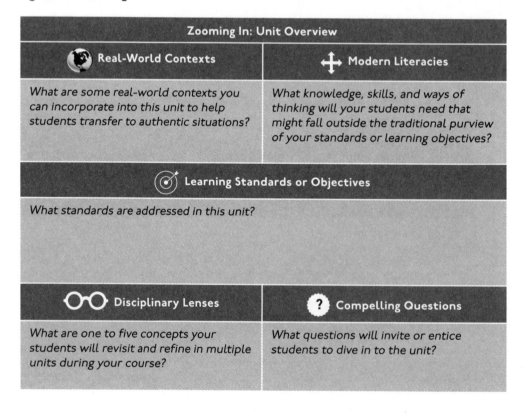

Zooming In: Unit Overview	
⚓ **Anchor Concepts**	💬 **Conceptual Relationship Questions**
What few concepts will anchor all of the specific contexts and situations in this unit?	*What conceptual relationship questions will your students need to explore to be successful during this unit? Consult our list of conceptual relationship question stems for more guidance.*
✳ **Subconcepts**	🐉 **Facts and Skills**
What additional concepts will your students need to navigate the specific contexts and situations you provide?	*What specific facts and skills or processes will your students need to be successful in this unit?*
Summative Assessment	**System of Ongoing Assessment for Transfer**
Which disciplinary lens(es), modern literacy, anchoring concepts, and sub-concepts will students apply on the summative assessment? *What real-world, novel scenario will students unlock on the summative assessment?*	*How will students transfer their learning from academic, similar scenarios to increasingly dissimilar, real-world scenarios?*

online resources 🔗 Download this Unit Planning Template at www.learningthattransfers.com.

The disciplinary lenses we selected in Chapter 3 supply our students with disciplinary practices that they should apply throughout the school year as they move toward disciplinary expertise. The lenses are concepts that capture the ways of knowing, doing, and thinking that make each discipline unique. Concepts like *author, purpose,* and *audience* are always relevant when thinking like an author in the same way *context* and *point of view* are always relevant when one thinks like a historian.

By focusing on a handful of these concepts throughout the course of the year, we'll ensure that students' new learning can always be placed in an appropriate conceptual file folder. Whether or not you choose one disciplinary lens concept to return to for the entire year or have a handful that you cycle in and out for each unit, the important thing is to revisit them more than once. They are typically rich and complex concepts, and students' understanding and application of them should evolve over the course of the year, which is why we've included a space for them in both the course overview and the unit plan.

DESIGN STEP

Take a moment to place one or two of the disciplinary lenses you selected in Chapter 3 in the corresponding space in the unit planner (Figure 6.1), as shown in the figure below.

- *What are one to five concepts your students will revisit and refine in multiple units during your course?*

Figure 6.2   **Disciplinary Lenses for the Unit**

 **Disciplinary Lenses**

Selecting Anchoring Concepts

Anchoring concepts:
The focus or building blocks of a unit of study; the essential conceptual elements of our content that span over an entire unit.

While disciplinary lenses provide students with enduring tools to think and reason through problems in our course, they won't suffice as the primary material to think *about*. For this, we need **anchoring concepts**, the essential conceptual elements of our content that span over an entire unit, as well as **subconcepts** that allow students to navigate more specific contexts and examples and usually bring a sharper focus to the anchoring concepts and the disciplinary lenses. Typically, though not always, anchoring concepts ground a particular unit, while disciplinary lenses span the entire year. Consider Figure 6.3 for some examples of anchoring and subconcepts.

There is not a right or wrong way to define concepts, and we implore teachers to use these categories to ensure meaningful dialogue and to bring about a rich curriculum for

Figure 6.3   **Example of Anchor Concepts and Subconcepts**

Discipline	Anchor Concept	Subconcepts
History	Liberty	rights, responsibility, self-determination
Math	Bias	data distribution, sampling, inference, variability, measures of center
Science	Living Things	needs, characteristics, conditions, suitability, energy sources, survival
English language arts	Persuasion	claim, evidence, analysis

students, but *not* to have round and round debates about whether or not a particular concept qualifies as a certain type of concept. When selecting which one(s) are useful for a particular unit, consider how you'd like students to think about or view the anchor concepts and subconcepts they'll be exploring for that individual unit or sequence of units.

The graphic in Figure 6.4 presents a visual to help think about the utility of selecting three levels of concepts: disciplinary lenses, anchor concepts, and subconcepts. In a high-school US history course, the teacher has selected the disciplinary lenses of *point of view* and *context* to help students to reason about history throughout the year. Whenever students approach a new primary or secondary source, she asks them to contemplate the author's point of view and the historical context in which it was created in order to aid in comprehending it. Whenever students are investigating a specific historical event or development, she reminds them to look for the ways various groups or individuals would view the situation differently. What would women think? How might this impact Native Americans? Immigrants? African Americans? She asks them to use what they know about the time period in general—the context—to understand the particulars of any given moment. What else was going on at the time?

Scan here for more examples of lenses and concepts.

Using disciplinary lenses to guide students' thinking is an excellent first step toward teaching for transfer. They are so transferable that they can be applied to nearly every lesson throughout the year. But in order to bring depth to the course, the teacher also needs anchoring concepts, such as liberty and power, to organize the content students are thinking about. And a robust set of subconcepts brings greater richness and a clearer direction to the course.

While the disciplinary lenses are meant to be employed as a habit of mind through every unit of the course, the anchoring concepts move in and out of focus as the year unfolds. For instance, this US history teacher might choose to teach the American Revolution through the anchoring concept of liberty using the following questions:

- What is the relationship between self-determination and liberty? Can a people be "free" without the power to determine their own destiny?

- To what extent was the American Revolution a fight for individual rights?

Or she might anchor this unit in terms of power:

- What does tyranny look like? Were British policies toward the American colonists tyrannical?

- What is the relationship between tyranny, authority, and revolution?

Or she could devise yet another iteration of this unit with a focus on change and continuity:

- What is the relationship between progress and stability? Is it possible for a society to achieve both at the same time?

- How much really changed in America as a result of the American Revolution?

Each of these is an interesting path through the unit, but trying to walk them all at the same time would overwhelm teachers and create a fragmented experience for students. All of the anchoring concepts *could* be applied to the unit, but that does not mean they *should*. Some concepts must necessarily recede into the background to bring others into sharper focus in the foreground. It's not that the background concepts disappear.

> Some concepts must necessarily recede into the background to bring others into sharper focus in the foreground.

Figure 6.4 Concepts for United States History, 11th Grade

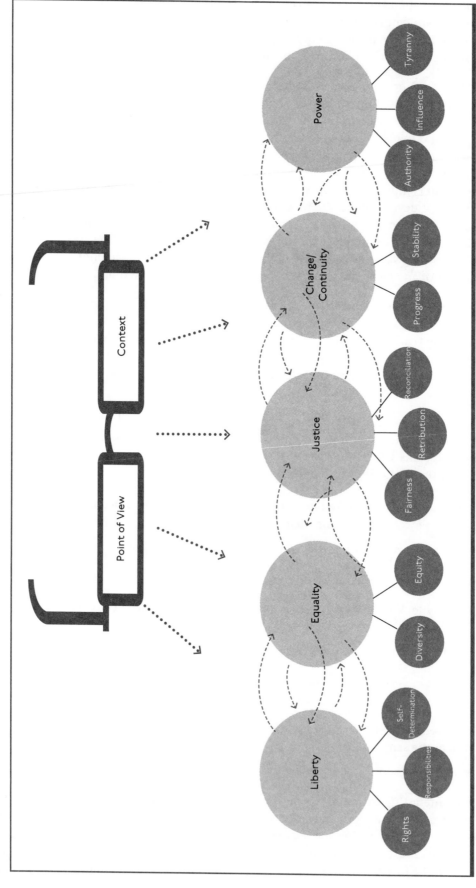

In fact, an astute student might draw them into the conversation even if they aren't asked to do so. But, unlike the disciplinary lenses, some of the anchoring concepts will be placed on the back burner in any given unit.

Most veteran teachers have likely detected patterns and areas of emphasis in the broader discipline they teach and in the course standards in particular, which will aid in determining anchoring and subconcepts. The thinking prompts in Figure 6.5 help when selecting a coherent, compelling set of anchoring concepts to guide.

Figure 6.5 Identify Anchoring Concepts

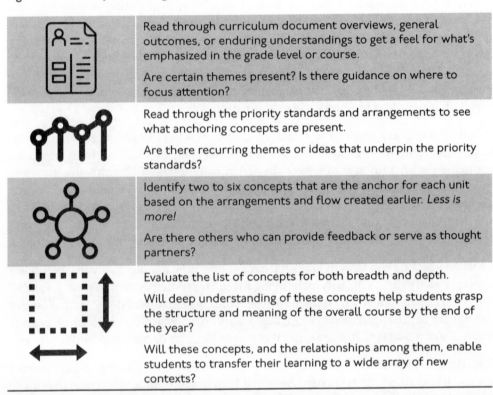

Read through curriculum document overviews, general outcomes, or enduring understandings to get a feel for what's emphasized in the grade level or course.

Are certain themes present? Is there guidance on where to focus attention?

Read through the priority standards and arrangements to see what anchoring concepts are present.

Are there recurring themes or ideas that underpin the priority standards?

Identify two to six concepts that are the anchor for each unit based on the arrangements and flow created earlier. *Less is more!*

Are there others who can provide feedback or serve as thought partners?

Evaluate the list of concepts for both breadth and depth.

Will deep understanding of these concepts help students grasp the structure and meaning of the overall course by the end of the year?

Will these concepts, and the relationships among them, enable students to transfer their learning to a wide array of new contexts?

DESIGN STEP

Take a moment to place a few anchoring concepts in the corresponding space in the unit planner, as shown in Figure 6.6.

Figure 6.6 Anchor Concepts for the Unit

Anchor Concepts

SPECIFY WITH SUBCONCEPTS

Disciplinary lenses function more like habits of mind that we want students to attend to in nearly every new situation in a course. Anchoring concepts are those concepts that are broad enough to anchor much of the content of a unit. Subconcepts often clarify the meaning of the anchoring concepts. They are neither too broad nor overly specific—they are sharp enough to provide nuance to our thinking.

For instance, *power* is an anchoring concept for many social studies courses. But alone, it may seem a bit blurry. When we look at subconcepts of authority, tyranny, and influence, the concept of power takes on multiple dimensions. When we learn something new, we flip through our prior learning for similar conceptual ideas. While very broad concepts like pattern or system allow for many potential prior experiences to be accessed, they might not provide enough meaning to be particularly helpful in grasping the nuance of a new context. Subconcepts are usually precise enough to provide useful understanding to unlock the new situation.

When selecting concepts in a geometry course, teachers might select transformation, proof, and sense-making as their disciplinary lenses while an individual unit could use the anchoring concepts of similarity, congruence, and symmetry. By using the subconcepts of dilation, rigidity, and construction students would have a firmer understanding of what it means to be similar, how to prove geometric figures are similar or congruent, and when to employ various theorems to make sense of a geometric figure and prove if it is similar to or congruent with another geometric figure.

Scan the QR code for more examples of completed unit plans.

Or when selecting concepts in English language arts, for example, many teachers select concepts such as bias, empathy, or bullying to read texts such as *Wonder* by R. J. Palacio. These are decent, but when coupled with subconcepts that speak deeper to the core of the human experience such as belonging, exclusion, insecurities, or maturity, provide a depth and richness that more general concepts like bias or bullying cannot provide.

The Human Experience Concepts that were introduced in Chapter 3 are another approach to connect our content in ways that help students understand who they are in the world. These can be used as disciplinary lenses, anchoring concepts, or subconcepts, it all depends on what you are trying to achieve with them. Human Experience Concepts can also serve as potential anchoring concepts for elementary teachers who plan integrated units for multiple subject areas. Figure 6.7 shows a few examples of these concepts.

The risk of offering these labels as a way to think about different layers of concepts will likely result in some frustration among those who want to know the "right answer" for whether or not a particular concept is a disciplinary lens, anchoring concept, or subconcept. We cannot emphasize enough how important it is that these labels simply serve as ways to think about grounding our units in transferable concepts, and ensuring we have both breadth and depth of transferable understanding in every unit. If there are debates or second guesses, we encourage planners to move on after a few minutes. Figure 6.8 illustrates a spectrum of concepts from less abstract to more abstract purely as a visual to help aid conversations and planning for both depth and breadth of transferable understanding.

In some disciplines such as science and mathematics, subconcepts are the smaller elements that make up anchor concepts, and a lot depends on the age or readiness level of students to determine whether something should be an anchor concept or a subconcept—where anchor concepts are the focus for that unit, they are made up of smaller subconcepts that perhaps students may have already studied, or subconcepts that add another dimension to the anchoring concept. For example, fraction may be

Figure 6.7 Sample Human Experience Concepts

Humanities and the Arts		Science, Health, and Physical Education	Mathematics
Friendship	Power	Survival	Question asking
Insecurities	Control	Equilibrium	Pattern seeking
Belonging	Chaos	Balance	Meaning-making
Truth	Ignorance	Interdependence	Communication
Courage	Identity	Force	Equality, equivalence
Fear	Bias	Attraction	Chance
Dreams	Beauty	Symbiotic	Precision
Experiences	Injustice	Interaction	Similarity
Family dynamics	Hate	Adaptation	Deviation
Redemption	Justice	Diversity	Balance
Authenticity	Systems	Systems	Flexibility
Story-telling	Freedom	Variation	Order
Ego	Belief	Cooperation	Solution

Figure 6.8 Different Types of Concepts

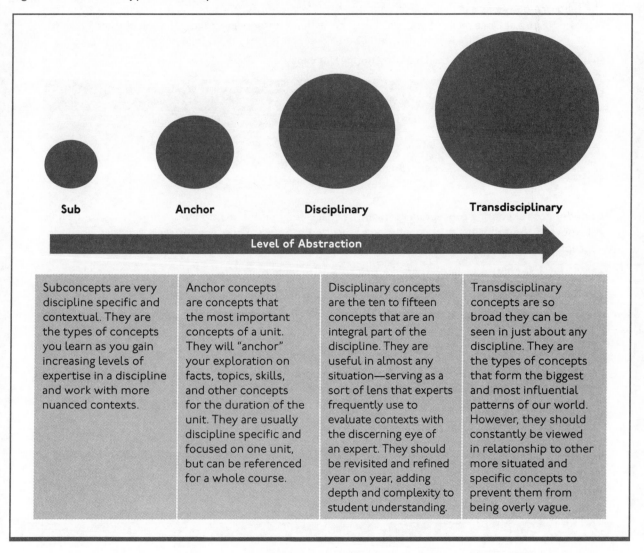

Sub   **Anchor**   **Disciplinary**   **Transdisciplinary**

Level of Abstraction

Subconcepts are very discipline specific and contextual. They are the types of concepts you learn as you gain increasing levels of expertise in a discipline and work with more nuanced contexts.

Anchor concepts are concepts that the most important concepts of a unit. They will "anchor" your exploration on facts, topics, skills, and other concepts for the duration of the unit. They are usually discipline specific and focused on one unit, but can be referenced for a whole course.

Disciplinary concepts are the ten to fifteen concepts that are an integral part of the discipline. They are useful in almost any situation—serving as a sort of lens that experts frequently use to evaluate contexts with the discerning eye of an expert. They should be revisited and refined year on year, adding depth and complexity to student understanding.

Transdisciplinary concepts are so broad they can be seen in just about any discipline. They are the types of concepts that form the biggest and most influential patterns of our world. However, they should constantly be viewed in relationship to other more situated and specific concepts to prevent them from being overly vague.

an anchor concept in upper elementary that could later become a subconcept under rational number or ratio as students' mathematical understanding increases.

For the humanities especially, it may even help to consider all the various synonyms and related terms for the anchoring concept to determine the nuance or more specific ways of expressing the ideas imbedded in our anchor concepts. For instance, the anchoring concept of *change* might produce the list of contenders for subconcepts listed in Figure 6.9.

Figure 6.9   Subconcept Examples for the Anchoring Concept of Change

incremental	turning point	disturbance	variance	stagnation
radical	transition	disruption	intentionality	stability
evolution	modification	equilibrium	permanence	progress
revolution	transformation	balance	impermanence	improvement

DESIGN STEP

The following questions can help you to consider and select a few subconcepts for each unit, which you can record in Figure 6.10. Once selected, you can place them in the corresponding space in the unit planner (Figure 6.1).

Figure 6.10   **Subconcepts for the Unit's Anchoring Concept**

Consider each anchoring concept on its own. The goal is to bring about a dynamism or potency to the unit. Ask yourself the following questions to build out two to four subconcepts or skills for each anchoring concept:

- What is it *about* the anchoring concept that I want students to investigate?
- Which smaller concepts will provide a richness to the anchoring concept?
- As I view each potential unit or chunk of content through the lens of this anchoring concept, what other, more specific ideas seem significant and relevant?
- What are the more nuanced, specific ideas embedded in this concept?
- What contrasting or opposing ideas relate to this concept? How might I use what this concept *does not mean* to illuminate what it *does mean*?

_____

_____

_____

Listing Facts and Skills

Keep in mind the ideas we put on paper now might change as more units and lessons are created. Curriculum work is iterative in nature. For now, don't worry if your list is perfect and don't agonize over each little choice. It is important, however, to build out a few clusters of concepts as a starting point.

Also keep in mind that these concepts are not meant to be a burdensome add-on to the existing course design. If you feel overwhelmed, wondering how it's possible to teach all the content *and* this list of concepts you've just brainstormed, stop to remember the purpose the concepts will serve. They are not meant to replace the existing content of a course, nor are they meant to be piled on to that content. Instead, the facts and skills defined by the standards will be taught often as the specific examples that students file into these conceptual file folders.

The goal is to help students create a stronger, more cohesive, organizational structure in their minds. The details of many standards documents or text books—facts, skills, examples—have customarily guided curriculum planning, leading to learning experiences that feel disconnected and insular. By anchoring and organizing surface level knowledge around transferable, organizing concepts that are frequently revisited, students are better equipped to make the kinds of connections that build schema.

Facts in this particular spot on the unit planner refers to specific details or information that do not transfer easily beyond a narrow set of circumstances, such as mathematical facts or formulas, historical names, dates, or time periods, specific artistic styles, or any other specific details that you want students to memorize or know with automaticity. Similarly, **skills** in this particular spot on the unit planner refers to specific abilities for students to *do* something, such as follow a set of procedures, again with automaticity. Each item on this list should ideally fit within one of the conceptual categories so that students can see how the world is organized.

Facts: Specific details or information that do not transfer easily beyond a narrow set of circumstances, such as mathematical facts or formulas, historical names, dates, or time periods, specific artistic styles.

Skills: Specific abilities for students to *do* something, such as follow a set of procedures, usually with an eye toward gaining automaticity or fluency with practice.

DESIGN STEP

If you have specific facts and skills to be learned with memorization, fluency, or automaticity, here is the spot to put them in the unit planner.

Figure 6.11   **Facts and Skills for the Unit**

 Facts and Skills

Drafting Conceptual Relationship Questions to Build Schema

Conceptual questions connect anchor and sub concepts in relation to each another so that students are able to unearth and discover these conceptual relationships as they move through carefully designed learning experiences. Following the ACT model, students first acquire a basic understanding of the anchor and subconcepts. Then, they connect the concepts to each other as they examine the relationships among them. This is where carefully crafted questions are essential. Conceptual relationship questions promote the type of thinking that builds the mental infrastructure necessary for learning transfer, helping kids build networks of meaning in their minds that can later be applied to a variety of novel situations. These questions also help promote clarity in learning and ensure we as teachers are aligning our learning experiences to the concepts and skills most important in our course, while affording students the autonomy to construct meaning for themselves.

Teacher clarity is a powerful driver of learning (Hattie, 2009). *Teacher clarity* involves clearly communicating the learning intentions and success criteria so that students know where they are going, how they are progressing, and where they will go next (Almarode & Vandas, 2018). We agree wholeheartedly that the intent of learning should be clear and visible to students to better promote student agency and ownership. We also believe this clarity can begin in the form of carefully crafted questions rather than overly detailed learning objectives.

Some learning objectives are overly specific and not really transferable. We want to be sure to keep the context out of the learning intention (Wiliam & Leahy, 2015). For instance, *Students will be able to analyze the themes of* Romeo and Juliet or *Students will be able to evaluate the failure of the League of Nations* do not point student attention to the deeper structural patterns and are therefore not terribly useful for transfer of learning.

Other learning objectives, such as *Students will be able to identify the main idea and supporting evidence of an informational text* or *Students will be able to solve two-step equations with 80 percent* accuracy, do not typically motivate students or promote thinking. Instead of inviting wonder, excitement, and intellectual collaboration, they tend to require compliance to a predetermined learning path and outcome. At their best, they give kids some sense of the topic or focus of the day, and sometimes more is lost than gained by creating checklists for learning instead of invitations to learning.

If a school or district requires or encourages posting learning targets or intentions, we propose keeping them relatively general without revealing the specific ways that concepts are connected. Notice how the statements below tell the specific concepts but do not tell students exactly how they are related:

- We are investigating how the temperature of the earth impacts the wind.

- We are exploring how characters, plot, conflict, and setting impact theme.

- We will determine the role of arrangements in permutations and combinations.

- We are examining how culture, equality, and government interact.

We prefer posting conceptual relationship *questions* to guide students in the learning journey. In fact, we used to write out the statements of conceptual relationship or generalizations in the unit planning process. We stopped doing that for several reasons, as we thought questions were more powerful. Here are a few of the reasons:

1. Adult-created statements of conceptual relationship can limit what teachers expose students to; in an effort to create the most direct path to the adult-written relationship, teachers often eliminate contradictions and complexity, both of which are essential for understanding our complex world.

2. Adult-created statements of conceptual relationship can limit student thinking to a narrow, preconceived focus for the teacher; we have seen teachers reject beautiful, creative, and valid ideas from students because they weren't in line with the "right" answer teachers were aiming for.

3. Predetermining the conceptual relationships leads teachers and students to think that this is the end-goal of the unit whereas, in fact, transfer of learning to novel situations is the end-goal.

4. Connecting two or three concepts does not build schema in the brain. Students eventually need to connect scores of concepts in their brains in order to build the patterns of thought that facilitate transfer. Layering on conceptual questions allows for students to continue connecting seven, eight, or more concepts, which has been done from kindergarten on up with our partner schools, as they discuss a web of connections among concepts.

5. Co-creating questions with students will help them gain a stronger sense of how they can construct their own lines of inquiry. The more experience they have, the more they can take ownership of them and make sense of a wider variety of ideas and conceptual relationships.

The conceptual question stems have been included in nearly every chapter of this book, as they are one of the most helpful planning tools in pointing students' attention to how the world is organized. This is not an exhaustive list of all the possible ways to pose conceptual relationship questions, but a decent starting point for crafting conceptual questions. We recommend at least three to five conceptual questions, each with different concepts, that allow students to see the relationships between the disciplinary literacy concepts, modern literacy concepts, anchor concepts, and subconcepts within each unit. Eventually, we want students connecting all of the concepts in the unit, which we will detail in Chapter 8.

DESIGN STEP

Place any relevant questions you may have already written into this part of the unit planner (Figure 6.1). Remember, fill the blanks with *concepts* and not details.

- How are _____ and _____ connected?
- What is the relationship between _____ and _____?

(Continued)

(Continued)

- How does _____ impact/affect/influence _____?
- What effect do _____ and _____ have on _____?
- How do _____ and _____ interact?
- What is the role/purpose of _____ in _____?

The following question stems work well for early elementary or as scaffolding questions before reaching the ones above:

- What is the difference between _____ and _____?
- What happens when _____ interacts with _____?
- Why does _____ make _____ [do whatever it does]?
- Why does _____ need _____?

Figure 6.12   **Conceptual Relationship Questions for the Unit**

? Conceptual Relationship Questions

We recommend co-constructing some of these questions as well as other types of questions with students at the start of a unit. Once they get the hang of it, students introduce new questions and reframe old ones as the unit goes on in order to shape the course of learning for themselves and others. Chapter 8 details one our favorite strategies for creating questions—Question Formation Technique from the Right Question Institute.

We intentionally want our questions to be vague, particularly about the type of connections between and among concepts, as we want the students to be the ones to determine and articulate the particular kind of relationship. We find that many guiding questions reveal too much for students, taking away their intellectual independence and innate curiosity of finding out.

Take for instance the following early childhood question: *How do our investigations impact materials?* As students are investigating different states of matter, the students should come to understand that investigations often *transform* materials. Chapter 8 will feature a strategy of offering different types of relationships to students where they can consider a variety of ways that concepts interact to deepen their thinking and understanding.

Writing Compelling Questions to Invite Learning

Compelling questions are a great way to invite students into the unit of study and consider the relationship between disciplinary literacies, modern literacies, and the world outside of school. We can use real-world problems and intriguing questions to motivate students to hone the disciplinary and cross-disciplinary ways of knowing, thinking, and doing necessary to transfer their learning to complex situations. These compelling questions and authentic contexts can serve as the jumping off point for inquiry. Consider, for example, the use of compelling questions to promote learning in a high school algebra course, as depicted in Figure 6.13.

Figure 6.13   **Compelling Questions to Drive Learning in High School Algebra**

Will we ever be able to prevent a pandemic?			
Disciplinary Lenses	**Interdisciplinary and Modern Literacy Concepts**	**Anchoring Concepts**	**Contexts for Exploration**
Proportionality	Data literacy	Growth and decay	The Plague
Function	Viral infection	Logarithm	Ebola
Representations	Communication	Geometric sequence	COVID-19

This question, "Will we ever be able to prevent a pandemic?" is an effective launching pad for the unit in many ways:

- It is *understandable*: Students can develop initial hypotheses without needing much instruction or new knowledge from the teacher.

- It is *open*: There is more than one way to reason through the answer, and it requires deep conceptual organization.

- It is *authentic*: It's a question that even experts are grappling with, rather than one that is already settled and is rooted in a situation outside of the classroom.

- It is *important*: Answering this question has implications for real-world action.

The following types of questions are also compelling ways to invite learning at the start of a unit. Consider which might be a good fit for students, courses, or disciplines.

Debatable Questions

Questions that ask students to "pick a side" or answer "yes or no" often make good compelling questions because they give students two concrete positions with which to frame their learning and spark debate about the best answer. For instance, compare these two questions, one framed in an open-ended manner and the other framed as a debate:

- Why was agriculture an important invention for mankind?

- Was agriculture the single most important invention in human history?

While both questions ask students to consider the significance of agriculture in human history, the second is more engaging, urgent, dynamic, and fun. It invites continual thought as students revise their positions in light of new information, whereas the first question allows students to feel "done" with their thinking if they can identify a single reason that agriculture was important.

A compelling question doesn't have to be a question at all. For instance, a life science teacher might ask students to investigate the claim that Russian scientists have found 40,000 worms buried in permafrost that came back to life and started moving and eating once the frost melted, as shown in Figure 6.14.

The teacher could ask students to review the claim and then rank it on a scale from "very believable" to "not at all believable" at the start of the unit. As they learn more about the science behind this claim, they can revisit the ranking scale a few more times and justify their answers based on the science. Then they can transfer their learning to completely different contexts involving adaptations of species and eventually solve a challenging new problem in life science. We like to pose these along a spectrum and

Figure 6.14   Russian Worms in Permafrost

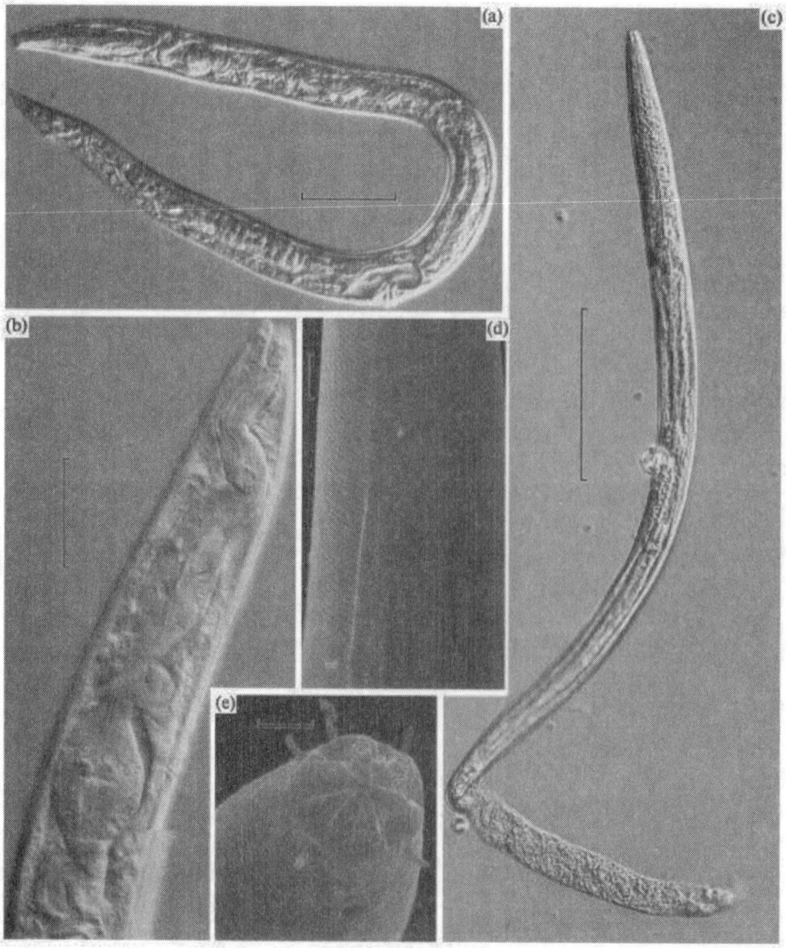

SOURCE: Shatilovich et al. (2018).

ask students to revisit their thinking as they gain more conceptual understanding involved in the compelling question. See Figure 6.15 for an example of a spectrum we have used to teach DNA and genetics.

Figure 6.15   **Compelling Question as a Continuum**

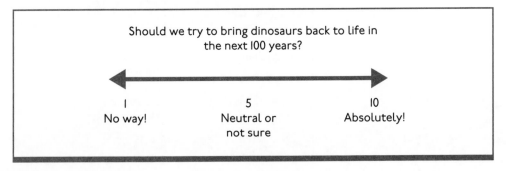

Ethical Questions

Another great source of compelling questions are the increasingly difficult ethical questions we face in the 21st century. As technology, especially artificial intelligence, becomes more advanced and integrated into our daily lives, ethical reasoning is going to become just as important to computer programmers as it was for philosophers. Take, for instance, the increased automation of driverless vehicles. Should cars be programmed to ensure the safety of the driver even if it means injuring or endangering pedestrians? Or should they seek to preserve as many lives as they can and potentially endanger the driver?

One doesn't need to have a degree in philosophy to incorporate ethical reasoning and inquiry into their classroom. At its core, ethics is an exploration of what one *should* or *shouldn't* do. In addition to helping hone students' ethical reasoning skills, ethics questions can go a long way in generating student investment. They can open the door to rich conversations about values, justice, and society.

Cross-Disciplinary Approaches

Often, a question can be made even more compelling when it spans multiple disciplines and allows for multiple entry points. Depending on what you selected for cross-disciplinary alignment in Chapter 4, the compelling questions can enhance planning. For instance, tenth-grade courses in modern world history and English language arts could investigate the relationship between freedom and security in a wide variety of personal, societal, and literary contexts. When launching the unit, teachers might ask students to consider several iterations of the core conceptual question as depicted below in order to engage students and help them see the wide applicability of the conceptual framework at play. Figure 6.16 contains examples of compelling cross-disciplinary questions.

A compelling question is, *Should freedom be restricted in order to ensure safety?*

- Should parents impose curfews to keep teens out of trouble?
- Should the state prohibit teen drivers from transporting non-family members in their vehicles?
- Should governments punish those who engage in hate speech?
- Should governments ban handguns?

Figure 6.16   Cross-Disciplinary Approaches to Compelling Questions

Compelling Question	Course	Anchor Concepts	Modern Literacy Concepts
Should freedom be restricted in order to ensure safety?	World history	Rights, power, justice	Digital citizenship—Privacy, access
	English language arts	Censorship, culture	
Should scientists be allowed to genetically modify humans?	Biology	Cause/effect Stability/change	21st century skills—Communication, critical thinking
	Math	Patterns, chance	
Should you tell a lie if it will help protect someone?	Social studies	Laws, responsibilities, fairness	Socioemotional skills—Honesty, integrity
	English language arts	Argumentation, persuasion	

DESIGN STEP

COMPELLING QUESTIONS

Whichever approach you choose, the goal of the compelling question is to invite learning and help students see the concepts as "living" and urgent, rather than inert. One well-crafted question can pique students' interest, keep them engaged through even the more mundane aspects of a unit, and motivate them to work hard when things get tough. Taking the time to stage the unit with a question that draws students in is well worth it! Brainstorm your compelling questions in Figure 6.17, then transfer your final questions to the Unit Planner in Figure 6.1.

Figure 6.17   **Compelling Questions for the Unit**

? Compelling Questions

ASSESSING FOR TRANSFER

The next chapter takes a comprehensive look at designing a system of assessment for learning that transfers. The key idea for unit planning is to ensure that transfer tasks are an ongoing part of our students' journey. We want to ensure our students are able to apply their understanding to new situations, and therefore we must foster and refine their ability to do so throughout the unit. If our performance task or summative assessment is the first time we ask students to transfer their understanding, they will undoubtedly struggle.

We will plan opportunities for transfer throughout a unit in the next section. First, we want to preliminarily select which of our disciplinary lenses, modern literacies, anchoring concepts, and subconcepts are the ones we want to measure on the summative task. One of the most widespread and useful ways to think about the relationship between assessment and instructional planning is backward design, as popularized by *Understanding by Design* (Wiggins & McTighe, 2005). The goal of backward planning is to design goals and acceptable evidence of those goals prior to mapping out learning experiences. That way we can create, structure, and sequence our lesson plans in a way that will most effectively prepare students for the end of unit summative or performance task.

Based on our standards or learning outcomes and our conceptual relationship questions and their respective concepts, we should have a pretty good idea of what students should understand and be able to do at the end of the unit. Using these as a guide, consider performance tasks that require students to apply their conceptual understanding in a *dissimilar, real-world context*. We have already brainstormed some contexts in Chapter 4, and although they may change, a dissimilar, real-world context serves as a goalpost that allows us to intentionally move students forward as we plan our units.

You might remember chemistry teacher Julia Briggs from an example in Chapters 3 and 4. When planning a unit about solubility, displacement, chemical persistence, and environment for her middle school science students, Julia *first* identified a complex, real-world problem that related to these concepts: declining birds of prey populations near ecotourism sites. Knowing that her ultimate goal was for students to transfer their understanding of chemistry to this novel problem, she was able to plan backward to ensure students were ready for the task.

The graphic in Figure 6.18 provides further clarity about how the learning transfer spectrum relates to assessment design. Notice that assessments may be more or less "real world" and they may also demand more similar or more dissimilar transfer. Innovation happens when students transfer their knowledge to complex, real-world situations that are very dissimilar from contexts previously studied. But in order to help students build toward innovative thinking, teachers must use other types of transfer as a scaffold.

Figure 6.18   Learning Transfer Spectrum Explained

	Dissimilar	
Academic	The assessment requires students to apply their conceptual understanding to situations that are very different from what they have done in class. They are engaging in complex transfer.	Real World
	The assessment involves a single discipline and does not involve a real-world challenge or authentic audience. Students do not observe their impact on the world or community.	The assessment requires students to apply conceptual understanding from multiple disciplines, solve real-world challenges, present their findings to an authentic audience, and observe their impact in the world.
	The assessment requires students to apply their conceptual understanding to situations that are similar to those they have studied in class. They are doing simple transfer.	
	Similar	

Some disciplines, such as social studies and language arts, naturally lend themselves toward the real-world side of the spectrum, as they are human-centered disciplines. But it is more than the context that determines where on this spectrum the task will fall. We move toward the real-world side of the spectrum when students use their conceptual understanding to

- Solve complex, *real* challenges
- Utilize concepts from multiple disciplines
- Present their findings to authentic audiences
- Impact the world around them

Real challenges are not the same as realistic, but made up, scenarios such as simulations. These are a great starting point and do a good job of getting students engaged, thinking from different perspectives, and applying their learning. Depending on the role students take on in the task or scenario, these simulated scenarios usually fall somewhere in the middle of the academic and real-world sides of the spectrum. Simulations or models that inform real-world problem-solving can certainly be viewed as further along the spectrum than those that do not directly impact the world.

On the other hand, learning that transfers naturally engages students in thinking about real areas of their lives, school, community, or the world that could be improved. These challenges usually require interdisciplinary thinking and modern literacies to be successful. They're not about finding one correct solution, but about being able to synthesize complex understanding in order to have meaningful impact. The current generation of students, the *why* generation, value impact and genuine experiences and are looking to make the most out of all experiences, including those within school (Perna, 2018).

DESIGN STEP

ASSESSING FOR TRANSFER

Take a moment to think about which concepts will be assessed on the summative task and brainstorm a real-world, novel scenario that students will unlock on the summative task. We will go into more detail on this in the next chapter, but for now, some initial thinking will be invaluable to guide the unit storyboard in the next section. If possible, jot down some additional scenarios that move students toward the real-world, novel scenario as part of our ongoing assessment for transfer.

Figure 6.19   **Brainstorming Assessment for the Unit**

Summative Assessment	System of Ongoing Assessment for Transfer
Which disciplinary lens(es), modern literacy, anchoring concepts, and subconcepts will students apply on the summative assessment?	*How will students transfer their learning from academic, similar scenarios to increasingly dissimilar, real-world scenarios?*
What real-world, novel scenario will students unlock on the summative assessment?	

THE UNIT STORYBOARD: PLANNING FOR SIMILAR TO DISSIMILAR TO REAL-WORLD TRANSFER

The storyboard part of our unit planner, introduced in Chapter 2, is a tool to plot out a series of learning experiences in a transfer-focused unit plan and shown again in Figure 6.20. It helps us to envision how students will run through each step of the ACT model over the course of the unit. We will more carefully design these steps in the next chapter and plan more specific learning experiences in Chapter 8. For now, you may want to jot some ideas down for each context but remember that we will return to this section in both of the next two chapters.

This section provides important framing and considerations to be aware of when sequencing learning experiences that acquire, connect, and transfer learning to increasingly complex situations, culminating in student taking action in the world. As we go through each section, use the template to jot down ideas that will serve as a springboard for this part of the planner when we design a system of summative and formative assessments in the next chapter.

Acquire: Making Meaning of Anchoring Concepts

We want to begin our units with lessons geared toward helping students acquire understanding of individual concepts. We like two analogies to think about the role that concepts play in the learning journey. In one way, concepts are like file folders helping students to file away details and specifics into the same file folder based on shared attributes. Another way we think of them is like building blocks or Lego bricks, which can be stacked and connected in countless ways, making innumerable varieties of unique structures. Even if we want students to eventually have freedom to build whatever knowledge structures they'd like, they must first have the "blocks" to do so. Anchoring concepts serve as a frame for students' understanding of the rest of the unit's subconcepts, facts, and skills—so by establishing them first, students will be able to better orient themselves as they move through each learning experience.

The overall features for this phase of the learning journey should involve three tenants. We outline several specific instructional strategies in Chapter 8, but we also want to take a little time to detail the types of activities that are most effective during this phase, so educators can design, adapt, or curate custom sets of strategies, too.

A. **Focus on a Concept's Attributes:** Every concept is comprised of a unique set of attributes. Some are more relevant or noticeable than others, but our ability to notice and organize these attributes is a central part of our cognition. For a very basic example, while toucans and bald eagles look quite different, our ability to generalize their attributes (beak, wings, talons, flies, etc.) are what help our brain file both of them in the "bird" folder. So, when introducing a new concept, we need to help students pay close attention to the most important and relevant attributes of that concept. This will ensure that they can engage more meaningfully with the concept of study, not just memorize it.

B. **Inductive Thinking:** Our brains are wired to seek out patterns. Providing students with activities that encourage them to evaluate or categorize examples will help them understand the relevant attributes across several examples. The

Figure 6.20 Storyboard Template

Sequence and Structure: Designing Student Learning Experiences

Acquire	Connect	Similar Transfer	Dissimilar Transfer	Student Action
Students acquire Understanding of anchoring concepts	**Context #1** Initial inquiry and hypothesis testing	**Context #2** Transfer and refine	**Context #3** Transfer and refine	**Context #4** Novel, real-world application
Anchor Concepts: *What are the individual anchor concepts your students will need to acquire to begin the learning experience?*	**Context:** *What context will you provide for your students that will help them begin to understand the relationship between and among the concepts they've acquired?*	**Context:** *What similar context will your students explore that will require use them to transfer their understanding of the conceptual relationships?*	**Context:** *What dissimilar context will your students use that will require them to transfer their understanding of the conceptual relationships?*	**Project:** *How will you provide opportunities for students to transfer their understanding to issues facing their class, school, community, or beyond?*
Note: *This does not mean that every single concept of the unit has to be taught upfront. Students often acquire understanding of additional concepts when they transfer to new situations. Consider which ones they'll need to begin their learning journey.*	**Questions:** *What conceptual relationship question will you pose to help guide and scaffold your students' inquiry?*	**Refine:** *How will you encourage your students to refine their understanding of the conceptual relationships? Will they need to know new concepts to understand the new context?*	**Refine:** *How will you encourage your students to refine their understanding of the conceptual relationships? Will they need to acquire understanding of new concepts to access the new context?*	*Consider frameworks like Design Thinking and Integrative Thinking that scaffold students' ability to engage in meaningful, real-world work.*
Feedback Plan: How will you and students use assessment as feedback about learning?	**Feedback Plan:** How will you and students use assessment as feedback about learning?	**Feedback Plan:** How will you and students use assessment as feedback about learning?	**Feedback Plan:** How will you and students use assessment as feedback about learning?	**Feedback Plan:** How will you and students use assessment as feedback about learning?

From Similar Transfer

To Dissimilar, Real-world Transfer

Scan this QR code to access the Learning That Transfers storyboard database opportunity to compare different examples of the same concept improves the comparison processes that takes place in their mind (Alferi, Nokes-Malach, & Schunn, 2013). Instead of having a rigid mental model of a concept that might look different depending on the context (the water cycle as a system in earth science class versus a governmental system in government class), inductive thinking encourages students to focus on concepts' attributes, helping them more easily categorize new examples into the right "conceptual folder."

C. **Consolidate Understanding:** Once students have had the opportunity to acquire and make meaning of individual concepts, they should consolidate their understanding. While it is important students construct their own understanding through inductive thinking and analogical reasoning, it is equally necessary for students to elaborate on their understanding and that teachers ensure students are on the right track. Chapter 8 provides useful strategies that, once students complete, teachers can use to assess student understanding of the concepts. If students misconstrue a concept during this phase, chances are much lower they'll be able to understand its relationship to other concepts in the Connect phase.

THINKING PROMPT

What are some key points you want to remember about the acquire phase of the learning journey?

_____

_____

_____

_____

Connect: Exploring the Relationship Between Concepts

Sadly, most instruction unfortunately remains at the surface level (Cuban 1984; Kane & Staiger, 2012). While gaining an awareness and understanding of individual concepts and their key attributes is important, learning can't stop there if we want students to transfer what they've learned in a meaningful way. Once students have a firm grasp on the key attributes of the individual skills or concepts they are learning, we need to shift their focus to the relationship between or among multiple concepts.

The best way to do this is to provide students with a context where they can observe the conceptual relationship. It might be a poem in language arts, an experiment in science, a time period in history, or an equation in mathematics. Regardless of what the context is, conceptual questions help scaffold their learning experience and focus their attention on the deeper patterns at play in the situation.

If too much time is spent teaching students surface-level information, they won't have the opportunity to foster a working understanding of disciplinary ways of knowing, doing, and thinking. Instead, they'll only be able to recite facts, topics, and examples. On the flip side, if students are pushed into transfer too early, they might lack the adequate schema and understanding to successfully apply conceptual relationships to new situations, or even misconstrue the relationship between concepts entirely.

The key elements for this phase are conceptual questions and related contexts. Additionally, we find visual-spatial thinking an excellent tool for students to consider when exploring how concepts are connected in relationship. Again, we outline three considerations for the connect phase of learning, with more detailed strategies outlined in Chapter 8.

A. **Conceptual Questions:** The powerful thing about conceptual relationship questions is their ability to guide students' attention toward the various types of relationships and connections concepts have between and among themselves. The way each of the stems is constructed focuses students' attention on the interaction between the concepts, not merely the concept themselves.

Scan the QR code for context inspiration.

B. **Contexts:** To ensure the conceptual questions we ask will help guide students to the desired conceptual understanding, it is vital we curate and provide rich and engaging contexts for students. Whether it is a TED Talk, experiment, poem, historical document, or real-world data set, the contexts we supply for students need to be equally compelling and clear. They need to be accessible enough for students to notice the conceptual relationship with some prompting but challenging enough that they have to investigate and inquire to do so. While this curation process is one of the most time-consuming parts of the unit creation process, we've compiled a list of sources and websites that can help you get started.

C. **Visual-Spatial Thinking:** Metaphors and analogies are a vital part of our cognition, language, and conceptual systems. Our mind regards ideas as objects and, like objects, we can use our visual-spatial perception to help organize, orient, and make sense of complex ideas (Lakoff & Johnson, 2008; Reddy, 1979). These are all things that can easily be reoriented or reorganized in different ways. Asking students to articulate something abstract as the "relationship between concepts" can seem difficult without strategies to make it more accessible. Being able to *see* those relationships, draw connections between them, and even use spatial reasoning as a means to orient them can make those abstractions more concrete and clearer for the student using them and for anyone else they might be explaining their thinking to, which is why we love whiteboards, sticky notes, and just about any way to make student thinking visual and moveable. Retired primary teacher, co-author of *Tools for Teaching Conceptual Understanding for Elementary*, and member of the Learning Transfer Team Nathalie Lauriault even has her students explore concepts through movement. Providing opportunities for nonlinguistic representation across different modes allows students to leverage prior knowledge and explore conceptual connections in a variety of ways.

THINKING PROMPT

What are some key points you want to remember about the connect phase of the learning journey?

_____

_____

_____

_____

_____

Similar and Dissimilar Transfer: Unlocking New Contexts

Once students have explored the initial context and articulated their understanding of a conceptual relationship, they can transfer their understanding to other contexts to determine if their thinking holds up. By using their understanding of the conceptual relationship generated in the previous phase of learning, students will be able to unlock new contexts. At the same time, by unlocking those contexts, students' understanding of the conceptual relationship will either be enriched, complicated, or challenged, leading them to a more nuanced understanding.

During this stage of learning, students apply their understanding of the conceptual relationship to a completely new situation. Figure 6.21 shows a few typical types of transfer. This is not an exhaustive list, but a few ways to think about how we can plan intentionally for similar transfer.

Transfer should be something that students are engaging in regularly. It helps to have their first few transfer tasks be low stakes, so students have ample opportunity to familiarize themselves with the mechanisms of transfer and gain a more nuanced understanding of the conceptual relationships within a unit.

Like any skill, the more opportunities students have to transfer their learning to new contexts, the more adept they will become at it. That isn't to say we can teach transfer as a discrete skill, but rather students will become more accustomed to and comfortable with the idea that, in a class that teaches for transfer, retention won't be enough. It is the norm. It isn't only expected but also encouraged.

Figure 6.21   Typical Types of Transfer in the Core Disciplines

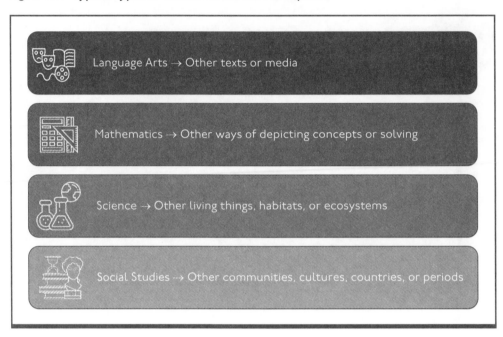

THINKING PROMPT

What are some key points you want to remember about the transfer phase of the learning journey?

_____

_____

_____

_____

_____

Student Action in the Real World

The goal of designing units for learning that transfers is to help students apply that understanding to the world in meaningful ways. The more opportunities students receive to embed their learning in real-world, authentic contexts, the more meaningful and transferable it will become. Ideally, we would have the time and flexibility for every unit to move students toward meaningful student action, but if that's not possible, it's important to be discerning and reflective about which units are best suited for authentic learning experiences and community projects.

We need to leave intentional space in our curriculum for students to impact their school, community, and even society in meaningful ways (Weil, 2016). Real-world, dissimilar transfer shouldn't be the afterthought, but the north star of our instructional design. We should consider what could be possible if we backward planned learning in ways that oriented learners toward meaningful, real-world action and engagement.

PRESERVING SPACE FOR STUDENT VOICE, CHOICE, AND PASSIONS

The Unit Storyboard serves as a scaffold to help teachers curate concepts, contexts, and provide ample opportunities for transfer. It is the "structure" element of our "freedom within structure" philosophy. Whereas the ACT model and Unit Planner are meant to provide a useful frame for learning, student voice, choice, and passion are how we can ensure students have the freedom necessary to take ownership of their learning.

The terms *voice*, *choice*, and *passions* have been the focus of numerous books, articles, and debates in recent years. Although cognitive load theory tells us too much choice can hinder learning and performance, thoughtfully planned learning experiences that increase student voice and choice in the classroom lead to increased motivation and agency in the learning environment (Marzano et al., 2017; Schneider et al., 2018). Like Marzano et al. (2017), we believe there are distinct differences between voice and choice.

Student voice is characterized as the students giving feedback to the teacher, and the teacher is receptive and willing to use that feedback when making decisions for their classroom community. Often times teachers seek student feedback, but students are not aware of how the teacher used their feedback and don't perceive their input as being valued. It is critical that teachers only request feedback when they know they will use it.

Jessica Mundy and Jessie Porter, language arts teachers at Little Mill Middle School in Forsyth County, continually demonstrate the importance of seeking student input and using this feedback to guide project and planning decisions. When designing their "My Voice" extended writing project, Mundy and Porter invited various groups of students in to describe what they had liked about being given choice in the past, what didn't work, and then solicited input on the project design. This feedback directly influenced the design, pacing, and overall options in the project. Students not only felt appreciated by having their feedback requested but also felt empowered to share their thoughts and feelings with both teachers because they saw their input was valued and used to inform decision-making.

NEXT-DAY STRATEGY

Try out a new activity and ask students how they like it. The next time you try a similar activity share with students how you used their feedback to adjust and improve the learning experience. This might seem simple, but students will feel validated that their input was taken into consideration, and they will be more likely to give honest feedback in the future.

Voice allows students to express their thoughts to the teacher. Choice, however, is characterized by students being co-creators of the learning process. They are actively making decisions and advocating for themselves throughout their learning experiences. This sense of autonomy is what leads to increased motivation. In today's classrooms, choice and student agency are no longer nice-to-have features. As our understanding of childhood advances, and as our students mature, the need for autonomy and chance to direct their learning is critical (McCombs, 2010).

Again, in the middle school language arts example, the teachers provided students with choice in their My Voice writing project. All students explored the anchoring concepts of audience, author's purpose, perspective, responsibility, and growth; however, students were the ones who determined the specific contexts of their storyboard. Instead of making all students do the same project around the same topic, students chose from a variety of short- and long-term options as well as the topic of their project(s). Mundy and Porter consistently conferenced with their students throughout the semester to guarantee they were making progress toward their personal goals.

Providing voice and choice does not mean students get free reign and the teacher is left with a pile of paperwork at the end of a unit. We want to provide freedom within structure. Restrictive structures and rules can feel rigid and limiting, while a total lack of guidance can quickly become confusing and disorienting as opposed to empowering. Instead of seeing these approaches as opposing binaries, we prefer to focus on the affordances of each. We ask ourselves, *What are the benefits of structure? What are the benefits of freedom? How can we leave space for both when we design learning experiences for students?*

> What are the benefits of structure? What are the benefits of freedom? How can we leave space for both when we design learning experiences for students?

Educators define the story line for a course, its anchoring concepts, and which modern literacies are most needed. All choices in content, process, or product should relate back to those critical concepts and skills we have identified. The good news about transferable concepts as opposed to isolated skills and facts is that they allow for authentic voice *and* choice.

Choice, like transfer, falls along a spectrum from simple choice to real choice. In Figure 6.22 we address the differences between these types of choices. Allowing students to make choices in their learning increases agency and the sense of autonomy, even choices we think are simple like choosing where to sit or if they want to learn more about topic A or topic B. Just the notion of perceived autonomy is enough to increase motivation and performance in learning (Schneider et al., 2018).

Figure 6.22   Student Choice Spectrum

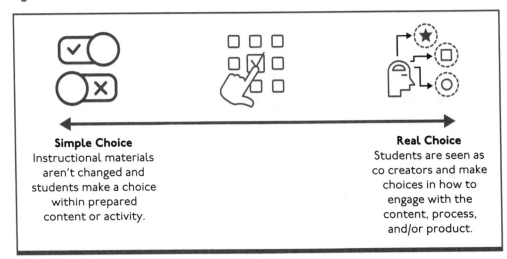

Simple Choice
Instructional materials aren't changed and students make a choice within prepared content or activity.

Real Choice
Students are seen as co creators and make choices in how to engage with the content, process, and/or product.

Knowing that simple choices can have a positive impact on student motivation should give educators inspiration to begin increasing opportunities for student voice and choice in their classrooms. We recommend starting slowly by providing a few options. This will ensure students do not become overwhelmed cognitively by too many options, and it allows you as the educator to help create structures and a workflow based on students' needs. As students become more comfortable, increase the number of options, and eventually remove the guardrails and allow students to determine their own options when appropriate.

THINKING PROMPT

Reflect on your instruction as a whole. Overall, where do you feel you fall on the choice continuum? How might you move along the continuum?

_____

_____

_____

_____

_____

Teaching that emphasizes concepts over specific facts is inherently more personal and equitable. For example, a science teacher in rural Georgia realized that her students would understand the concepts of *structure* and *function* by starting the unit with the question: *Why wouldn't we go mud riding in a Prius?* Because the *structure* of a Prius does not match the *function* of mud riding. She used this engaging example to help students make meaning of the concepts of structure and function. When we think in terms of organizing concepts, we can think about concrete examples from students' own lives and background knowledge that help students make meaning of these organizing ideas.

This allows students to leverage their rich bodies of prior knowledge in the classroom. Too often, students believe what they learn in school has no relevance to what they do outside of it. While we can plan for specific local or global challenges that students can tackle, we can also leave room for students to explore problems or challenges they find interesting, especially after we've worked together as a class to use the ACT model, acquire–connect–transfer, to answer a compelling question or solve a real problem. In trying to create more personalizable lessons where students are able to help create their own learning experiences, consider the role inquiry might play (Zhao, 2018).

In the book *Dive into Inquiry* (McKinzie, 2016), *inquiry* has four phases: structured, controlled, guided, and free. Figure 6.23 illustrates these phases. The inquiry process moves from a teacher-centered setting in structured inquiry where students all respond to the same question and do the same activities and slowly becomes more student centered in guided inquiry. At this phase, students create their own paths to find solutions to a class question. Once students are at free inquiry, they are in control of their learning

Figure 6.23   Four Phases of Inquiry

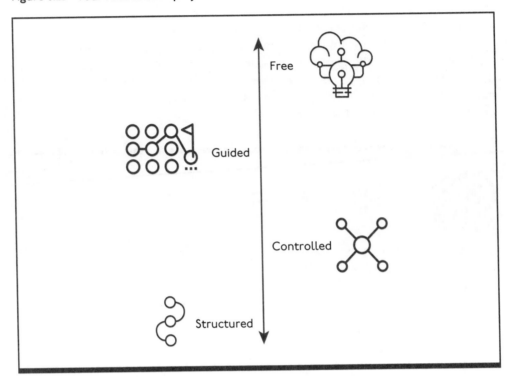

and the teacher is a partner giving feedback along the way. Like choice and transfer, the phases of inquiry fall along a spectrum. As educators we can meaningfully assist students in progressing along this continuum by including their preferences and views in the planning process.

Using inquiry in the classroom poses an opportunity for the teacher to structure lessons that embrace disciplinary expertise and modern literacies in tandem. Students learn content through questioning and investigating, and, as they grow in maturity and experience, students are able to take on more freedom in the inquiry process.

THINKING PROMPT

What are some key points you want to remember about providing student voice and choice in the learning journey?

_____

_____

_____

_____

_____

Moving Students to Meaningful Action

While we believe meaningful and targeted types of choice, voice, and inquiry are viable at all stages of learning, the Student Action section of the storyboard is where it is centered. As students move from more structured to freer phases of inquiry, they should be taking more direct ownership of the content and context of their learning. The power and beauty of teaching for learning transfer is it allows for educators to systematically grow student schema around broader concepts while encouraging ownership and inquiry. Instead of seeing these as pedagogically conflicting values, it places them on a continuum. The more facts and skills students have, the more deftly they are able to design and monitor their own learning and progress. Because knowledge is organized at a conceptual level instead of a topical one, creating connective tissue between the content and students' passions, hobbies, and interests is much easier.

This might sound idealistic or far-fetched at first, but students in our digital age take this kind of ownership on all the time. They learn new strategies in *Fortnight*. They study elaborate designs in *Minecraft*. They learn complex dance routines on TikTok. The key is baseline levels of knowledge and skill. Once students have developed that, there is no limit to what they can do and find online. Additionally, there is a wealth of digital tools and platforms students can learn to curate, share, and present their learning in dynamic and authentic ways.

Consider how students could freely combine the products in Figure 6.24 and processes in Figure 6.25 with the content of your course or unit to take ownership of their learning during the Student Action phase.

Figure 6.24 **Products for Student Action**

Product	Explanation
Podcast	Students select a topic of interest, conduct research, and record a podcast exploring a topic or presenting an argument.
Community Service Project	Students find a topic or issue in their community they're passionate about and look to improve it through research and a plan of action.
Museum Exhibit	Students conduct research and curate resources while learning to think like an archivist, curator, or museum worker.
Documentary	Students select a topic of interest, research it, and showcase their understanding through a well-designed documentary.
Social Media Campaign	Students conduct research on a topic of interest, learn how effective social media campaigns are conducted and marketed, before launching one themselves in support of their cause.
Class Blog	Students write about a variety of topics on a class blog that is publicly accessible to either the school, community, or world.
Live Performance	Students conduct a live group or solo performance where they showcase new knowledge or skills they've obtained.
TED Talk Event	Students help design and execute a TED Talk style event with relevant guest speakers, influential faculty members, or fellow students.
Research Symposium	Students conduct a research or inquiry project on a topic with personal significance to them. They then present their findings to the school, community, or even a panel of expert volunteers.
E-Book or E-Zine	Students use an application like Canva or Book Creator to design a e-zine or e-book that can be shared with an authentic audience.

Figure 6.25 **Processes for Student Action**

Process	Explanation
Design Thinking	Students follow the Design Thinking framework of Empathize, Define, Ideate, Prototype, and Test to create a product.
Integrative Thinking	Students use the Integrative Thinking tools and processes to understand a complex problem and develop a potential solution.
Storyboarding	Students envision how their product or design will look in a sequence of images or snapshots to plan.
Empathy Mapping	Students conduct interviews and complete empathy maps to understand what people are seeing, thinking, hearing, and feeling in their school or community.
Kanban Board	Kanban board is a physical or digital project management system that helps teammates communicate where they are in their process.
Expert Interviews	Students can reach out to experts in their selected field or industry and schedule a Zoom or Meet interview with them to learn about their topic.
Journey Mapping	Students create a Journey Map to visualize and simulate how a potential user would interact with their product or design.

THINKING PROMPT

What are some key points you want to remember about the real-world application or student action phase of the learning journey?

_____

_____

_____

_____

_____

CONCLUSION

The goal of this chapter is to provide a framework to help organize all the thinking and reflection we have done so far. It is important to stress that the Unit Planning Template is a tool, not a prescription for student learning. The boxes are there to help categorize and organize elements of instructional design in ways we feel are useful.

They can and should be swapped, deleted, or re-arranged in ways that suit each particular vision or learning context.

What is important is that there is a clear vision for the unit and related learning experiences. When a clear vision for learning is established, it is much easier to be flexible about how one reaches the destination. We encourage and value improvisation, reframing, and adaptation as much as we encourage developing structure for a unit. One does not need to throw away all their previous lessons, strategies, or tools to teach for transfer. As long as there are concepts established, questions asked, and contexts provided, you have all the key ingredients.

The important thing to keep in mind with unit design is the ultimate goal is to help move students toward meaningful student action through the application of conceptual structure and schema. That does not mean every unit has to end in a massive community service project. It simply means that when picking concepts, drafting questions, curating contexts, and designing summative assessments, we remain conscious that the true goal of learning is to help students build understanding that can be transferred to meaningful, real-world situations.

Equally important is that student learning moves them toward increased autonomy. When we are discerning about the amount of prior knowledge students have with concepts, leverage the digital affordances offered by technology, and have built a culture of transfer, students can take their learning to the next level. We simply need to give them the trust, time, and tools to do so effectively and efficiently. When designing unit planners that establish structure and value freedom, powerful, transferable understanding is not just possible, it's achieved by design.

THINKING PROMPT

What is your refined thinking about the following questions?

- How are **unit planning choices** and **learning transfer** connected?
- What is the role of **questions** in the **unit planning process**?
- How do **authentic contexts**, **concepts**, and **meaningful real-world** connections interact?

_____

_____

_____

_____

_____

CHAPTER SEVEN

Assessments

What Is the Role of Assessment in a Classroom Focused on Transfer?

"Too often the educational value of doing well what is done, however little, is overlooked. One thing well done prepares the mind to do the next thing better. Not how much, but how well, should be the motto. One problem thoroughly understood is of more value than a score poorly mastered."

—Booker T. Washington

Why does this chapter matter?	Creating a system of assessment that focuses on feedback about transfer can empower both students and teachers.
What will I be able to do by the end of this chapter?	I will be able to design a system of feedback about the quality of teaching and learning in my classroom, including summative and formative assessments of transfer.

As the old refrain goes, whatever gets measured gets treasured. In the classroom, this means what we assess and how we assess it—our measurements—reveal a lot about our values and goals. A daily quiz after students read a passage sends the signal that retaining details from the text and preparing well each day are important. Vocabulary tests at the end of the week send the message that the language of the discipline matters. Speed drills in math tell students that automaticity is valuable. If we truly treasure transfer, then the best way to convey this to students is through our assessment practices.

In fact, if there was one single shift that had the power to transform a coverage-based classroom into a transfer-focused one, this would be it: assess for transfer. And, conversely, if there was one single practice that had the power to prevent a classroom from becoming transfer focused, it would be a lack of assessing transfer. Even if individual lessons include learning transfer, ultimately both teachers and students will direct their energy toward the goals that are explicitly assessed.

Again, when we talk about assessment in this book, we are not talking about singular events such as the test at the end of the unit or one awesome project at the end of the term. We are talking about a way of monitoring the quality of our teaching and the quality of students' learning through constant feedback loops aligned to our goal

> What we assess and how we assess it—our measurements—reveal a lot about our values and goals. If we truly treasure transfer, then the best way to convey this to students is through our assessment practices.

of transfer. This includes summative assessments where students apply their learning to novel, real-world situations to impact the world around them. It also includes formative assessments that are carefully aligned to the summative task, which form the "meat" of every unit.

Perhaps most importantly, we assert here that assessment is primarily a student-directed process. Students must steer the vision of quality thinking and quality work. Students must determine, for themselves, how well they understand and how proficiently they have applied their skills. Students must recognize their strengths and weaknesses; they must seek and use feedback for improvement. In other words, our students must become independent learners and self-sufficient thinkers and problem-solvers.

However, while assessment is student directed it must also be teacher designed. In our role as classroom leaders, it is our job to cultivate student independence through a system of feedback that informs their view of themselves as learners. *Am I on the right track? Do I understand? Does this seem right?* Ultimately, students must answer these questions for themselves if they are ever to solve the big, important problems they will face in their lives beyond school. It is the teacher's role to provide experiences that help students hone their instincts and hold themselves to high standards of quality. By guiding students' assessment of themselves, rather than doing that assessment for them, we honor their full dignity as human beings and help them gain the confidence they will need to tackle life's greatest challenges. At the same time, we alleviate our own burden, shifting more responsibility to the students themselves. It's a win-win.

> If there was one single shift that had the power to transform a coverage-based classroom into a transfer-focused one, this would be it: assess for transfer.

THINKING PROMPT

The following concepts anchor this chapter, culminating in application. Take a moment to think before you read on. What is the meaning of each of these concepts and how are they related to one another?

- Systems

    _____
    _____

- Feedback

    _____
    _____

- Novelty

    _____
    _____

- Authenticity

    _____
    _____

- Alignment

    _____
    _____

- Summative assessment

  _____

  _____

- Formative assessment

  _____

  _____

- Transfer

  _____

  _____

- Student empowerment

  _____

  _____

Consider your current thinking on the following questions as well:

- How can we create systems of feedback that empower students?
- Why is novelty an essential component of assessing transfer?
- What role does authenticity play in assessment? How does it impact student empowerment?
- What does alignment between summative and formative assessments look like?

_____

_____

_____

_____

_____

CHAPTER STRUCTURE

This chapter is organized around the following sections:

- A system of feedback
  - Assessment as feedback about teaching
  - Assessment as feedback about learning
  - Designing a comprehensive system of feedback for both teachers and students
- Summative assessments of transfer
  - Novel situations: the essential ingredient
  - Designing summative transfer tasks
  - Identifying novel scenarios
  - Authentic value beyond school
- Planning for formative assessment of transfer
- Putting it all together

ASSESSMENT AS A SYSTEM OF FEEDBACK

Assessment as Feedback About Teaching

Professor John Hattie asserts that assessment is feedback to teachers about teachers (Hattie et al., 2017). It's a profound and counterintuitive idea worth reading again: Assessment is feedback to *teachers* about *teachers*. Of course, assessment serves other purposes, too. But we think this is an essential place to start. Before we design assessments for our students, we need to establish a clear vision of our mutual success.

THINKING PROMPT

Take a few moments to think for yourself: What will it look like (and not look like) to help students successfully acquire, connect, and transfer the concepts of your course? What does the teacher's success look like in terms of student behaviors and thinking? Jot your ideas down in the chart provided in Figure 7.1.

Figure 7.1 **Success Criteria for Teachers Brainstorming Chart**

		In Students' Written Work	In Classroom Discussions and Activities	Other
Acquire	If I have successfully taught a new concept, what will I see?			
	If I have not been successful in teaching a new concept, what will I see?			
Connect	If I have successfully enabled students to connect concepts to one another to form a mental model, what will I see?			
	If I have not done this successfully, what will I see?			

		In Students' Written Work	In Classroom Discussions and Activities	Other
Transfer	If I have successfully taught students to transfer their understanding to new situations, what will I see?			
	If I have not done this successfully, what will I see?			

Of course, there is quite a bit of room for teachers to develop their own answers to these questions and for the answers to vary from grade to grade, course to course, teacher to teacher. However, there are a few general hallmarks of successful acquisition, connection, and transfer of new learning as shown in Figure 7.2.

Figure 7.2 **Criteria for Successful Acquisition, Connection, and Transfer**

As a result of successful lessons focused on *acquiring* understanding of concepts, students should be able to

- State the meaning of the concept(s) in their own words

- Elaborate on what the concepts mean and do not mean, distinguishing them from other similar or overlapping concepts and addressing common misconceptions (*In other words . . . ; This is different from . . . ; Although many may assume that this means _____, it actually means _____.*)

- Recognize examples and non-examples and generate their own examples and non-examples

- Illustrate the concept through use of metaphor, symbol, or visual

As a result of successful lessons on *connecting* concepts in relationships, students should be able to

- Explain the complex relationships among several concepts using precise words, diagrams, and other visuals

- Distinguish between simplistic relationships or truisms (*Word choice impacts poetry; Kindness and empathy are both important.*) and complex, insightful relationships that make claims about how the world works (*To fully understand a poem, we have to consider the connotations, not just definitions, of each word*

(Continued)

Figure 7.2 (Continued)

> *the author has chosen. Empathy is a prerequisite of kindness.*), arriving at the latter and avoiding the former
>
> - Provide specific examples from a range of contexts that illustrate the connections among concepts
>
> As a result of successful lessons on *transfer*, students should be able to
>
> - Recognize which concepts apply in a given situation
>
> - Use conceptual relationships to move beyond the surface-level features of a situation and instead focus on its deeper structure
>
> - Develop theories about why a new scenario is unfolding the way it is, generate hypotheses about unknown aspects of a new scenario, make predictions about what will happen next, construct arguments, and develop solutions to novel problems based on their understanding of the deeper conceptual structure at play
>
> - Apply prior learning with caution, noting important underlying differences between two situations and how these differences impact transfer
>
> - Use insights gained from new situations to alter and refine their mental model of the concepts and their relationships

When we view assessment as feedback to teachers about teaching, we are on the look-out for these student behaviors in the midst of a lesson as well as in the more formal work we collect from students. We listen with the ears of an assessor during discussions and conversations, observe with the eyes of an assessor as students write and create, probe with questions accordingly, and provide corrective feedback or change course in our lessons to move students closer to success. If we wait until an assessment "event"—a big test or quiz, the final project—we've already lost our chance to coach students toward transfer.

Therefore, we suggest that teachers approach each lesson with one or more of the criteria in Figure 7.2 in mind. What, exactly, is the purpose of the learning activity students will experience? Is the goal of this lesson to help students distinguish between two commonly conflated concepts such as *equation* and *expression* in mathematics, or *narrator* and *author* in English language arts? Or is the goal for students to recognize examples and non-examples of each without being prompted to do so? Which students are stuck in an overly simple view of the relationship among concepts, and what will I do to help them increase the complexity of their ideas? Having a clear picture of the learning we intend to foster, and continuously monitoring our own effectiveness, is a key piece of teaching for transfer.

Assessment as Feedback About Learning

The flip side of thinking about assessment as feedback for teachers about teachers is to think about assessment as feedback to students, by students, about students. In other words, just as teachers must use assessment tools to constantly monitor the effectiveness of their teaching, students must use assessment tools to continuously monitor the effectiveness of their own learning efforts. When students monitor their progress in the learning journey, they are what Hattie (2012) refers to as assessment-capable learners. This means students are able to explain what they are going to learn, how they will demonstrate their learning, what success in learning looks like, and discuss their growth and next steps in the learning process.

This can be a big shift for both teachers and students. Traditional schooling separates the role of learner and assessor. Students are there to learn; teachers are there to assess. Teachers set the expectations; students strive to meet them. Teachers judge; students are subject to judgment. The teacher poses the questions and holds the answers. Even when teachers ask students to self-assess, it is often done only as a reflective exercise. The assessment that matters—and ends up in the grade book—is usually still that of the teacher.

But separating learning from assessing obstructs student ownership of learning in the worst possible way. Instead of enabling young people to take charge of their own intellectual development, we send the message that learning is a transaction whereby students exchange effort for percentages or letters written atop their paper. In doing so, we rob students of the deep satisfaction—the thrill of discovery, the triumph of invention, the bonds created through collaborative pursuit of a common goal—that learning can bring.

The problem is that students are not innately good at self-assessment. Of course, neither are adults. The art of measuring one's own understanding or judging one's own proficiency is not one easily mastered. And yet, we must ask ourselves, what is the cost of *not* being able to do these things? Imagine the musician who cannot tell when a note is out of place or his instrument out of tune, or the chef who cannot tell if she has added the right amount of salt to a dish. Expertise and transfer both require an ability to self-assess and self-correct. Without this ability, students are relegated to a life of intellectual dependency, forever reliant upon other experts to tell them what they know and don't know, what they can do or not do.

It is worth the investment of time and energy, then, to teach students to recognize the traits of effective learning summed up in the ACT model—what it looks like to effectively acquire new conceptual understanding, connect concepts in relationships, and transfer their conceptual models to new phenomena. Not only will this enable students to be lifelong, independent learners, but it will also alleviate the burden of being students' sole source of feedback. Once students understand what learning looks like, they can assess themselves and provide useful feedback to their peers, enabling them to take fuller ownership of their own learning. When students no longer need the teacher to tell them whether or not they've learned something or performed well, we free them (and ourselves!) from the transactional nature of traditional schooling.

> When students no longer need the teacher to tell them whether or not they've learned something or performed well, we free them (and ourselves!) from the transactional nature of traditional schooling.

Consider the rubric for conceptual understanding and transfer in Figure 7.3. Often, rubrics are designed to be task specific, meaning that teachers spend time constructing new rubrics for each separate project or performance throughout the year and kids spend time decoding new rubrics each time they approach a new task. The inefficiencies of this approach leave both students and teachers worse for the wear and impede students' ability to self-assess. However, the rubric in Figure 7.3 is task independent, establishing criteria for successful transfer of learning no matter the lesson, unit, or course. This rubric can be used to assess student learning using a wide variety of pieces of evidence—an entire portfolio of journal entries and reflections, short quizzes and major projects, exit slips or discussion comments—rather than a single piece of work. No one has to wait until the unit is over or a piece of work is polished to get a sense of

Figure 7.3 Rubric for Conceptual Understanding and Transfer

	Off Track	Novice	Apprentice	Practitioner	Expert
Acquire	My understanding of the concepts is **inaccurate.**	My understanding of the concepts is **partial.**	My understanding of the concepts is **fully developed.**	My understanding of the concepts is **complex.**	My understanding of the concepts is **precise, complex, significant and transferable.**
Connect	Conceptual connections show **misunderstandings** or confusion. Examples used inappropriately or not at all.	Conceptual connections are **vague** or **simplistic.** **Few** examples used to illustrate ideas.	Conceptual connections state a **complete, precise** relationship. Examples are used to illustrate ideas.	Conceptual connections are **complex** or **sophisticated.** **Relevant, significant** examples are used to **justify** ideas.	Conceptual connections are complex, precise, and **significant.** **Powerful** examples compellingly justify ideas.
Similar Transfer	I do not understand how new, similar situations relate to my ideas about the conceptual connections.	I **partially** understand how new, similar situations confirm, complicate, or contradict my ideas about the conceptual connections.	I **fully** understand how new, similar situations confirm, complicate, or contradict my ideas about the conceptual connections.	I understand the **complexities** or **nuances** of how new, similar situations confirm, complicate, or contradict my ideas about the conceptual connections.	I understand the **complexities and nuances** of how new, similar situations relate to my understanding AND can judge how **significant** the new information is to my understanding of conceptual connections.
Dissimilar Transfer	I do not use my understanding of the conceptual connections to respond to dissimilar situations OR I use conceptual connections inaccurately.	I use my understanding of **individual concepts** (not the connections between concepts) to respond to dissimilar situations.	I use my understanding of the **connections** among concepts **implicitly** to respond to dissimilar situations.	I use my understanding of the connections among concepts **explicitly and appropriately to** respond to dissimilar situations.	I explicitly **evaluate the transferability** of my understanding of the connections among concepts to dissimilar situations and **account for nuanced differences** in my response.

online resources 🔗 Download template at www.learningthattransfers.com.

the learning that has taken place. In essence, it allows for every learning product to be considered as evidence of student progress toward the goal of transfer.

The beauty of using one consistent rubric to assess conceptual learning in your course is that both teachers and students know exactly how to recognize the criteria of successful performance. For students, this aids in the development of metacognition and self-awareness. *Is my understanding partial and superficial, or thorough and complex? Am I uncovering sophisticated relationships among concepts through rigorous use of facts and examples, or are my ideas overly simple and poorly supported? Can I transfer my learning to new situations?* These are questions that students must continue to ask themselves if they hope to be lifelong independent learners and innovators. For teachers, this consistent rubric saves precious time and energy, allowing them to recognize successful learning more easily and provide feedback that transcends a specific task. We encourage you to download the template in Figure 7.3 and modify its contents to fit your needs.

Designing a Comprehensive System of Feedback for Both Teachers and Students

Focusing on what successful *learning* looks like—no matter the particular unit or content—and taking the time to establish a systematic way of tracking student performance is the first step in building an ecosystem of assessment that works. Consider the routines described in Figure 7.4.

Figure 7.4 **Assessment Routines**

	Student Self-Assessment	Teacher Feedback and Data Collection
Pre-assessment	At the start of the unit, the teacher introduces the anchoring concepts he has selected as the unit's focus. He asks students to write down everything they already know about these concepts and develop a hypothesis or two about how the concepts relate to one another. Then he has them examine the first two rows of the rubric in Figure 7.3 and explain to a partner where they think their understanding falls on this scale.	The teacher circulates throughout the room as students write down what they already know, noting trends and common misconceptions. He will use these trends and misconceptions to inform his upcoming lessons. As students discuss their ratings with a partner, the teacher listens in. If students are wildly off base in their self-assessments, he reminds them of the meaning of the criteria in the rubric. "Take a look again. Is this idea really complex?"
Ongoing Formative Self-Assessment	At the beginning of each lesson, the teacher frames the daily learning targets in terms of acquiring, connecting, or transferring knowledge. Students take a few minutes to set a goal for themselves based on the rubric and write it down. At the end of class, they check back in with their goal. Did their understanding grow more precise or complex? Did they overcome a misunderstanding? Did they successfully account for the nuances in a new situation before transferring?	Every few days, the teacher asks students to submit a representative artifact of their learning—a journal entry, diagram, written response, problem set, short quiz—with a quick explanation of what they think it demonstrates about their understanding and ability to transfer. The teacher examines the artifacts and provides feedback on students' work and their self-assessment of that work. He asks himself, "What does this body of evidence suggest about the effectiveness of my lessons? Where to next?"

(Continued)

Figure 7.4   (Continued)

	Student Self-Assessment	Teacher Feedback and Data Collection
Ongoing Formative Peer Assessment	*Several times per unit, students present their current thinking about the concepts and their relationships to one another. Peers ask questions and provide feedback to help each other move forward on the rubric.*	*As students critique each other, the teacher guides their thinking with probing questions or by providing exemplars to help them calibrate their vision of success. He listens carefully to students' feedback and models effective feedback of his own.*
Summative Assessment	*The teacher designs a complex task requiring dissimilar transfer and includes the language of the transfer rubric in his grading scheme for the task. The last step of the task is for students to grade themselves and justify their ratings.*	*When he goes to grade students' work, the teacher simply confirms or modifies students' self-score. Or, if the student's self-assessment is too far off base, the teacher offers descriptive feedback and returns the task to the student for further consideration.*
Reflection	*Students wrap up their study in each unit by tracing the evolution of their thinking with regard to the concepts of the unit. They account for their successes, reflect on the challenges they faced, and contemplate the significance of their learning. They also explain which learning experiences were most useful to them and why.*	*The teacher reflects on the effectiveness of his teaching throughout the unit and takes students' reflections about the effectiveness of specific activities and lessons into account.* *He shares some of his reflections and opens up about what he learned—about teaching and about the concepts themselves—throughout the unit.*

Notice that the burden of assessment falls heavily on the students themselves. While traditional approaches to assessment—tests or quizzes plotted on the calendar as accountability events—often create a mountain of work for the teacher and renewed anxiety for students as each assessment event draws near, a consistent system of monitoring learning across all tasks can minimize work for teachers and empower students to take charge of their own learning. The more students are involved in monitoring their own progress, the greater agency and motivation they have in the learning environment.

Scan here for assessment templates and examples.

As you develop a system of feedback for your own classroom—hopefully one that encourages student ownership of learning and assessing while also providing plenty of actionable data for the teacher—consider our digital resources found here.

SUMMATIVE ASSESSMENTS OF TRANSFER

In addition to effective assessment routines that inform daily teaching and learning, we also need well thought-out summative assessments to guide the learning of each unit. Having a clear performance task in mind helps us to plan backward and align our teaching to our goals. Of course, this is not a new idea. The authors of *Understanding by Design,* among others, have long advocated for this approach (Wiggins & McTighe, 2005). However, backward planning is particularly essential in a transfer-focused classroom. The same approach was used to create the health unit shown in Figure 7.5. The teacher has designed this unit around the following conceptual questions:

- How do drugs and alcohol impact my ability to determine my own destiny?

- What is the relationship between self-determination, drugs and alcohol, and media messages?

Figure 7.5   Sample High School Health Unit

Unit 3: Self-determination in the context of drugs and alcohol

Disciplinary lens: **Self-determination and Agency**	Modern literacy focus: **Media Literacy—Motives and Manipulation**	Anchoring concepts, subconcepts, skills: *Drugs and alcohol* *Abuse and addiction* Compare & contrast treatments of the same topic in several primary sources (CCSS.RH.9-10.9)

How do drugs and alcohol impact my ability to determine my own destiny?

What is the relationship between self-determination, drugs and alcohol, and media messages?

Context #1	Context #2	Context #3	Context #4
Alcohol and alcoholism	Tobacco and e-cigarettes	War on Drugs	Novel, real-world application: Opioids
Students read about alcohol's *effects on the body* and then examine and compare a series of movie clips that depict teenage drinking in order to *assess the implicit messages that teens receive about alcohol use,* including its relationship to *self-determination and agency.*	Students examine and compare two advertising campaigns: the *Truth anti-tobacco campaign and e-cigarette advertisements in* order to **contemplate the role of media and marketing in drug use** and **evaluate how each campaign impacts teens' self-determination and agency.**	Students learn about different types of drugs (hallucinogens, depressants, stimulants) and the federal government's attempts to reduce drug use and drug-related crime through the **War on Drugs, including an analysis of the "Just say no" campaign.** Then they engage in a Q&A session with a survivor of drug addiction to better **understand how drugs impact an individual's ability to choose their own destiny.**	Students research the *opioid crisis* in the United States, **evaluating the media messages related to opioids** and comparing them to media portrayals of the War on Drugs. Then they work in groups to **design a peer education campaign that uses social media** to educate teens about the **relationship between opioid use and self-determination,** including ways that teens can be savvy consumers of media when it comes to opioids.

From similar transfer   To dissimilar transfer

From simple understanding   To sophisticated understanding

Students first investigate these conceptual relationships in the context of alcohol and alcoholism before looking at tobacco and e-cigarettes and then a range of "harder" drugs, such as cocaine and heroin, while looking at the War on Drugs. With each new context, students practice transferring their understanding of the concepts and then refining that understanding in light of new learning.

Finally, as a summative assessment, the teacher asks students to research the current opioid crisis, evaluate the media messages they find, and design a peer education campaign to educate fellow teens about the ways in which opioid use might impact their ability to determine their own destiny.

Notice that in many ways, students' study of Contexts #1 through #3 serve as rehearsals for their investigation of opioids in Context #4, the summative assessment. So, by the time students arrive at the end of the unit, they have received plenty of formative feedback on their ability to transfer their understanding of the concepts to new contexts.

This is no accident. In designing this unit, the teacher *first* envisioned the transfer task described in Context #4. Then, knowing that she wanted students to research the opioid crisis and design their own social media campaign to educate teens about the ways in which opioid use could impact their self-determination, she worked backward to build up a sequence of experiences that would prepare them for the task. She identified several other drug and alcohol contexts in her standards—alcohol, tobacco, other "hard" drugs—and arranged them from the simplest context to the most complex context in order to guide students toward a sophisticated understanding of the concepts.

Notice, too, that the summative assessment asks students to apply their understanding to a novel (not yet studied), real-world context. Students did not study the opioid crisis prior to the summative assessment, but rather investigated this crisis as part of the assessment. This is key!

Novel Situations: The Essential Ingredient

In a more traditional classroom, students rarely encounter unfamiliar material on assessments. For instance, a student who has studied photosynthesis in biology expects to answer questions about photosynthesis on the exam. The student who has read *Hamlet* expects the topic of the final essay to be about Hamlet. Even math students expect the problems on a test or quiz to mirror those seen previously in class.

In a transfer-based classroom, though, unfamiliar material is the backbone of assessment. The student who has studied photosynthesis knows that she will be expected to apply her learning beyond what she learned in the classroom in order to demonstrate transfer. So, too, the student who has read *Hamlet* knows that he will need to apply his learning to a different text or scenario.

In a classroom focused on transfer, the summative assessment must involve a novel context. Most teachers aspire for students to conduct higher-ordered thinking such as analysis, evaluation, and synthesis of complex ideas. Even if we present analytical,

> In a transfer-based classroom, though, unfamiliar material is the backbone of assessment.

evaluative, or synthesis questions about a situation or context that we previously studied in class, we cannot be sure the students are not simply recalling *our* analysis, evaluation, or synthesis (Brookhart, 2010). We must provide a novel situation for students to tackle in order to measure both higher-ordered thinking skills as well as their conceptual understanding.

Think back to our World War I example in Chapter 2. Students studied the relationships among the concepts of sovereignty, power, freedom, and security in the context of the period between World War I and the Cold War. However, on their assessment, students were given the task to analyze articles and use their understanding of these relationships to argue for or against the United States' use of drone strikes in Pakistan. This is often the hardest change for teachers. *How can I measure students' learning about World War I by asking them questions about Pakistan?* It is also one of the hardest changes for students. *How can I prepare for a test on material I've never seen in class? Why bother to learn about World War I when the test is all about Pakistan?*

In making this shift, it helps to distinguish the types of knowledge that transfer from those that do not, and to assess these types of knowledge accordingly. Figure 7.6 illustrates this distinction in the context of Anderson et al.'s (2001) revised Bloom's taxonomy. Notice that conceptual knowledge, procedural knowledge, and metacognitive knowledge are all transferable, meaning they can be applied to new scenarios using higher-order thinking skills in the cognitive dimension. Therefore, these types of knowledge can and should be measured through transfer tasks that assess students' ability to apply their learning to novel, real-world contexts. The transfer task concerning drone strikes in Pakistan is not really *about* Pakistan, it's about the underlying conceptual structure of sovereignty, power, and conflict.

Notice, too, that factual knowledge operates differently. This is not to say that factual knowledge is unimportant or plays only a minor role in a transfer-based classroom. Quite the contrary. Fact-rich contexts are the only way students can draw conclusions about the relationships among concepts. We build our understanding of concepts by observing the ways they interact within factual case studies or scenarios. We prove the validity of our conceptual relationships by supporting them with factual instances that show them to be true. Even though the facts don't transfer, they help *justify* the choices and connections we make when engaging in transfer. For this reason, in Chapter 2's transfer task about drone strikes, students were asked to *support* their argument for or against drone strikes using their understanding of the concepts *and* their knowledge of World War I. *Why bother to learn about World War I when the test is all about Pakistan?* Because one way to substantiate your claims about Pakistan is through your knowledge of World War I. We need organizing concepts, however, in order to make the intellectual leap between and among different situations.

Figure 7.6 adapts the revised Bloom's taxonomy table to explicitly explain how conceptual knowledge, procedural knowledge, and metacognitive knowledge unlock novel situations. As you read through the table, consider *how* each type of knowledge can be employed for learning transfer. Factual knowledge, or specific details of an area of study, does not transfer, while the other three do. Conceptual, procedural, and

Figure 7.6   Assessing Transfer in the Context of *A Taxonomy for Learning, Teaching, and Assessing*

The Knowledge Dimension	The Cognitive Process Dimension					
	1 Remember	2 Understand	3 Apply	4 Analyze	5 Evaluate	6 Create
A. Factual Knowledge						
B. Conceptual Knowledge			Given a novel scenario, students can • Recognize the concepts that **apply** *and* **evaluate** the extent to which the relationships among concepts apply • Use their understanding of concepts and conceptual relationships to **analyze** what is happening in the novel scenario • Use understanding of concepts to **generate hypotheses and make predictions** about the new scenario • Use understanding of concepts to **create** solutions to novel, real-world problems • Reshape understanding of conceptual relationships based on new findings			
C. Procedural Knowledge			• **Evaluate** the extent to which known procedures apply to a new scenario • Flexibly **apply** and **adapt** known procedures to meet the complex demands of a new, real-world scenario			
D. Metacognitive Knowledge			• **Evaluate** one's own application of conceptual and procedural knowledge through self-monitoring and self-correcting practices			

TRANSFER

SOURCE: Stern et al. Knowledge framework adapted from Anderson et al., 2001.

metacognitive knowledge work together when we transfer our learning to unknown contexts. First, a few brief definitions of each term.

- **Conceptual knowledge** involves grasping the larger structure of relationships among concepts.

- **Procedural knowledge** refers to knowing how to do something in a particular field of study.

- **Metacognitive knowledge** involves recognizing how thinking and learning works as well as monitoring one's own thinking (Anderson et al., 2001).

However, no transfer task can effectively assess *all* the factual content of a given unit. Although students should use facts and examples to justify their application of concepts, they will necessarily pick and choose the facts that best serve them in the task at hand. To assess the broader range of factual knowledge that students have learned, other assessments are necessary.

Because of this, it often helps to create an assessment "blueprint" to map out which components of a unit will be assessed through the summative transfer task and which goals should be assessed elsewhere. Consider the health unit discussed earlier. The transferable goals of the unit revolved around the concepts of self-determination, drug abuse and addiction, media literacy, and the skill of comparing treatments of the same topic in various primary sources. The factual components of the unit include details about alcohol and alcoholism, tobacco and e-cigarettes, and various other drugs and their impacts. After mapping these elements out, the teacher was able to visualize the types of assessment she would need in this unit as shown in Figure 7.7.

Isolating the factual knowledge she needed students to master from the transferable goals of her unit helped the teacher design a short pen-to-paper test to evaluate students' understanding of the facts while using a summative transfer task to assess students' ability to transfer their conceptual, procedural, and metacognitive knowledge.

Once this distinction was clear for the teacher, she could make it clear for students, too. Leading up to her assessments of factual knowledge, the teacher could cue students about what to expect and the best way to prepare given that the goal of the assessment was to measure their understanding of the facts they had learned. On the other hand, she could also help students see the very different nature of a transfer task. The transfer task would primarily measure students' application of conceptual relationships and procedures to a novel, real-world situation.

Of course, students would need to recall some of the facts they had learned about alcohol, tobacco, and other drugs when examining opioids. In fact, comparing the fact patterns of these case studies to the fact patterns of opioids is a key step in determining the extent to which their prior knowledge of concepts applies to the new scenario at hand. Here again, we are reminded of the essential role that factual knowledge plays in learning transfer. *Are opioids more or less addictive than tobacco? How can we account for the fact that opioids are often prescribed by doctors for medical purposes, while alcohol and tobacco are not? Where do opioids fit in with drugs like marijuana and heroin?* The answers to these factual questions will impact the way students transfer what they already know to their research about opioids.

Conceptual knowledge: Grasping the larger structure of relationships among concepts (Anderson et al., 2001).

Procedural knowledge: Knowing how to do something in a particular field of study (Anderson et al., 2001).

Metacognitive knowledge: Recognizing how thinking and learning works as well as monitoring one's own thinking (Anderson et al., 2001).

Figure 7.7   Example Assessment Map for Drugs and Alcohol Unit

The Knowledge Dimension	The Cognitive Process Dimension					
	1 Remember	2 Understand	3 Apply	4 Analyze	5 Evaluate	6 Create
A. Factual Knowledge	• Describe alcohol's impact on the body. • Explain the connection between tobacco use and cancer. • Recognize the characteristics of drug and alcohol addiction.		• Compare the impacts of hallucinogens, stimulants, and depressants on the body. • Analyze the impact of drug and alcohol addiction on personal health, interpersonal relationships, education and employment options, etc.		• Evaluate media messages about drugs and alcohol for factual accuracy.	

B. Conceptual Knowledge			• Apply conceptual relationship among the following concepts to novel situation: opioids
			
			  o Drugs and alcohol
			  o Addiction
			  o Self-determination
			  o Personal agency
			  o Media motives and manipulation
			
			• Design a peer education campaign to explain the relationship between opioids and self-determination.			

C. Procedural Knowledge			• Compare and contrast treatments of the same topic in several primary sources (CCSS.RH.9-10.9). • Evaluate media messages to determine the motives of the content creator.			
D. Metacognitive Knowledge			• Evaluate one's own consumption of media messages to avoid being manipulated. • Design a peer education campaign to help others be savvy consumers of media messages related to opioids.			

TRANSFER

SOURCE: Stern et al. Knowledge framework adapted from Anderson et al., 2001.

To this end, it is sometimes helpful to provide teacher support for understanding the facts of a novel situation on a summative assessment. For instance, after teaching a unit on the America Revolution eighth-grade history teachers asked students to apply their understanding of *power*, *systems*, *freedom*, and *revolution* to the civil war in Syria. They provided several articles about the political system in place prior to the war, reports on human rights abuses in the country, and statements by Syrian rebels about the freedoms they sought. Students were asked to write short articles in response to the question, *Why did Syrians rebel against their government in 2011?* Since the teachers' goal was to measure transfer of conceptual knowledge, they allowed students to ask questions and discuss the basic facts of the situation in Syria as part of the assessment. *Where is Syria? Who is Bashar al-Asad? What is a drought?* The answers to these questions helped students understand the facts of the novel situation without robbing them of the chance to apply the concepts for themselves. By providing some support as students encountered the facts of the novel situation, teachers made sure that they were measuring what they intended to measure: conceptual transfer.

Designing Summative Transfer Tasks

Once we've isolated the transferable components of a unit, we can begin to imagine a summative task that measures these goals. Start with the unit elements that you put together in the previous chapters: the focus standards or outcomes, the anchoring concepts and their connections with each other and the subconcepts (conceptual knowledge), procedural knowledge, and metacognitive knowledge. The summative assessment, or assessment at the end point of a period of study, should determine students' ability to apply their learning in each of these important areas to a completely novel situation.

Figure 7.8 is the first section of our summative assessment planner. It brings together the transferable goals of a unit.

The critical piece in this section is to be sure we have clarity on the success criteria for conceptual, procedural, and metacognitive understanding. For instance, will students be using their conceptual understanding to make predictions about a novel scenario, advocate for a position, or develop a solution to a problem? Specifying the type of transfer students will engage in and describing successful performance will ensure that the task is focused and aligned with your goals. With clear criteria in mind, we can design an assessment that elicits the type of thinking we're looking for from students.

The next section of our summative assessment planner, depicted in Figure 7.9 with the health unit example, involves planning explicitly for the transfer task that students will tackle at the end of a unit of study. We will apply our learning after reviewing each piece step by step and completing a few reflection prompts.

After we establish our success criteria, we can ask ourselves these questions:

- What novel situation or problem would serve as an engaging scenario for application of the concepts and procedures of this unit?

- How can students impact the world by conveying their ideas to an authentic audience?

- How will students reflect on this task and explain how and why they transferred their conceptual and procedural knowledge?

KEEP IN MIND . . .

In a classroom focused on learning transfer, we must articulate success criteria around acquiring, connecting, and transferring concepts and their relationships. Most of our templates are meant to spark your own creativity and we encourage you to adapt them to your context. Just be sure that success criteria around conceptual organization are included in your adaptations. We often find that this critical piece is missing from most assessments and even books about deeper learning or transfer of learning.

Figure 7.8   Target Goals and Success Criteria for Summative Assessments

Summative Assessment
Conceptual + Procedural + Metacognitive Understanding

Focus Standard(s) or Learning Outcome(s):	
Disciplinary Lenses, Anchoring Concepts, & Modern Literacy Concepts:	Conceptual Questions:
Procedural Concepts (skills):	Procedural Questions:

Success Criteria:

- Conceptual Understanding: I can explain a strong relationship between two or more concepts in my own words and provide powerful, clear examples (factual knowledge) that prove that relationship.

- Procedural Understanding: I can apply procedures and skills flexibly, adapting them as necessary to fit the new situation.

- Metacognitive Understanding: I can explain the complexities and nuances of how new information confirms, complicates, or contradicts my understanding of concepts. I use a range of tools to monitor my thinking and select appropriate strategies to respond to the situation.

 Download template at www.learningthattransfers.com.

Identifying Novel Scenarios

For many teachers, identifying a novel scenario around which to build a transfer task seems daunting at first. While it's true that some of the most engaging, meaningful transfer tasks are built around complex, ever-evolving real-world situations that require a good deal of new learning for both teachers and students, there are plenty of novel scenarios that will feel "closer to home" and more accessible as you get started. You may be surprised to realize that many "novel situations" are actually embedded in the content and standards that you already teach.

For instance, in the health unit depicted in Figure 7.9, the novel situation of the modern opioid crisis was pulled directly from the teacher's standards. However, instead of teaching this content directly, she embedded this learning in the transfer task and asked students to research opioids as part of their summative assessment.

Figure 7.10 shows how a seventh-grade social studies standard can be "mined" for novel situations. Here, the concepts are bolded, skills are underlined, and specific contexts (facts and examples) are in brackets. Notice that the standard asks students to explain how Pan-Africanism and nationalism led to independence in Kenya and Nigeria. A teacher might choose to teach these concepts in the context of Kenyan independence and then ask students to transfer their understanding to the situation in Nigeria. Or he might use Kenya and Nigeria as case studies in class and assess students' ability to transfer what they've

Figure 7.9   Sample Summative Assessment Plan: High School Health (Opioids)

Summative Assessment:
Conceptual Knowledge + Procedural Knowledge + Metacognitive Knowledge

Focus Standard(s) or Learning Outcome(s):

ORH.C.2 There has been a dangerous increase in misuse and abuse of Opioid pain killers among young adults ages 18–24 (OASAS CDS Data, 2015).

ORH.C.3 Be aware that the misuse of Opioid painkillers such as morphine, codeine, oxycodone, and hydrocodone commonly obtained for common occurrences or procedures (e.g., sports/athletic injuries, oral surgeries) or for pain management for pervasive illnesses (e.g., cancer) can become highly addictive. Most people who are prescribed these drugs do not develop addiction.

ORH.C.13 Due to the behavioral consequences of Heroin and other Opioid addiction, the user may not be able to meet their college or work responsibilities. In order to fund the habit that becomes more expensive over time because of tolerance, users sometimes engage in illegal activities such as stealing, selling drugs, and promiscuous behavior.

ORH.C.22 Be active and advocate for awareness, prevention efforts, policies, laws, and supports that decrease the prevalence of and access to harmful substances everywhere as well as the dangers associated with Heroin and Opioid abuse.

Disciplinary Lenses, Anchoring Concepts, & Modern Literacy Concepts:	Conceptual Questions:
• Self-determination • Agency • Drugs & alcohol • Abuse & addiction • Media literacy	*How do drugs and alcohol impact my ability to determine my own destiny?* *What is the relationship between self-determination, drugs and alcohol, and media messages?*

Procedural Concepts (skills):	Procedural Questions:
• CCSS.RH.9–10.9 Compare & contrast treatments of the same topic in several primary sources (media messages) • Author's motive • Author's message	*What is the role of media messages in both reducing and perpetuating drug and alcohol abuse?* *How does an author's motive impact messages about drugs and alcohol?*

Success Criteria:

- Conceptual Knowledge: I can explain a strong relationship between drugs and alcohol, self-determination, and media messages in my own words and provide powerful, clear examples (factual knowledge) that prove that relationship.

- Procedural Knowledge: I can compare and contrast media messages regarding drugs and alcohol using concepts of author's motive, bias, manipulation, and message.

- Metacognitive Knowledge: I can explain the complexities and nuances of how new information confirms, complicates, or contradicts my understanding of concepts. I use a range of tools to monitor my thinking and select appropriate strategies to respond to the situation.

Engaging, novel scenario:	How students will impact the world:
• Research the opioid crisis in the United States • Compare media messages about opioids with those from the War on Drugs (previously studied in class)	• Design social media campaigns to educate peers about the relationship between opioids and self-determination and how to be savvy consumers of media about opioids

Explanation/reflection piece:

- After the task, students examine the media messages of other groups, compare them to their own, and reflect on the effectiveness of their own work as compared to others

- After the task, students explain how their understanding of the concepts and knowledge from throughout the unit impacted their product and process in the transfer task

SOURCE: Stern et al., 2021. Standards from Ficarra, 2016 (New York State Education Department).

Figure 7.10 Identifying Contexts Within a Social Studies Standard

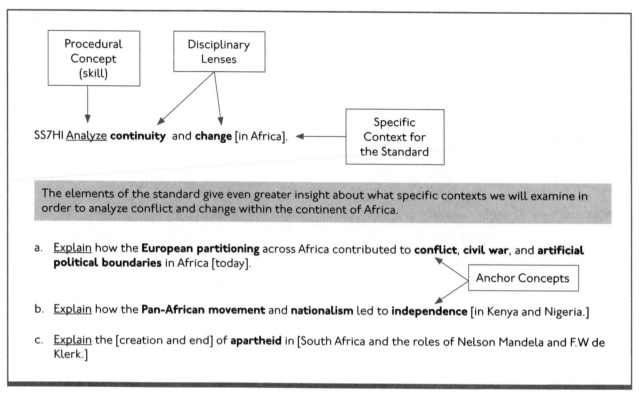

SOURCE: Stern et al., 2021. Standard from Georgia Standards of Excellence (2016).

learned to the situation in South Africa under apartheid (also mentioned in the standards). Although not mentioned directly in this standard, other African independence movements, such as that in Algeria, could easily be used as well. All of these options are either stated or fall directly within the purview of the standard as it is written. After all, the broader standard here asks students to "analyze continuity and change in Africa." Thus, while the situation that students encounter on their assessment is novel to them, it does not necessarily need to be novel to the teacher or outside the current curriculum.

Of course, there are many novel situations *beyond the scope of this standard* where the concepts of Pan-Africanism and nationalism play an important role. Students might study Cuba or Jamaica, for instance, and realize that these forces have been influential outside of the African continent. Or students might examine these concepts as they appear in hip hop and other Black art forms. Or perhaps they might examine the Pan-Arab movement to determine how closely it follows the pattern of Pan-Africanism. Although the standards are a great place to start when it comes to identifying novel situations for assessment, often times the most engaging and relevant situations are those that move us out of the prescribed curriculum and into current issues developing in real time. Because of this, we encourage teachers to view the learning standards as the floor, not the ceiling. The standards provide a strong foundation, but we should not limit student thinking and learning to these benchmarks.

Like social studies, we can mine our math standards for clues to which concepts, skills, relationships, and even contexts should be explored in a unit a study. Take for example the two Algebra 1 standards in Figure 7.11. Notice the bolded terms represent the disciplinary lenses, anchoring concepts, and subconcepts students will explore. Facts are in brackets. Conceptual relationships—connections between concepts—and conceptual understandings—profound knowledge of individual concepts—are also illuminated to demonstrate the gold mine of information we can find in our standards if we dig deep enough.

Figure 7.11 Identifying Concepts Within a Mathematics Standard

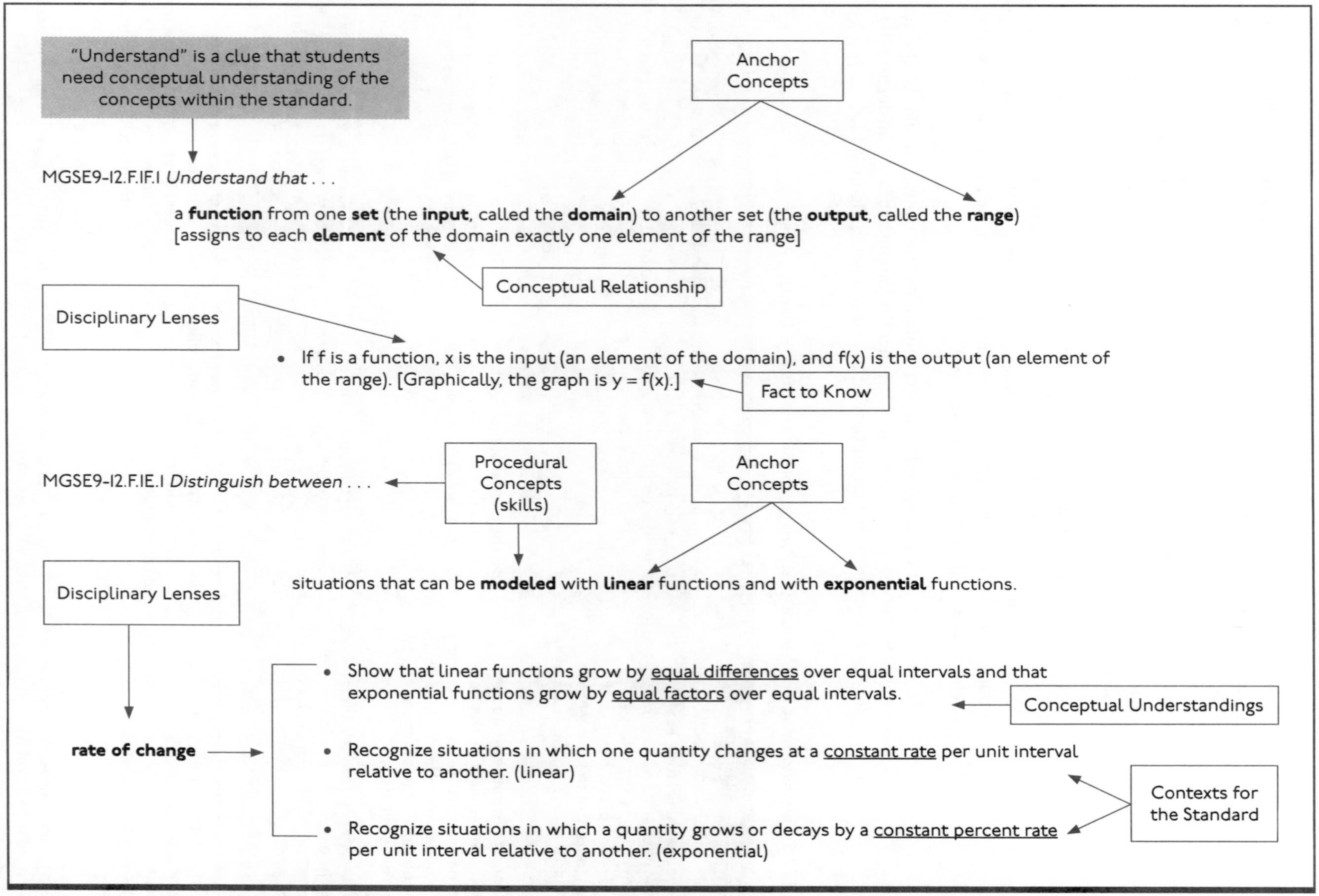

"Understand" is a clue that students need conceptual understanding of the concepts within the standard.

MGSE9-12.F.IF.1 *Understand that . . .*

a **function** from one **set** (the **input**, called the **domain**) to another set (the **output**, called the **range**) [assigns to each **element** of the domain exactly one element of the range]

Conceptual Relationship

- If f is a function, x is the input (an element of the domain), and f(x) is the output (an element of the range). [Graphically, the graph is y = f(x).]

Fact to Know

Disciplinary Lenses

Anchor Concepts

MGSE9-12.F.IE.1 *Distinguish between . . .*

Procedural Concepts (skills)

situations that can be **modeled** with **linear** functions and with **exponential** functions.

Anchor Concepts

Disciplinary Lenses

rate of change

- Show that linear functions grow by equal differences over equal intervals and that exponential functions grow by equal factors over equal intervals.
- Recognize situations in which one quantity changes at a constant rate per unit interval relative to another. (linear)
- Recognize situations in which a quantity grows or decays by a constant percent rate per unit interval relative to another. (exponential)

Conceptual Understandings

Contexts for the Standard

SOURCE: Standards from Georgia Standards or Excellence (2019).

The first standard MGSE9-12.F.IF.1 shows the relationship students should see between functions, inputs, and outputs. This standard is foundational to student understanding but alone is not the heart of a unit. This is why it is paired with the second standard in Figure 7.11, MGSE9-12.F.LE.1. After students acquire understanding of function, domain, and range they will connect and transfer their understanding to linear and exponential functions. Here students will compare how different types of functions grow, how to best model these functions, and when data are indicative of linear or exponential relationships.

Unlike the social studies standard in Figure 7.10 that specifically articulated Africa as the context, math standards are not always this explicit. The contexts indicated in 7.11 illustrate the ways in which students will interact with the concepts and skills, but it is up to the teacher to determine the case studies, rich tasks, or real-world problems that will include these interactions.

In order to generate possible transfer situations from these standards, the teacher needs to think a bit on their own. Consider the various types of transfer and the types of novel situations that might be used to assess them in Figure 7.12.

Figure 7.12   Brainstorming Novel Situations: Function(s), Rate of Change, Domain, Range

Type of transfer:	On an assessment, students might . . .	So a novel situation might look like . . .
Develop theories to explain new phenomena: recognize the underlying structure of a new situation as it relates to the concepts; use the concepts to theorize about what is happening and why	Examine graphs, equations, or data tables, recognizing the domain and range of each, and determining which ones are functions	Graphs, data tables, and equations that **are** functions alongside graphs, data tables, and equations that are **not** functions
Generate hypotheses about unknown aspects of the new scenario: use their understanding of conceptual relationships to "fill in the gaps" in the fact pattern of the novel situation	Use their understanding of functions to interpolate missing data (the range) for a given domain	Graphs of changes in population over time for endangered species with missing data over a span of years
Make predictions: explain what might happen in a new scenario based on known conceptual patterns	Logically predict the domain for a given range beyond the dataset provided	A compilation of yearly earnings for minimum wage jobs between 2000 and 2015 is provided and students make predictions about average yearly and hourly earnings in 2020
Solve problems: develop solutions to novel dilemmas by drawing on conceptual knowledge of how situations with similar underlying features have been resolved	Recognize when situations present linear or exponential relationships and find solutions based on this understanding	Volunteer logs are presented to students for town clean-up activities. Students determine the appropriate model for the data, and use this model to determine how many volunteers are needed at the next community event
Construct arguments: take a position on a novel issue and defend their view using the known relationships among concepts	Argue if a data set is linear or exponential based on a table of values	Students gathering data in order to argue whether or not they should invest in a portfolio that provides constant or variable returns

These two examples show clearly how assessing for learning transfer is completely compatible with standards-based or mastery-based assessment. All the same, as we plan our assessments, we must continuously remind ourselves and our colleagues that the standards are benchmarks, not limitations on student learning. We are not preparing students to be *good* standardized test takers, but to be innovators who will lead meaningful lives and make the world a better place for others.

THINKING PROMPT

What novel situation or problem could serve as an engaging scenario for application of the concepts and procedures of your unit? How might students have the opportunity to do one of the following tasks based on the example in Figure 7.12?

- Develop theories to explain new phenomena

- Generate hypotheses about unknown aspects of the new scenario

- Make predictions

- Solve problems

- Construct arguments

_____

_____

_____

_____

_____

One common misconception involves open-ended questions. When constructed-response questions require students to explain or describe the conceptual relationships but don't include a novel situation, it is not enough. Our assessments must include opportunities for students to transfer their understanding to novel, meaningful contexts for us to truly measure their ability to transfer.

For example, a mathematics class includes a unit centered on the anchoring concepts of *scale*, *graphs*, and *data*. Students are exploring the conceptual question, *How can we use the scale of the graph to change how data is interpreted?* By writing out answers to this question, students might demonstrate their understanding of the conceptual relationship but not necessarily their ability to transfer that understanding to new phenomena. *Explaining* a relationship is not the same as recognizing the applicability of that relationship to a new situation and using knowledge of the relationship to gain insight into a novel scenario.

Instead of simply asking his students to explain the conceptual relationship, the teacher draws on his chosen modern literacy concepts *environmental impact* and *communication* and presents students with various graphs of greenhouse gases emitted by different human food sources. He asks students to interpret the data by determining which food source is a greater contributor to greenhouse gases. In order to successfully interpret the graphs, students must recognize the differences in the scales used before comparing them. Students who do not account for the differences in scale have not achieved transfer because, despite understanding the relationship in an abstract way, they can't yet leverage that relationship to make sense of new phenomena.

See Figure 7.13 for the novel scenario in this example along with a few other examples.

Figure 7.13   **Examples of Novel Scenarios**

Subject	Anchoring Concepts	Novel Scenario
Mathematics	scale, graph, data	Students compare two **graphs of greenhouse gases** emitted by different human food sources and use their understanding of scale to effectively compare the two graphs.
Science	separation, purification, physical and chemical change, physical and chemical properties	Students investigate situations where **access to clean drinking water** is limited or impossible and make suggestions for filters or other methods of purifying the water to make it safe for drinking.
Psychology	confirmation bias, fundamental attribution error, belief perseverance	Students examine a social media post and string of responding comments regarding a current **conspiracy theory** popular on the internet. They must apply their understanding of contribution bias, fundamental attribution error, and belief perseverance to determine the psychological basis for people's belief in the conspiracy theory.
English Language Arts	speaker, context, audience, purpose, message	Students compare **two different news segments** from ideologically conflicting sources on the same topic. They must leverage their understanding of the relationship between speaker, audience, purpose, and context to determine how and why the segments showcase different perspectives.

With a novel situation in mind, the next step in the planning process is to determine how students will communicate their findings to an authentic audience to impact the world around them. In the case of the scale, graph, and data math unit, the teacher asked himself how students' conclusions about the environmental impact of food sources could be used to change people's beliefs and actions. Should students present this information to their families to guide household food consumption? Should they contact members of the US House of Representatives Committee on Agriculture, or address someone from the meat and dairy industry? After brainstorming a variety of stakeholders and decision-makers in the arena of environment and food, he settled on the director of food services for his school district as the target audience because she met the following criteria:

- **Influence or power:** This director of food services has the ability to act upon students' recommendations.

- **Visibility of impact:** If the students succeed, the impact would be visible to them via concrete changes in the school lunch menu; it is easy to follow up with the director to determine students' impact on the lunch program.

- **Scope of impact:** Targeting this audience will allow students to have a greater impact (an entire school district) than, say, targeting their parents would have.

- **Feasibility:** The director of food services is more likely to make time to hear students' concerns and visit the classroom than, say, a member of the House of Representatives.

After scheduling the director of food services to visit his classroom and hear students' ideas, the teacher decided that group presentations would be the best format for engaging this audience.

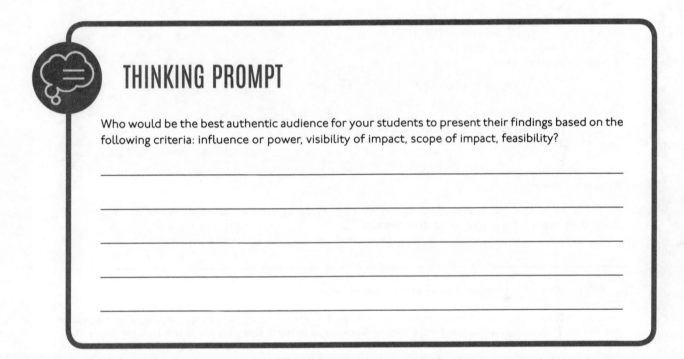

THINKING PROMPT

Who would be the best authentic audience for your students to present their findings based on the following criteria: influence or power, visibility of impact, scope of impact, feasibility?

_____

_____

_____

_____

_____

The final element of planning the transfer task is determining how students will explain and reflect on how they transferred their conceptual, procedural, and meta-cognitive knowledge to the novel situation. In addition to answering the conceptual questions already planned in your unit, this might involve a discussion or written response to prompts like the following:

- How did your understanding of _____ help you complete this task?

- Describe what was happening in your mind as you applied the concepts to this situation.

- What challenges or difficulties did you have in applying the concepts to this scenario?

- How was this scenario similar and dissimilar to other contexts we've studied?

Take a moment to put these together in your own summative assessment planner.

DESIGN STEP

Figure 7.14   **Novel Scenario for Summative Assessments Planning Template**

Engaging, novel scenario:	How students will impact the world:
*What is the new situation that requires students to apply their understanding of the connections between **anchoring concepts, subconcepts, modern literacies** (**conceptual knowledge**)?*	*What artifact, product, invention, or performance will allow students to transfer the targeted skills (**procedural knowledge**)?*
*How can students leverage their application of **disciplinary lenses** in order to unlock this scenario? Which practitioner role will they be taking on for this task (e.g., historian, journalist, data scientist)?*	*What real-world, authentic audience will students engage with to have an impact beyond the classroom?*
	How will students observe their impact?

Reflection Piece:

*How will students monitor their thinking and learning (**metacognitive knowledge**) as well as reflect upon their experience in this unit and in this task?*

Once we have identified a novel situation, determined how students will impact the real world, and planned for explanation and reflection, we can create a narrative to frame the transfer task in student-friendly terms. For instance, when presenting the summative transfer task to his students, the third-grade math teacher included the information in Figure 7.15.

Notice that, while the novel situation introduces a complex, real-world scenario for students to grapple with, the disciplinary role they take on, authentic audience they address, and parameters around the item they create all add layers of complexity to the task. The fact that students will be presenting their ideas to the director of food services for their school district means they must also account for the cost, nutritional balance, and kid-friendliness of the food sources they investigate, not just their environmental impact. If they were taking on the role of newspaper reporters writing articles about food production or policy experts advising their state government on food-tax policy, the task would take on a whole new form. However, the

Figure 7.15   **Student Assignment, Math Example: Environmentally Friendly School Lunches**

The Situation	Your Mission
The production of food for humans often causes greenhouse gases to be emitted into our atmosphere. However, many people are unaware of this fact and do not know which foods are most harmful to the environment. It can be difficult for people to make informed choices because that data about this issue is often hard to compare. As a student who understands **graphs**, **scale**, and **data**, you are uniquely equipped to determine which foods are least destructive to the environment. Use what you have learned in this class to think like a statistician and compare the provided graphs of food-related greenhouse gas emissions.	You will present your findings to the director of food services for our school district, who is concerned about the nutritional balance and cost of school lunches, using a PowerPoint presentation in order to convince her to adopt an environmentally friendly school lunch menu. This will be a team project. Working in a group of three, you and your teammates will analyze the provided graphs and draw conclusions about which foods should be included in the school lunch menu and which should be avoided. You should base your recommendations on the data in the graphs **and** your own knowledge of which foods kids would like to eat for lunch. Your presentation should include the data from the graphs as well as a proposed lunch menu for one week of school lunches using low-emissions foods. The proposed menu must be realistic in terms of cost and must also provide balanced nutrition.

Success Criteria and Reflection Piece

Successful presentations will

- Clearly **explain** the data in the graphs

- Accurately **compare** the greenhouse gas emissions of the production of different foods based on the graphs, accounting for **scale**

- Creatively describe how environmentally friendly foods could be used to make tasty, kid-friendly school lunches that are possible within nutritional and budget constraints

As you prepare, be sure to monitor your own thinking to make sure you are interpreting and presenting your graphs accurately. After your presentation, you will write a one-page reflection about how you used your understanding of graphs, scale, and data in this project.

 Download blank template at www.learningthattransfers.com.

heart of each of these tasks would still involve students transferring what they know about graphs, scale, and data to a novel, real-world scenario that empowers them to impact the real world.

Also notice that complex, real-world problems are often interdisciplinary in nature. The goal of convincing the director of food services to adopt an environmentally friendly school lunch menu requires students to engage with health topics such as nutrition, additional mathematics concepts such as budgeting and cost, and concepts such as argument and evidence from English language arts. On the other hand, if students were to take on the role of food-tax policy advisors, they might utilize social studies concepts such as representative government and stakeholders.

AUTHENTIC VALUE BEYOND SCHOOL WALLS

As you may have gathered already, there is a wide range of "novel situations" in which to apply a given set of concepts. For instance, in the math example we just examined, students could just as easily have transferred their understanding of *graphs*, *scale*, and *data* to examples of graphs in their textbook or equations from a test bank or fictitious data sets created by the teacher. Is this still transfer? The simple answer is, yes. Anytime we ask students to use their understanding of the relationships among concepts to unlock a new-to-them scenario, we are asking them to transfer. Much of transfer is what we would call **academic transfer**, or situations that are new to the students (not previously studied in class) and require students to apply their learning to a more targeted and controlled setting. They typically reflect more school-related tasks such as timed essays, standardized tests, etc. These provide a safe space for students to test out their ideas and receive feedback on their understanding and application to new situations. But we must keep in mind that our ultimate goal is for students to engage in real-world, dissimilar transfer that helps them apply what they learn in school to the world around them.

Both a textbook exercise and the environmentally friendly school lunch performance task measure transfer, but the second example has greater *authenticity*, meaning it asks students to grapple with a real rather than artificial context. Authentic assessments present scenarios connected to life outside of the classroom and ask students to produce work of "utilitarian, aesthetic, or personal value" (Newmann et al., 2001). In the school lunch task, students have the opportunity to make an impact on more than just their grade; successful performance might actually lead to a change in the lunches they eat and a reduction in greenhouse gas emissions connected to these meals.

Academic transfer: Situations that are new to the students (not previously studied in class) and require students to apply their learning to more targeted and controlled settings and reflect more school-related tasks such as timed essays, standardized tests, etc.

When designing transfer tasks, we always strive to present students with scenarios that allow them to impact the world around them. This allows students to see the relevance of their learning and, perhaps more importantly, empowers them through the experience of making a positive contribution to their community. The Learning Transfer Spectrum in Figure 7.16 illustrates how we can gradually move students toward increasingly dissimilar and more impactful transfer. If the math teacher measured students' ability to transfer their conceptual understanding using graphs in the textbook, this example would be plotted on the left-hand, or "academic," side of the spectrum; the school lunch example would fall further to the right, or "real-world" side.

Of course, we do not mean to imply that academic transfer is "bad" and only real-world transfer is meaningful. Students need to practice academic transfer in order to become proficient in the disciplines they study in school. And transfer needs to be built gradually, increasing in complexity, dissimilarity, and real-world impact. So, while we advocate for summative assessments that focus on real-world scenarios, we also advise teachers to give students plenty of practice with academic transfer as part of the essential "training wheels" of a unit.

Figure 7.16   The Learning Transfer Spectrum

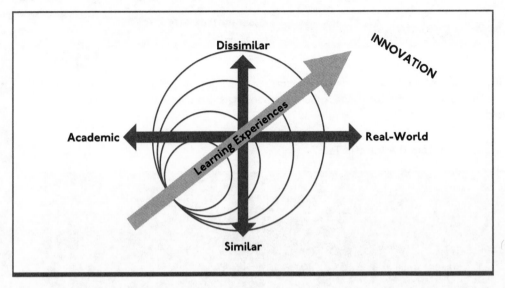

SOURCE: Adapted from Stern et al., 2017.

Another essential feature for real-world transfer means an authentic audience is involved in the process. This can come in the form of other classes, parents, or experts in the community or abroad especially with the use of technology such as video calls. If students present their learning to an authentic audience but then nothing happens with these findings, this task falls somewhere closer to the middle, right side of the spectrum. But if their learning, for instance, has actual positive outcomes such as designing a solution for cleaning up or reducing plastic waste, then it is farther toward the real-world side of the spectrum. It has made an impact in the world around them.

The final part of our vision deals with frequency. Assessing for transfer should not be relegated to a fancy project after the unit test or a stand-alone event. Students need regular opportunities to transfer their understanding to unlock novel situations. They should be moving between similar and dissimilar transfer on a frequent basis, so it becomes second nature for them to analyze a problem and look for connections to attempt or solve the problem. This brings us to the role of *formative assessment* in the transfer-focused classroom.

PLANNING FOR FORMATIVE ASSESSMENT OF TRANSFER

Once we've designed a summative transfer task, our next step is to map out a progression of formative assessment tasks that will help students track their own readiness and ensure they are prepared for the summative assessment when we get there. Here is where the unit storyboard or learning sequence chart from our unit planner comes into play.

Figure 7.17 shows the last phase of the unit planner and demonstrates how we can plan a unit from the acquire stage all the way through to student action. But, instead of filling out the table from left to right, we will use backward design to help us build students' abilities to transfer to a meaningful and authentic task.

DESIGN STEP

We can begin completing the real-world student action column on the right, and **then** move from the left to right to ensure students are prepared for the task. See the planning steps below the table to guide you through the backward design process.

Figure 7.17   **Planning Backward From the Transfer Task**

Sequence and Structure: Designing Student Learning Experiences				
Planning Step 2	**Planning Step 3**	**Planning Step 4**	**Planning Step 5**	**Planning Step 1**
Acquire	Connect	Similar Transfer	Dissimilar Transfer	Student Action
Students acquire understanding of anchoring concepts	Context #1: Initial inquiry and hypothesis testing	Context #2: Transfer and refine	Context #3: Transfer and refine	Context #4: Novel, real-world application

Step 1: Start by summarizing the real-world transfer task in the final column labeled "student action."

Step 2: Then, fill in the anchoring concepts of your unit in the **acquire** column. Check for alignment. Do these concepts and the relationships among them help students unlock the novel situation? Will you be able to measure students' understanding of these concepts through the transfer task? If the concepts and transfer task are not aligned, tweak them to ensure alignment. Keep your standards and other established goals in mind as you do this.

Step 3: Next, describe an initial context in which students can **connect** the concepts in relationship. We like to begin with simpler contexts and build up to more complex contexts that look increasingly dissimilar to the way students first explored the concepts. Note that students do not need to acquire every concept of the unit at the beginning. In fact, it is often helpful to begin with a handful of anchoring concepts and then layer in other ideas that add complexity and richness as the unit goes on.

Step 4: Now students should be ready for similar transfer. Think of a context that is similar to the initial context but still a new situation or scenario for students to apply their understanding. Sometimes we add a couple of similar contexts in this column so that students continue to practice transfer. We can use videos, graphs, political cartoons, statistics, or even photos for students to apply their learning to this new scenario; it doesn't have to take a ton of time. We often layer on more concepts that students might need as the situations become more and more complex. In this case, we need to be sure students acquire understanding of those new concepts even as they are transferring their learning of the initial or anchoring concepts.

Step 5: Students should be ready to increase the dissimilarity of the transfer task. What situation or couple of situations might serve as an important bridge for students to reach the novel, real-world scenario that we outlined in the far right "student action" column? Again, we may find that new **concepts** arise out of these new contexts or scenarios, and we need to be sure that students acquire understanding of those new concepts as they refine their understanding of the initial ones, and connect them all together to form a larger structure or organization in their minds.

For instance, the math teacher we described earlier determined that students would present their findings and recommendations for a more environmentally friendly school lunch menu based on their understanding of the concepts of *data*, *graphs*, and *scale*. This situation presents quite a bit of modern literacies such as *communication* or advocating for a position, as well as *environmental impact*, *nutritional balance*, and *budget*.

To prepare students to tackle the eventual complex, real-world scenario, the teacher might begin by teaching students the terms "data," "graph," and "scale," and provide several exercises from a math textbook to reinforce these concepts. Notice the completed sequence of concepts and contexts in Figure 7.18. Then, he might layer in the concept of *communication* and ask students to use their knowledge of graphs and scale to effectively communicate data to the rest of the class (Context #1 in Figure 7.18). Later in the unit, he might bring in the concept of *environmental impact* and ask students to begin comparing data presented in graphs with different scales (Context #3 in Figure 7.18). The concepts of *nutritional balance* and *budget* are unique to the transfer task, so he waits until students begin that project to introduce those elements.

Figure 7.18   **Planning Backward From the Transfer Task Example**

Sequence and Structure: Designing Student Learning Experiences				
Acquire	**Connect**	**Similar Transfer**	**Dissimilar Transfer**	**Student Action**
Students acquire understanding of anchoring concepts. Concept attainment lesson on each concept, followed by textbook exercises: Graph Scale Data	Context #1: Initial inquiry and hypothesis testing How does the scale of a graph impact how data is interpreted? New concept: **communication** Students work in groups to gather **data** about their classmates' hobbies, favorite foods, etc. and **graph** the results; they explain to the class what **scale** they chose and why this was the best scale for **communicating** their findings.	Context #2: Transfer and refine How does the scale of a graph impact how data is interpreted? Students examine two **graphs**, each depicting the same **data** but using different **scales**; they discuss why someone would choose each scale when trying to **communicate** about data (*If we wanted to show ____, we would choose graph A because . . . But if we wanted to show ____ we would choose graph B because . . .*).	Context #3: Transfer and refine How does the scale of a graph impact how data is interpreted? New concept: **environmental impact** Students compare several **graphs** that show the **environmental impact** of personal actions such as using an electric dryer to dry clothes (vs. hanging them to dry), driving a car (vs. public transportation, walking, or biking), etc. Before they can effectively compare, students must notice the differences in **scales** of the graphs.	Context #4: Novel, real-world application New concepts: **nutritional balance, budget** Students examine **graphs** (remembering to attend to **scale**!) of the **environmental impact** of different food sources in order to determine which foods are most environmentally friendly and **advocate** for a new school lunch menu that lessens our impact on the environment based on this **data**, as well as their understanding of **nutrition** and **budgetary constraints**.

Notice that early on, the teacher directs students' attention to the concepts of *scale*, *graph*, and *data*. He asks them to specifically discuss the scale they selected for their graphs in Context #1 and has students explicitly discuss the impact of different scales in Context #2. However, in Context #3, he intentionally presents students with graphs that have different scales *without* mentioning this to students. This is because he is using this context to assess students' ability to independently and spontaneously transfer. It is one thing for students to engage in *teacher-directed transfer,* meaning that they can transfer their knowledge of conceptual relationships when prompted to do so. It is another for them to engage in *self-initiated transfer,* meaning they can recognize when to transfer their understanding of conceptual relationships on their own. Since he wants students to engage in self-initiated transfer in the summative assessment, he uses Context #3 as a formative benchmark to determine their readiness to do this.

DESIGN STEP

Now we are ready to refine our unit storyboard section of the unit planner that we began in Chapter 6. Download the Unit Planner at LearningThatTransfers.com and complete the storyboard section for a unit in your context.

Finally, once we have sketched out a progression of learning experiences in which students practice transferring and refining their understanding of the concepts, we check again for alignment. Let's take a moment to reflect on how well all of the pieces of our learning progression work toward success on the summative assessment.

DESIGN STEP

CHECK FOR ALIGNMENT

Ask the following questions:

- Which concepts do students need to understand to perform the transfer task? When will I introduce each of these concepts?
- If I read my plan backward, am I moving from complex, real-world transfer toward simpler transfer?
- How will I know if students are ready for the transfer task? What evidence of learning will I look for each step of the way?
- Do all the pieces add up?
- Does this entire plan match up to standards and other goals?

_____

_____

_____

With a clear vision of the summative assessment, as well as intentional, aligned scaffolds built into each learning context of the unit, we're ready to return to the systems of feedback at work in our classrooms as shown in Figure 7.4. Consider the following components of that system:

- **Pre-assessment:** How will students make visible their prior knowledge of these concepts? How will I adjust instruction according to what I see?

- **Ongoing formative self-assessment:** When will students assess their own conceptual understanding? What rubric or criteria will they use? How will I provide guidance and feedback about students' self-assessments? How will I use students' self-assessments to adjust instruction?

- **Ongoing formative peer assessment:** When will students assess each other's conceptual understanding? What rubric or criteria will they use? How will I provide guidance and feedback about students' peer assessments? How will I use students' peer assessments to adjust instruction?

- **Summative assessment:** How will students use self-assessment strategies throughout the transfer task? What type of feedback will I give (and not give) during the task? How will I monitor the effectiveness of my teaching through this task?

- **Reflection:** How will students reflect on their learning process to improve learning in the future? How will I reflect on my teaching in order to improve my teaching in the future?

DESIGN STEP

Now we are ready to complete a comprehensive feedback plan for our unit storyboard using the feedback and assessment models detailed throughout this chapter. Include your plan for each part of the ACT model, as shown in the example in Figure 7.19. Download the full Unit Planner template by visiting LearningThatTransfers.com and complete the feedback plan for a unit in your context.

PUTTING IT ALL TOGETHER

Imagine the math class in action during this unit. Students begin by writing and drawing as much as they can about the concepts *graph*, *scale*, and *data*. As they do so, students realize that, collectively, they know quite a bit about these terms already. The teacher clarifies what is meant by "scale" in math terms, which differs quite a bit from a scale in music or a bathroom scale that students might have at home. Students practice reading graphs with different scales and create their own graphs from data tables in the textbook before discussing the conceptual question in small groups: How does the scale of a graph impact how data is interpreted? In the following lessons, students watch their understanding grow. They create their own graphs and make their own decisions about scale. They evaluate graphs provided by the teacher. All the while, they are keeping track

Figure 7.19   Example of Planning for Formative Feedback

Sequence and Structure: Designing Student Learning Experiences				
Acquire	Connect	Similar Transfer	Dissimilar Transfer	Student Action
Students acquire understanding of anchoring concepts.	Context #1:	Context #2:	Context #3:	Context #4:
	Initial inquiry and hypothesis testing	Transfer and refine	Transfer and refine	Novel, real-world application
Concept attainment lesson on each concept, followed by textbook exercises:	How does the scale of a graph impact how data is interpreted?	How does the scale of a graph impact how data is interpreted?	How does the scale of a graph impact how data is interpreted?	New concepts: **nutritional balance, budget**
Graph	New concept:	Students examine two **graphs**, each depicting the same **data** but using different **scales**; they discuss why someone would choose each scale when trying to **communicate** about data (*If we wanted to show _____, we would choose graph A because . . . But if we wanted to show _____ we would choose graph B because . . .*).	New concept:	Students examine **graphs** (remembering to attend to **scale**!) of the **environmental impact** of different food sources in order to determine which foods are most environmentally friendly and **advocate** for a new school lunch menu that lessens our impact on the environment based on this **data**, as well as their understanding of **nutrition** and **budgetary constraints.**
Scale	**communication**		**environmental impact**	
Data	Students work in groups to gather **data** about their classmates' hobbies, favorite foods, etc. and **graph** the results; they explain to the class what **scale** they chose and why this was the best scale for **communicating** their findings.		Students compare several **graphs** that show the **environmental impact** of personal actions such as using an electric dryer to dry clothes (vs. hanging them to dry), driving a car (vs. public transportation, walking, or biking), etc. Before they can effectively compare, students must notice the differences in **scales** of the graphs.	
Feedback plan:	Feedback plan:	Feedback plan:	Feedback plan:	Feedback plan:

Scan the QR code for this math example adapted for elementary, middle, and high school.

of their evolving understanding of the conceptual question in their math journals. They trade journals with a partner every few days and help each other pinpoint next steps according to a rubric they helped create. The teacher conferences with students individually and in groups, giving both verbal and written feedback to help them self-assess more accurately. By the time of the summative assessment, students are confident in their understanding of "graph," "scale," and "data," as well as "environmental impact" and "communication." They buzz around the room with excitement as they await the director of food services, equally ready to wow her with their presentations and hold her accountable for the improvements they want to see in the school lunch program.

Of course, the teacher was the *designer* of this experience, but the design left room for students to be the *directors* of their own learning. By creating a transfer-focused system of feedback about teaching and learning, including carefully aligned formative and summative assessments, the teacher signaled very powerfully what his values and goals were: transfer of learning, student empowerment, and using math to create a better world.

THINKING PROMPT

Let's return to the anchoring concepts that underpin the content of this chapter:

- Systems
- Feedback
- Novelty
- Authenticity
- Alignment
- Summative assessment
- Formative assessment
- Transfer
- Student empowerment

What meaning do these concepts hold for you and how are they connected? Look or think back to your response earlier in the chapter. How have your ideas changed? Consider the following questions as well:

- How can we create systems of feedback that empower students?
- Why is novelty an essential component of assessing transfer?
- What role does authenticity play in assessment? How does it impact student empowerment?
- What does alignment between summative and formative assessments look like?

_____

_____

_____

_____

_____

CHAPTER EIGHT

Instructional Design

Building a Community for Learning That Transfers

"To teach in a manner that respects and cares for the souls of our students is essential if we are to provide the necessary conditions where learning can most deeply and intimately begin."

—bell hooks

Why does this chapter matter?	A coherent sequence of learning experience allows students to move fluidly in and out of the acquire, connect, and transfer phases of learning.
What will I be able to do by the end of this chapter?	I will be able to design an instructional calendar and use specific instructional strategies that allow students to acquire, connect, and transfer their conceptual understanding to novel situations.

Chapter 7 provided a thorough guide on creating a meaningful system of assessments as feedback about learning—so that we can all improve the learning experience and journey for our students. Cohesive planning facilitates transfer. We can sequence learning experiences that gradually and intentionally prepare students to transfer their learning to increasingly complex scenarios. Finally, we are ready to design powerful instruction for a transfer-focused classroom.

THINKING PROMPT

Before we begin, let's reflect on our current thinking in response to the following questions:

- How **intentionally** do you plan for learning that transfers?
- What is the role of the **student** in a transfer-focused classroom? What is the role of the **teacher**?
- How does **classroom community** impact **student thinking**?

(Continued)

(Continued)

- How do **student independence**, **metacognition**, and the **ACT model** interact?

_____

_____

_____

_____

_____

CHAPTER STRUCTURE

The structure and strategies in this chapter are organized around the ACT model of acquire, connect, and transfer. We begin with ideas for establishing thinking classrooms, as this is the foundation of independent learning that transfers. Then we move through several specific instructional strategies that facilitate learning through acquiring, connecting, and transferring conceptual organization to new situations. The chapter closes with plotting out learning experiences on an instructional calendar as well as designing daily or individual lesson plans. The content follows the order below:

- Highlighting the importance of intellectual growth

- Acquiring understanding of single concepts

- Connecting concepts in relationship

- Transferring conceptual relationships to new situations

- Designing instructional calendars

- Designing lesson plans

HIGHLIGHTING THE IMPORTANCE OF INTELLECTUAL GROWTH

Learning is more than the accumulation of facts and figures. To truly learn something requires connecting it to our prior knowledge and examining how it relates to what we already know. It requires making meaning, consolidating, and navigating something new or complex. Most educators know this. The trouble is, much of today's schooling communicates to students that learning is an accumulation of disconnected bits of information, to be memorized for the sake of a test, and then forgotten shortly thereafter. It's not that retrieval and automaticity aren't important, but what's the use of storing things in your long-term memory that you'll never need after you graduate?

We sometimes need to reorient students to a different understanding of the concept of *learning*. Classroom teachers have numerous routines in relation to materials—such as passing out papers, turning in assignments, and locating materials after an absence— in both the physical and digital classroom. Most teachers understand the power that these routines have to save time and create a culture of efficiency.

The same benefits apply to routines about thinking and learning. Students need to be explicitly taught how to monitor their learning, practice during instructional time, receive feedback on their use of the routines, and then practice using them some more. Teachers don't need an exhaustive list of strategies to promote reflective and metacognitive thinking. The handful that follow are a core set. When we teach students to use them well, monitoring their progress becomes as natural and seamless as our other classroom organization systems.

Sharing the What, Why, and How

In Chapter 6, we discussed the role of learning intentions, success criteria, and conceptual questions in our unit planning. Here we will take a slightly different approach and use these to promote student ownership and metacognition.

The what, why, and how of learning should not remain hidden until right before the unit exam or summative assessment. It should be shared, explicitly or through discovery, early on in the unit of study so that students clearly know the expectations and possibly develop a sense of intrigue about the content. Figure 8.1 gives a quick synopsis of how students can think about the what, why, and how of learning. Notice in "What are you learning," we again emphasize that we can share learning intentions *or* conceptual questions as a way to share the what of learning.

Figure 8.1   What, Why, How Explained for Students

Question	Meaning
What are you learning?	What are the intentions or conceptual questions of the unit or learning experience? What is the big picture or end destination for this learning experience?
Why are you learning it?	Why is this relevant to learn? How does this learning experience connect to past and future learning experiences? How will learning this help me in the real world?
How will you know when you've learned it?	How will I be able to monitor my progress toward the learning intention? What will success look like if I have reached the learning intention or answered the conceptual question?

SOURCE: Adapted from Almarode, J., & Vandas, K. (2018) *Clarity for Learning.* Corwin.

Students can track their understanding of what they're learning and how they're doing in journals, on graphs, or with magnets, for example. What matters is that students clearly know what they're learning, how they will demonstrate mastery, and they have a process to monitor this themselves. The sentence stems in Figure 8.2 are useful to help craft success criteria that remain focused on teaching for transfer. Because students understand what it means to acquire, connect, and transfer, they easily use these stems as a guide to what it means to be successful in a particular learning experience.

Figure 8.2   Sentence Stems to Promote Clarity

We are acquiring an understanding of _____ and _____.

We are connecting _____ and _____ in context of _____.

We are transferring _____ and _____ to _____ context.

We are practicing the skills of _____ and _____ so that we can _____.

We are building fluency or memorization of _____ so that we can _____.

Students need tools to reflect on how their learning is progressing. These next two strategies are for this purpose and—if used well—empower students to take ownership and become advocates for their learning.

At First, I Thought . . . But Then . . . So Now, I Think . . .

Students bring preconceived notions and misunderstandings to learning experiences all the time. Unless we confront these misconceptions head on, students will learn what we want them to learn, and at the end of unit forget it and go back to believing what they originally thought (Bransford et al., 2005). A simple strategy to use throughout the entire of the unit is "at first I thought . . . now I think" (adapted from Ritchhart, Church, & Morrison, 2011). Figure 8.3 depicts how to setup and use this strategy with students.

Tip—In early elementary grades, do this together as a class discussion or on posters.

Figure 8.3   At First . . . But Then . . . So Now . . .

At first I thought . . .	But then . . .	So now I think . . .
Students identify the knowledge and understandings they had at the beginning of the lesson, week, or unit. This could be knowledge of individual concepts or skills, understanding of the relationships between concepts, or facts and examples students knew that relate to the concepts of study.	Students write down what acquire strategies or contexts they explored that shifted or deepened their thinking.	Students articulate their new understanding after going through each concept attainment lesson or transfer context.

This strategy should be used as students move through acquire, connect, and transfer phases of learning. The right side of the table will allow students to see how their thinking has not only grown in sheer information but also deepened in conceptual understanding. Imagine how much more confident students might feel and the quality of the thought that would result if they made a habit of monitoring their learning in all classes. These strategies would trickle into everyday life any time students approach complex tasks.

No matter what phase of the ACT model students are in, we cannot assume it is happening because we delivered an engaging lesson. Every strategy in this chapter needs to be demonstrated multiple times and scaffolded to support student learning. One of the best ways to help students understand the power and purpose of these strategies is through teacher modeling.

Teacher Modeling

Through modeling, teachers help students clarify what they are doing as well as why they are doing it. Furthermore, modeling supports students by preparing them to tackle both simple and complex tasks and behaviors, including addressing unclear concepts, making generalizations, and problem solving (Harbour et al., 2015).

From an instructional perspective, "modeling" is defined as a twofold process that includes demonstrating a desired skill or behavior while simultaneously describing the actions and decisions being made throughout the process in an attempt to have students imitate the skill or behavior and illustrate when it is appropriate to use the desired action (Harbour et al., 2015). It is necessary to explicitly model our thinking for students when we first start this shift to teaching for transfer and building conceptual understanding. When we model a strategy, we grant students access to our minds and show what quality thinking looks like.

After establishing a positive community of learners and making thinking routine, we are ready to explore strategies through the ACT model. The next few sections provide strategies, tools, routines, and protocols to use during the acquire, connect, and transfer phases of the learning journey. These sections are not exhaustive and we encourage you to consider how some of your favorite teaching strategies might be adapted to explicitly help students make meaning, consolidate, and deepen their understanding of concepts and their connections.

ACQUIRING UNDERSTANDING OF INDIVIDUAL CONCEPTS

This book centers the ACT model of three essential phases for learning that transfers. In the classroom, we should prompt students' attention to each phase so that they can begin to organize their learning and transfer this understanding to new situations. This section provides specific strategies, seen in Figure 8.4, that can be used to help students acquire understanding of individual concepts. In this phase, it is that critical teachers help students extract and leverage their prior knowledge and develop a working understanding of individual concepts by making meaning of and consolidating their understanding of these concepts.

Scan the code for templates and examples of acquire phase strategies.

Learning That Transfers

Figure 8.4   Acquire Phase Strategies

Example Instructional Strategies	What It Looks Like in the Classroom
Four Corners	Students consider four options for the description of a concept. After think time, they go to the corner with the description that best matches their thinking.
Affinity Mapping	Students write down everything they know about a concept or skill on sticky notes. In small groups, they sort their sticky notes based on commonalities.
Notice and Wonder	Students view an image or quote and write down what they notice about the image. They follow this up with wonderings and discuss in small groups.
Concept Attainment	Students sort images of examples and non-examples into categories based on the critical attributes presented in them and then explain their rationale.
Jigsaw Method	Students are split into expert groups and home groups. Experts learn a specific piece of information about a new concept and share their findings in their home group.
SEE-IT	Students consolidate their understanding of the concept by explaining it in their own words, providing examples and non-examples, and nonlinguistic representations.
Frayer Model	Students consolidate their understanding of the new concept by determining the characteristics and providing examples and non-examples of the concept.
What's all true about *x*?	Students review concepts and discuss or write what critical attributes are always present or always true for that specific concept.

Review or Pre-Assess Familiar Concepts

The first few strategies in this section help to review previously learned concepts and serve to refine understanding. In addition to helping students identify what they initially remember about a concept or disciplinary lens, these strategies allow the teacher to identify misconceptions or determine if students already have a strong grasp of the concepts.

Acquire Strategy #1: Four Corners

1. Identify the concept.

2. Write or find four varying descriptions for the concept and put one in each corner of the room. These definitions can all be partially correct and should range from simple to complex thought. The point isn't for students to get the correct answer but for them to reveal the sophistication of their current thinking about this concept.

3. Provide the concept and each descriptive option to students. Allow students individual thinking time to reflect on their current understanding. We suggest having them write their option down so that they aren't compelled to go to the corner with their friends once we ask them to move.

4. Ask students to go to the corner that best matches their understanding of the concept.

5. Have each group discuss why they chose this corner. A representative from each group will share these reasons with the class.

6. Option: Turn this into a discussion by having students provide evidence for why their corner is the best option. Allow students to change corners if they feel a different group compels them to change their minds.

This strategy is great for identifying the varying nuance in student understanding of a concept. Figure 8.5 shows an example of four corners for the concept of fractions. Notice how the varying definitions might all be considered "correct," but they reveal a difference in the level of sophistication that students have about the concept of fractions.

Figure 8.5   Four Corners—Fractions Example

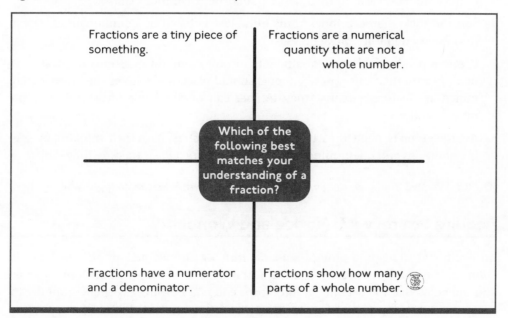

Acquire Strategy #2: Affinity Mapping

The next strategy is taken from *Gamestorming: A Rule Book for Innovators, Rule Breakers, and Change Makers* (Gray et al., 2010). Affinity mapping is a group brainstorming protocol meant to help teams discover patterns of thought and lets the group know where most of their thinking is focused.

This is a way for students to do what is commonly called a "brain dump." Students write down everything they remember about a concept. At this point they have not received explicit instruction. This is to gain insight into what students already know and can pull from their prior experiences. Dr. Pooja K. Agarwal, author of *Powerful Teaching* (2019), says the act of writing down everything we know or remember about a topic (dumping it from our brain) is a powerful learning strategy that will allow students to assess their current thinking and can lead to improvements in student learning (Retrieval Practice, 2019). Think of it like putting together a puzzle. We can dump out all of the pieces to start making sense of this bigger picture we have yet to put together.

Affinity mapping goes one step beyond free recall or brain dumps by having students discuss their ideas and organize them into categories. This allows students to see the thinking of their peers, discuss similarities and differences, and determine what questions they have for the teacher. For the teacher, this strategy provides great insight into the knowledge students bring with them and misconceptions they might have.

Affinity Mapping in the Classroom

1. Post the concept(s) on the board.

2. Ask each student to take two to five minutes to write down everything they know about the concepts. Write individual ideas on sticky notes or index cards. This is done individually and silently.

3. Have students post their sticky notes on chart paper for the corresponding concept or have students clear off their desks and lay out their index cards.

4. Sort the sticky notes or index cards into clusters based on commonalities. Don't throw away duplicate sticky notes.

5. Create a parking lot space for students to post common questions or ideas that don't fit into their categories. Students should place sticky notes they have determined are incorrect so that they teacher can discuss these ideas and clear up misconceptions.

6. Ask the group to name the categories for their clusters. Push their thinking by asking questions and questioning why students grouped ideas the way they did.

SOURCE: Adapted from *Gamestorming* (2010) by Gray, Brown, & Macanufo, pp. 56–58.

Acquire Strategy #3: Notice and Wonder

An additional strategy to prompt student thinking and activate prior knowledge is *notice and wonder*. Notice and wonder is a strategy that works across all content areas and can be used at the beginning, middle, or end of a learning experience. Similar to the popular thinking routine See, Think, Wonder (Ritchhart et al., 2011), students are asked to slow down to think deeply, and explore a situation, context, or text more deliberately. It's a simple strategy that can help promote perspective taking, use prior knowledge to contribute to the discussion, and spark creativity through observation and wondering. The following steps highlight how to get started.

1. Post a graph, image, or video for students to observe.

2. Ask students to jot down what they notice in their observation and what wonderings or questions they have.

3. Have students turn and talk with a neighbor to discuss both what they notice and what they wonder.

4. Share ideas with the whole class and create a class list of everything students notice and wonder.

Notice and wonder can be used to activate student thinking or to establish criteria or shared understanding. Figure 8.6 is an example of notice and wonder through what youcubed (2020) refers to as a "data talk." We show a captivating chart, graph, or

Figure 8.6   Notice and Wonder Data Talk

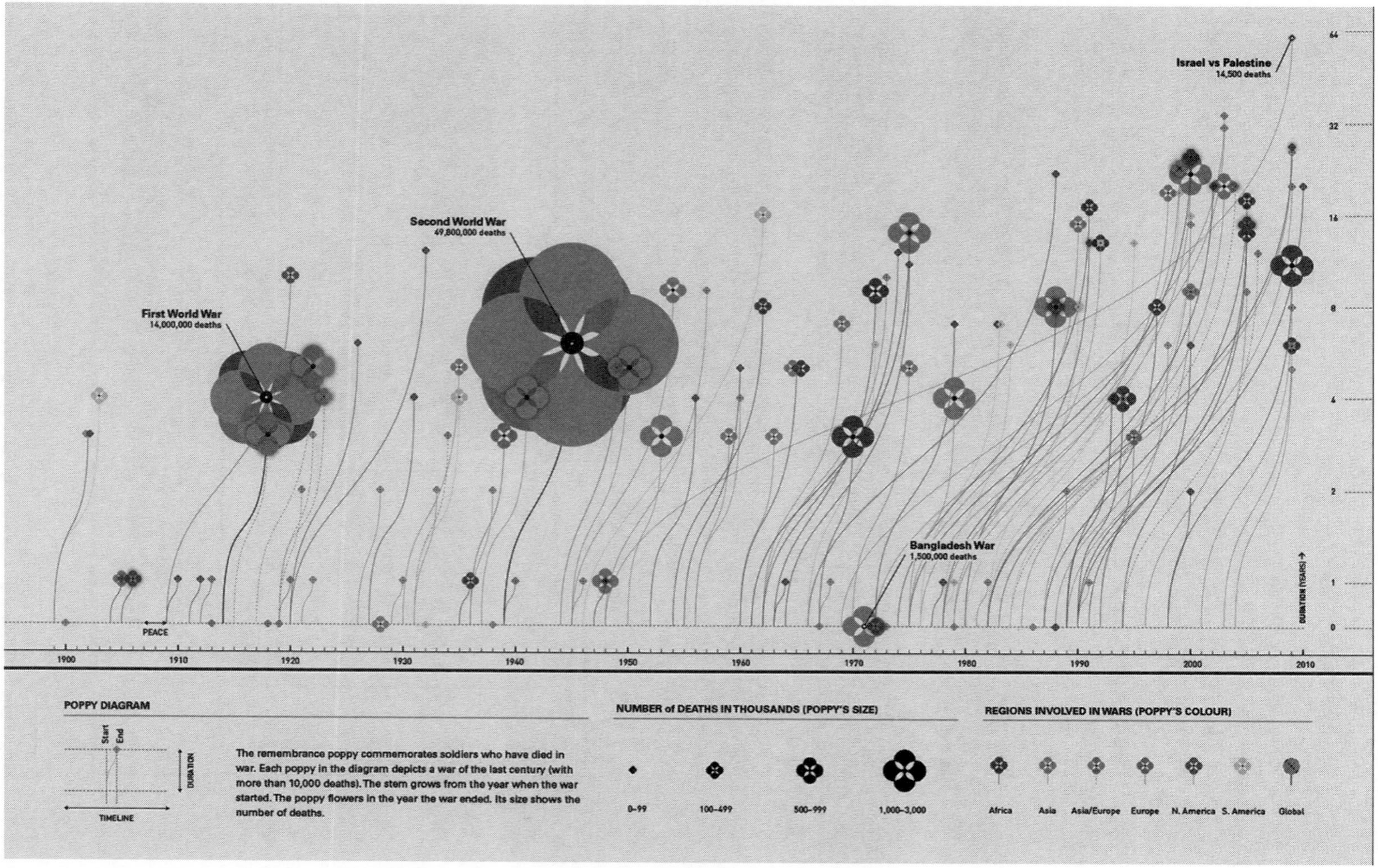

SOURCE: D'Efilippo, 2013, *The Infographic History of the World, Poppy Field.*

diagram that will prompt students' natural curiosities. Then ask, what do they notice and wonder about the image? In Figure 8.6, students might notice the nuance in colors or size of the flowers. This promotes discussion about what the size or color of the poppies represent and launches students into an interdisciplinary unit between math and history about the cost of war.

When students share their wonderings, we need to temporarily withhold correction as we want to elicit student thinking in a safe environment. Students will eventually see if they are correct or incorrect through examples, working through new learning experiences, and by receiving feedback.

Make Meaning of New Concepts

We help students to see how the world is organized by asking them to identify the critical attributes of a concept—usually by exploring illustrative examples. These attributes are the characteristics that distinguish one concept from another (Sousa, 2017).

Acquire Strategy #4: Concept Attainment

Concept attainment is our go-to strategy for building understanding of individual concepts. Sometimes seen as a card or picture sort, concept attainment requires students to look at examples and non-examples of a concept to determine the critical attributes, use these attributes to distinguish between the examples and non-examples, and discuss the criteria that allow something to be an example of the concept. Concept attainment can happen in a variety of ways. Figure 8.7 illustrates a template for posting three examples and asking students to notice what the three examples have in common. Discussion around these commonalities will reveal the critical attributes of the concepts.

Figure 8.7   Template for Concept Attainment

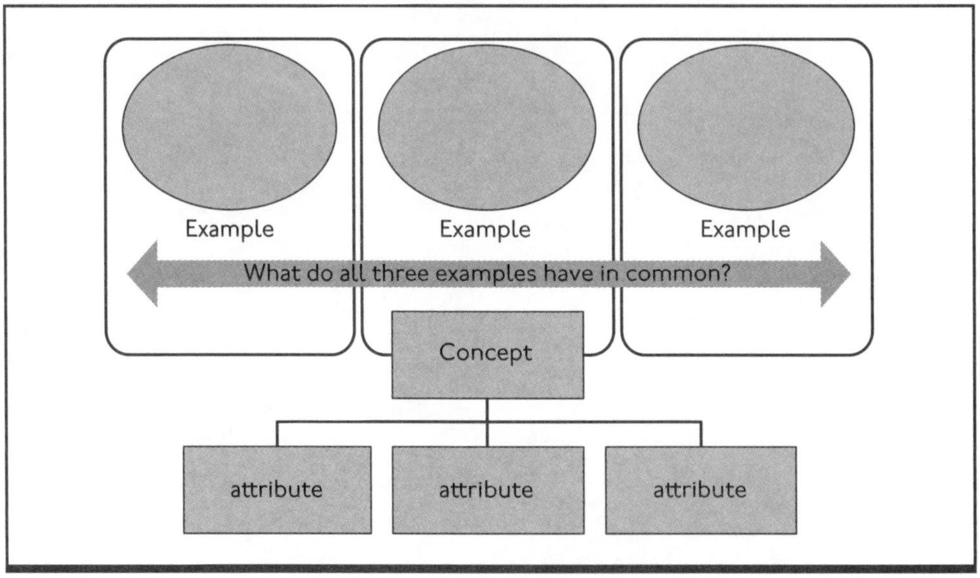

online resources   Download template at www.learningthattransfers.com.

An additional method is to create a presentation and have individual images on each slide. Early on, show students a few images in succession that are examples of the concept. Have students identify what attributes are present and as they move through more examples, students can narrow down their lists to the most critical attributes. After students have a good grasp of the critical attributes of a concept, put in non-examples and have students justify their reasoning for why this is a non-example based on the critical attributes they have derived.

Figure 8.8 shows a kindergarten science example and demonstrates two ways we can use concept attainment as a sorting activity. Students sort images or objects into categories based on the attributes they notice. This could be done with multiple concepts, such as living and nonliving, or into examples and non-example groups.

Figure 8.8   Concept Attainment Via Sorting

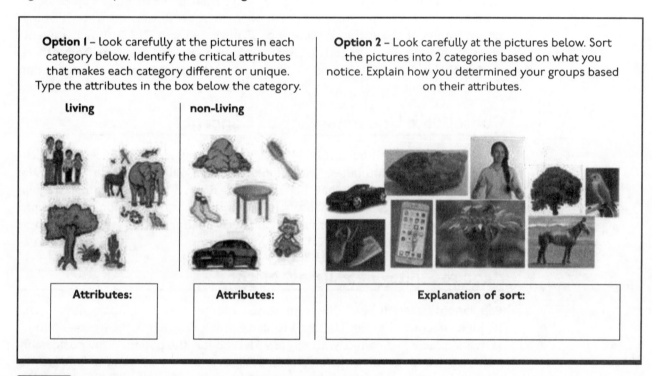

online resources   Download this template at www.learningthattransfers.com.

As illustrated in the pictures, concept attainment can be highly structured or more open ended. Choose the option that works best for your students. The following steps help to plan for concept attainment:

1. Identify the critical attributes of the concept(s) you want students to acquire.

2. Find examples of the concept(s); this can be images or tangible artifacts. TIP: Enter your concept into an image search as a way to find pictures. Make sure these examples clearly illustrate the critical attributes of your concept(s).

3. Find non-examples. At first, it should be obvious they do not align to the attributes of the concept.

4. Provide students with the images either on the board or as cards and have them analyze the images to determine the critical attributes of the concept so that they can distinguish the examples from the non-examples.

5. Find some images that will complicate students' thinking. These could be examples of the concept that don't necessarily fall within the determined critical attributes OR it could be a non-example that might be identified incorrectly as an example of the concept. The point is for students to use their working definition of the concept and its critical attributes to defend their position on if the image is an example or non-example.

No matter which method, concept attainment is an inductive approach that allows students to come up with the "definition" of the concept first before receiving explicit instruction from the teacher. By making sense of the concept on their own, students will retain their understanding better than if they simply copied down definitions first. The real magic occurs when students notice *differences* through non-examples of the shared attributes of a concept (Sousa, 2017). When students identify the unique characteristics that make one concept different from others, that is, the critical attributes, it enables better retrieval and recall of information from their memory.

Consolidate Understanding of Concepts

After students move through initial strategies of making sense of concepts via identifying their critical attributes, they should then consolidate their thinking of the concepts by elaborating on what they have learned and adding in nonlinguistic representations. This step is essential to strengthen student understanding of concepts. Consolidation helps ensure information isn't freely floating around in students' brains but is organized for better retrieval.

Acquire Strategy #5: Jigsaw Method

Popularized in recent years due to increased attention on disciplinary literacy and its high effect size in John Hattie's Visible Learning research is the Jigsaw Method. When implemented correctly, the Jigsaw Method has the potential to considerably accelerate learning with an effect size of 1.20, over three years of academic growth potential in a single academic year. This strategy is powerful, and it is one of the few that can be used across the acquire, connect, and transfer phases of learning. See other ideas for using the Jigsaw Method in a transfer-focused classroom in the companion website.

1. Identify the anchoring concepts of the lesson and the critical attributes for each concept.

2. Find examples that illustrate the critical attributes for each concept.

3. Divide students into home groups and assign each student an anchoring concept.

4. Move from home groups into expert groups, and have students make sense of their individual concept by determining the critical attributes. Students return to home groups and take turns sharing the critical attributes of their assigned concept.

5. Each student documents this information on a Frayer Model or SEE-IT table to keep in their notebooks.

6. Whole group discussion follows to answer any questions that arose throughout the process.

Jigsaw is not just breaking students into groups and then coming back to share what they did. It is a cooperative strategy that can help students acquire insightful understanding of individual concepts both through meaning making and consolidating.

Acquire Strategy #6: SEE-IT Model

This is a simple yet powerful strategy that moves students from meaning making to consolidating understanding. It requires students to elaborate on their understanding, come up with examples and non-examples of the concept, illustrate or provide a metaphor for this concept, and then talk about their understanding with the class. Figure 8.9 provides an overview of the steps for SEE-IT.

Figure 8.9 **SEE-IT Model**

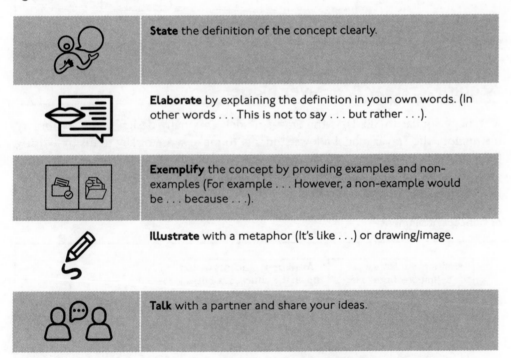

State the definition of the concept clearly.

Elaborate by explaining the definition in your own words. (In other words . . . This is not to say . . . but rather . . .).

Exemplify the concept by providing examples and non-examples (For example . . . However, a non-example would be . . . because . . .).

Illustrate with a metaphor (It's like . . .) or drawing/image.

Talk with a partner and share your ideas.

SOURCE: Adapted from Stern et al., 2017; originally adapted from Paul & Elder, 2013.

Figure 8.10 illustrates two student examples of SEE-IT. Notice how the right side of the services concept card has a hole in it. This was a genius idea from teacher Jeffrey Phillips and his colleagues who have their students hole punch each concept card and add it to a metal ring so that the concepts are easily accessible throughout the unit.

Figure 8.10   SEE-IT Student Examples

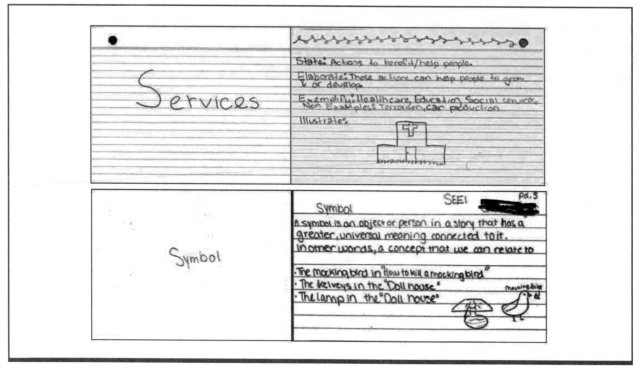

SOURCE: Hannah Eldon and Anna Christenson

Acquire Strategy #7: Frayer Model

A strategy similar to SEE-IT is the Frayer model. Originally designed for vocabulary instruction, the Frayer model allows students to make sense of key terms by writing the definition in their own words, describing the critical attributes, providing examples and non examples, and sometimes illustrating the concept. Figure 8.11 illustrates the Frayer Model we use most often.

Figure 8.11   Frayer Model for Concept Attainment

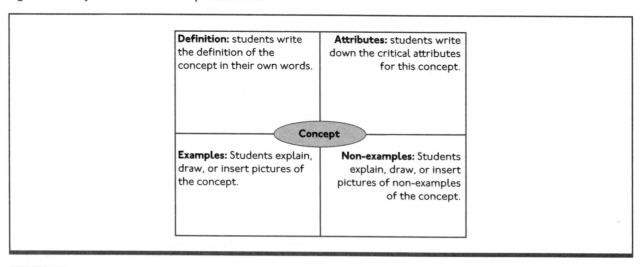

Download this digital template at www.learningthattransfers.com.

Acquire Strategy #8:
What's All True About *X* (Concept)?

The final strategy in this section comes from innovation expert Adam Hansen while on the *Conceptually Speaking* podcast (Episode 12). "What's all true about *x* (concept)?" is a powerful way to have students reflect on and consolidate their thinking about concepts by brainstorming all the things they know to be true about a concept (Stern & Aleo, 2020). It allows students to consider nuance and multiple dimensions of a concept, again, digging deeper than the initial definition from a textbook or dictionary. Therefore, we want students to brainstorm as many things as they can about the concept—perhaps giving them a number such as five or six facts or "all trues" about the concept.

Figure 8.12 is an example from a middle years' mathematics course discussing what is always true about ratios. This strategy can be completed independently or brainstormed independently and then discussed as a class. We want students to continue considering what else they know about a concept rather than stopping at an initial definition, often provided by a text book or teacher, and to be able to address any misconceptions or confusions that might arise.

Figure 8.12   What's All True About Ratios?

Concept	All True
Ratio	• Ratios show relationships. • A ratio compares two quantities with the same units or, if comparing two measures with different units, it is called a rate. • A ratio can be represented in multiple ways: a/b, a to b, a:b. • When set equal to another ratio, a proportion is formed. • Fractions and percentages are ratios. A fraction is a ratio comparing a part to whole relationship; a percentage is expressed as the parts per one hundred.

The exact strategy doesn't matter all that much. What is important is that students are making meaning and consolidating their thinking about individual concepts. They are *acquiring* conceptual understanding. Students must be taught how to use these tools and work through these processes before we can expect them to complete them independently. Often times they have not been asked to think this thoroughly about individual concepts and are used to writing definitions for vocabulary terms before moving on in their notes.

When we are moving toward consolidating our learning, as we all know, learners can either space practice over time or we can cram it all in at once. Of course, *spaced practice* over time leads to greater learning than cramming. So, we must space out opportunities to work with our concepts throughout an entire unit (Agarwal & Bain, 2019). The act of connecting and transferring our understanding of concepts to new situations serves as a way to practice and apply what we've learned over time.

When we make the shift to teaching for transfer our lessons and units no longer move in a linear, sequential fashion. Learning is iterative. We pose a conceptual question and take students through simple to complex contexts to deepen their understanding of concepts and the relationships between them. This iterative cycle, illustrated again in Figure 8.13, layers in new concepts and additional questions to add depth and nuance to student thinking.

Figure 8.13   Iterative Nature of Teaching for Transfer

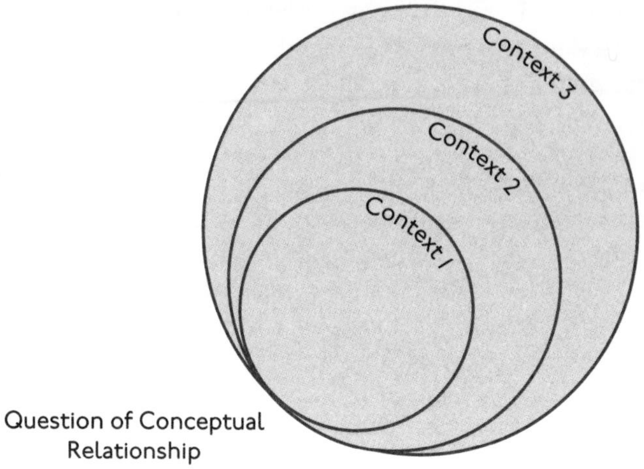

SOURCE: Adapted from Stern et al., 2017.

CONNECTING CONCEPTS IN RELATIONSHIP

Once students have a strong understanding of a few individual concepts, it is time to move to deeper levels of thinking by having the students connect concepts in relationship to one another. The conceptual relationship question stems (p. 36) are the most useful way to direct student attention to the connections between and among concepts. Paired with other powerful thinking tools, we can elevate the level of intellectual discourse in our classrooms.

Much of our focus on the acquire phase has been on understanding the importance of concepts—the nouns of transferable learning. However, the magic happens when students add the verbs, or the types of connections or relationships that help us to see how concepts interact. And this is not a one-and-done type of consideration. We can revisit our understanding again and again as new details and examples provide insight into the ways in which concepts interact.

The strategies for the connect phase of the ACT model, seen in Figure 8.14, are designed to scaffold and support this deeper thinking. This type of learning is like enjoying a multicourse dinner rather than going to a buffet. Not all information is shared at once but is deliberately paced through a variety of contexts to engage students in deeper, more complex thinking that will lead to meaningful experiences that transfer to future situations.

Figure 8.14   Connect Phase Strategies

Example Instructional Strategies	What It Looks Like in the Classroom
Types of Connections	Teacher provides a list of possible types of connections to scaffold student thinking about how concepts are related. Students discuss possible connections in specific contexts or situations.
Question Formulation Technique	Students generate open-ended questions about a concept focus, discuss with their peers, and research to find answers or solutions to these questions.
Conver-Stations	Students discuss specific questions or contexts while regrouping at each station in order to promote increased conversation between peers.
Socratic Seminar	Students participate in a structured discussion by providing evidence of their thinking about a context or conceptual relationship and building on their peers' thinking to demonstrate their understanding.
Hexagonal Thinking	Students physically manipulate concept cards, discuss, and look for multiple relationships between concepts and supporting factual details. They critically assess and describe the subtle differences between these connections and if the relationship is viable or not.
CLICK Thinking Tool	Students track their thinking throughout a unit keeping up with what they know about concepts, inquiries they have, and their new knowledge as a result of being part of the learning experience(s).
BOLT Map	Students create, edit, add to, and rearrange concept maps over the course of a unit or in a lesson to demonstrate the connections they see between and among concepts.

Scan the code for templates and examples of connect phase strategies.

Connect Strategy #1: Types of Connections

We can scaffold student thinking by providing a list of possible connections for students to consider. For instance, one can imagine this question posed to young students: *How are plants and animals connected?* The teacher could prompt them with the types of connections choices: Do they "compete" with each other? Sometimes. Do they "cause" each other? Not really. Do they "depend on" each other? Yes! Animals depend on plants as food to eat and also for shelter. Plants depend upon animals to help them pollinate or spread their seeds.

Figures 8.15 and 8.16 illustrate types of conceptual connections elementary and secondary students might see between concepts.

Figure 8.15   Elementary Types of Connections

Increase	Attract	Strengthen	Interdepend
Decrease	Repel	Block	Transform

Figure 8.16   Secondary Types of Connections Examples

Necessity	Supplementary	Opposition
Sustains	Contributes	Opposes
Expansion	**Negation**	**Causality**
Perpetuates	Diminishes	Generates
Interdependence	**Prevention**	**Transformation**
Reciprocate	Hinder	Evolves

online resources   Download Types of Connections Examples at www.learningthattransfers.com.

These tables are not exhaustive and purely represent sample types of connections to scaffold student thinking. Student understanding of the types of connections can evolve over time, too. So, it's important to show them that there is not really a "right" answer. For example, as students continue to explore the relationship between nature and humans, their understanding usually evolves. When reflecting on the connections they might say, "At first, I thought people *destroy* nature, then I realized people also *depend on* nature. All of that is true, but now I realize people *are* nature. It is not us *separate from* nature, but us *as one part of* nature. We are human animals, part of the circle of life, and we need to live in harmony with all other living and nonliving things found in nature."

Chapter 6 explained how inquiry and choice move along a continuum from guided to free and see the types of connections in a similar manner. This scaffold can and should be slowly removed once students have adequate practice looking for connections. They will eventually be able to look at contexts and through thoughtful discussion be able to present evidence as to which connections they see and why.

Connect Strategy #2: Question Formulation Technique

Once students practice thinking about conceptual questions and types of connections, their ownership in learning can grow by developing their own questions. Students learn more deeply and think more creatively than they often would when we provide the questions.

The Question Formulation Technique is a primary strategy from the Right Question Institute that was first introduced in the book *Make Just One Change* (Rothstein & Santana, 2011). Students develop their own compelling and conceptual questions to drive inquiry, which increases the relevance and meaning of the learning experience for them.

Question Formulation Technique Steps

1. **Create question focus**—start with a statement, phrase, image but not a question

2. **Produce questions**—students generate as many questions as possible without judging them

3. **Improve questions**—change between open and closed

4. **Strategize**—prioritize questions, create a plan to find a solution, and share findings

5. **Reflect**—students reflect on their new understanding and the process (Rothstein & Santana, 2011)

A critical step in the connect phase of learning is for students to articulate the connections between and among concepts. Classroom discussion is an excellent strategy to do this, and has an effect size of 0.82, which means it can potentially double the average growth of a year's worth of learning if done effectively (Hattie, 2020 [Visible Learning MetaX]). Classroom discussions should be structured while still allowing room for authentic student questions, clearly focused on the concepts under study, allow students to do the majority of the talking, and center around open-ended conceptual and compelling questions. Figure 8.17 provides a few guidelines we recommend for classroom discussions no matter what strategy or structure you use.

Figure 8.17   Guidelines for Classroom Discussions

Classroom Discussion Tips

- Use sentence stems or frames to help structure and scaffold student thinking.
- Give students time to think independently before discussing with peers.
- Utilize partners and small-group discussion for optimal engagement.
- Assign roles to partners or groups members to collect and organize thoughts and stay on task.
- Center discussion around a specific context or question to maintain focus.
- Provide time for individual reflection at the end of the discussion.

The power in classroom discussions is that students are learning with and from their peers. Their thinking is extended or complicated and the more students meaningfully discuss, the stronger their conceptual connections and understanding will be. When students are able to discuss authentic questions, it results in students talking for longer amounts of time, prompting them to elaborate on their ideas, which promotes higher levels of thinking (Soter et al., 2008).

Three strategies to promote classroom discussion are Conver-Stations, Socratic Seminar, and Hexagonal Thinking. These structures help guide student discussion and keep it focused. We like to post the conceptual question and compelling question plus provide reminders to use evidence to support their articulation of the conceptual relationships in their discussions.

Connect Strategy #3: Conver-Stations

Conver-Stations is a low-prep discussion strategy that capitalizes on small group discussion and student movement (Gonzalez, 2015). In typical rotations through stations, students move with the same group, which can lead to a decline in discussion quality by the last station. This strategy avoids this stagnation by regrouping students throughout the discussion. Figure 8.18 highlights two possible ways to run Conver-Stations. After choosing the method, determine how students will rotate. Will they move from table group to table group or rotate around the room like in a gallery walk rotation? We recommend providing students with a list of where they will go for each station to ensure smooth transitions.

Figure 8.18   Conver-Stations Structure

Option 1	**Same Question, Different Contexts**
	Students will answer the conceptual question by viewing it through the lens of specific contexts. In this version, the conceptual question remains the same in every station; only the contexts change.
Option 2	**Different Question, Same Context**
	Students analyze a context through different lenses based on the question posted. This allows students to find multiple meanings within one specific context.

Connect Strategy #4: Socratic Seminar

Socratic Seminar dates back to the time of Socrates who believed in the power of posing questions and teaching through student inquiry rather than lecture alone. In a Socratic Seminar, the purpose is to have students take a lead role and engage in discussion and dialogue around important concepts or questions. Figure 8.19 illustrates two possible entry points and steps for conducting Socratic Seminars. In addition to disciplinary literacy benefits, the modern literacy skills such as active listening, reasoning, and critical thinking are all core components of a Socratic Seminar.

Figure 8.19   Socratic Seminar Steps

Start with a compelling question.	Create corresponding conceptual relationship questions.	Identify multiple contexts that provide a variety of perspectives about the concepts in the question.	Collaborate with students to establish the norms of the seminar. Ask students to identify the purpose of the seminar, what strong evidence is, what it looks like to build on or disagree with a statement respectfully, etc.	Establish clear expectations for student roles and responsibilities throughout the seminar. The teacher should be monitoring and minimally interjecting.	Practice. This process isn't natural, and students must learn how to actively listen, build arguments, and even prepare for discussions. Choose the structure that works best for you—whole group circle, inner circle/ outer circle, two different circles—and allow students the opportunity to practice frequently.
Start with a central text or context.	Determine connections students should make between concepts in the context.	Create questions that will ask students about the connections between concepts in the text or context. They should be open ended.			

Connect Strategy #5: Hexagonal Thinking

Hexagonal Thinking is a powerful strategy that capitalizes on physical placement or manipulation of concept cards. Students place their hexagonal concept cards for the lesson, series of lessons, or unit and discuss how the concepts are related. Due to hexagons having six sides, students can look for multiple relationships and cannot repeat the same connection twice. Figure 8.20 depicts a hexagon discussion from an interdisciplinary STEM unit centered around the compelling question, *Should genetic modification be allowed on organisms?*

Figure 8.20   STEM Hexagonal Thinking

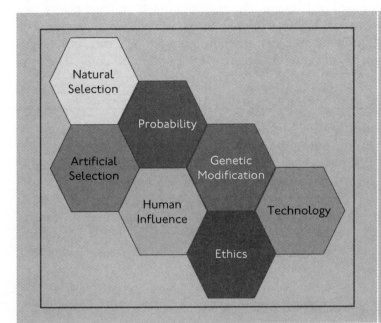

Humans influence an organism's likelihood of reproducing desirable traits through artificial selection.

The probability of certain traits surviving is greater with artificial selection than natural selection.

Humans increase the probability of desirable traits being preserved through artificial selection and an even greater likelihood through genetic modification.

Humans must ethically use technology in the genetic modification process.

Students determine if a relationship is viable or too far of a stretch based on their current evidence in learning and debate among themselves about the strongest representation of the concepts. The teacher should circulate around the room probing student thinking with questions like, *What would happen if I moved this card to here?* deepening student thinking and their ability to see multiple perspectives. Hexagon discussions or hexagonal thinking has been praised for its ability to spark discussion, engage students in thinking of multiple scenarios, and increase their critical thinking (Potash, 2020). Use the following steps to set up and implement a hexagon discussion.

Hexagonal Thinking Steps

1. Post a list of concepts and ask students to individually reflect on all of the connections they see.

2. Provide a set of hexagon concept cards to students.

3. Assign students to small groups and have them determine the best arrangement of cards based on their shared understanding.

4. Circulate among students asking probing questions and rearranging their cards to complicate and deepen their thinking.

5. Facilitate peer instruction by conducting a gallery walk or having students insert pictures of their arrangements and the connections they see into a shared slide deck.

6. Follow up with whole-group discussion. Expand on strong points that were made or address any misconceptions seen.

As students move through different contexts and make connections between concepts, help them to see how their thinking has deepened or grown throughout the unit or learning experience. Utilize concept maps and other types of graphic organizers to help students with verbalizing and visually representing the connections they are seeing. Initially, we can create these maps and organizers together as a class and post them on the wall.

The beauty of the next few strategies is that as student understanding grows so does the visual representation. Students can add to, erase or scratch out, and clarify connections between concepts as they move through the phases of the acquire, connect, and transfer model. As students make connections between concepts and deepen their thinking, they need to continuously reflect to see how their thinking has grown.

Connect Strategy #6: CLICK Thinking Tool

CLICK is a comprehensive strategy for the connect phase of learning that supports metacognitive thinking and motivation as students monitor their thinking and watch it grow and evolve. CLICK stands for **c**oncepts, **l**ist, **i**nquiries, **c**onnections, and new **k**nowledge and it focuses student attention as they dive into different fact-rich contexts over the course of a learning experience or unit. We want conceptual relationships to "click" and make sense to students as they are exploring different contexts. Figure 8.21 illustrates the basic essence of the CLICK Thinking Tool. This could be done individually in student reflection journals, in small groups, or as a whole class.

Figure 8.21   CLICK Thinking Tool

Conceptual or Essential Questions				
C	L	I	C	K
What concepts are central to this learning experience? *Ask the teacher if you're unsure. These are like your key vocabulary terms.	List everything you already know about these concepts. *Do this at the beginning of the learning experience.	What inquiries or questions do you have? *Write down questions throughout the learning experience.	What evidence from the contexts will help you answer the conceptual questions? *Write down ideas throughout the learning experience.	What do you now know about the relationship between these concepts? *Do this in the middle of the learning experience and at the end to reflect on what you have learned.

online resources ☞ Download this template at www.learningthattransfers.com.

Connect Strategy #7: Concept Maps

Students build organizational schema in the brain when they activate prior knowledge of conceptual connections and then elaborate on these connections as their thinking deepens and grows. Concept maps are one such way to visually represent the growing network of ideas in the brain and we use this strategy again and again throughout the learning journey.

Figure 8.22 shows an example of a concept map from an elementary mathematics classroom. In this unit, students were exploring the relationship between multiplication and division. Students created the maps together, discussing the connections they saw throughout a variety of learning experiences, adding on to their map or erasing and writing their refined thinking as their learning progressed. These ideas were formed through student discussion, not through lecture from their teacher. By formatively assessing and observing student discussion, their teacher was able to clarify misconceptions and ensure students were on the right track.

Concept maps are phenomenal tools to support critical thinking, promote discussion, prompt reflection, or act as a formative assessment of student understanding. This next strategy takes concept maps a step further.

Figure 8.22   Coal Mountain Concept Map

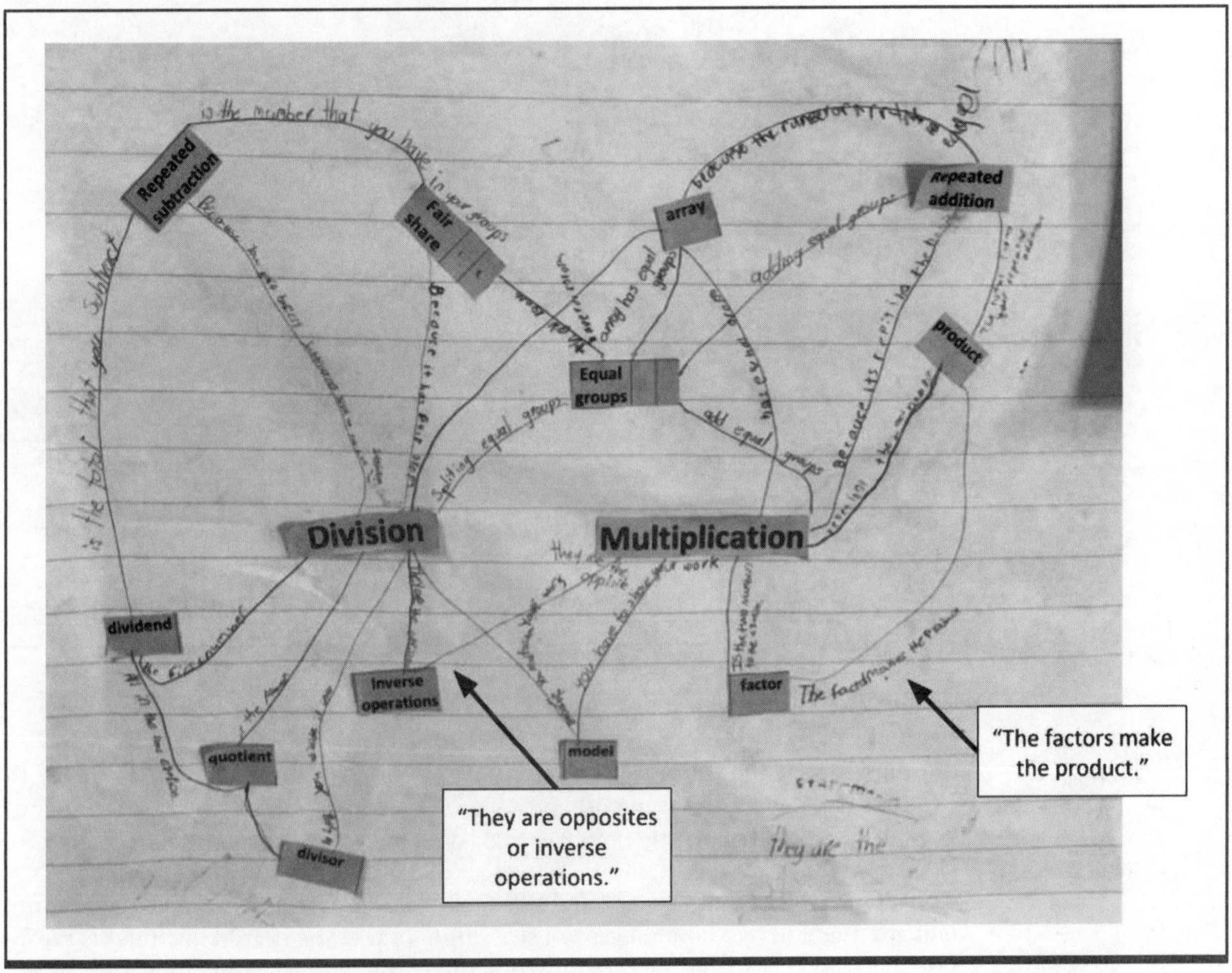

SOURCE: Coal Mountain Elementary, Forsyth County, GA.

Connect Strategy #8: Brainstorm, Organize, Link, Transfer (BOLT)

This strategy takes the concept map to the next level by explicitly asking students to transfer their conceptual organization to new situations. BOLT stands for **b**rainstorm, **o**rganize, **l**ink, and **t**ransfer and assists students in articulating the connections they see between and among disciplinary lenses and concepts and think about how these understandings and relationships might transfer to new situations.

We love to provide sticky notes or index cards for students to physically manipulate the arrangement of the concepts. They can then use dry erase markers or fuzzy sticks to draw lines linking the concepts together. The physical manipulation of concepts helps students think of different arrangements as seen in Figure 8.23.

Figure 8.23   BOLT Map to Connect Concepts

Brainstorm concepts related to the conceptual or compelling question. Students can also create branches to facts or examples of the concept that are relevant to the question.

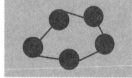

Organize these concepts based on how they are connected or interact with each other. As long as students can explain the connections, they can put them in any arrangement.

Link concepts by drawing a line between them. They can even indicate the strength of the connection by changing up the density of the line. Students must provide an example or describe how these concepts are related.

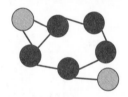

Transfer understanding by thinking of new contexts, connections, and examples. Students should write their transfer ideas in a different color or on a different color sticky note to show that it is a new thought.

A critical component to this strategy is to ask students about their arrangements: Why did they arrange the concepts in a certain way? Can they think of a different way to organize their concepts? Can they provide evidence for how the concepts are connected? Can they transfer their conceptual connections to a different context?

Concept maps can be freely formed like Figure 8.23 or given in a specific structure. Oliver Caviglioli has several free-to-use graphic organizers that help students create visual clarity by articulating relationships and connecting concepts. These maps are not only beneficial tools to help students express how the concepts are connected, but the structure and visual representation of the maps deepens understanding of the relationship.

Scan the QR code to experience Oliver's graphic organizers for yourself.

Taking the time to allow students to reflect on and articulate the connections between concepts is an essential investment for learning that transfers. Simple strategies like warm-ups and exit tickets can take on new meaning and greater purpose if we structure them in a way that activate and connect prior knowledge to new knowledge or consolidate our thinking from a lesson. The point is, we do this intentionally and do not assume that because we taught a lesson, students automatically saw the connections. It takes carefully planned experiences, scaffolding, and prompting to help students get used to this way of thinking; however, once they start, they won't be able to stop. Students will see connections inside and outside the classroom allowing them to transfer their understanding to new and novel situations.

We can deepen students' understanding and ability to transfer by gradually moving from academic to real world transfer where students are continuously applying their knowledge and skills to novel situations. With this gradual shift in breadth of transfer, we hope there is also a gradual shift in the onus of learning to a more student-directed environment by increasing voice, choice, and inquiry within the learning experiences.

TRANSFERRING CONCEPTUAL RELATIONSHIPS TO NEW SITUATIONS

Scan the code for templates and examples of transfer phase strategies.

Transfer is an intentional act of activating one's prior knowledge and figuring out how that knowledge unlocks a new situation. Each strategy included in this phase of the learning journey, listed in Figure 8.24, allows students to approach, solve, and reflect on increasingly complex situations.

Figure 8.24   Transfer Strategies

Example Instructional Strategies	What It Looks Like in the Classroom
What concepts live here?	Students activate prior conceptual understanding and analyze a novel situation by asking themselves, *What concepts live here?*
Unlock and Refine	Students access prior understanding to unlock new situations and then refine their understanding by considering the unique features of the new situation.
Divide and Slide	Students analyze a compelling question that has two obvious choices. They take a stance based on reasoning and evidence, then debate with a peer who has a different opinion.
Deliberation in the Classroom	Students learn the power of deliberation and examining multiple perspectives on issues or problems before making final decisions.
Pro-Pro	Students look for the pros or benefits of both possible solutions rather than looking for the cons of a solution.
Design Thinking	Students design real world solutions after empathizing with their intended audience.
From What to Wow	Students answer a series of questions that indicate their level of understanding of the learning experience and share questions or major insights from the experience.

Just because a student solves a new problem, reads a new text, conducts a new experiment does not mean they will gain the full benefits of learning that transfers. Students must intentionally call upon their conceptual organization when encountering a new situation. We can create a culture of transfer using the strategies found here.

Transfer Strategy #1: What Concepts Live Here?

To create learning experiences that leverage students' prior knowledge and create a culture of transfer, consider frequently posing the question, *What concepts live here?* alongside interesting quotes, pictures, videos, news headlines, historical documents, complex mathematical problems, etc. that can capture student attention (Paterson, 2019). Students can simply jot down or call out the concepts that they notice. This focuses student attention on the underlying structure of every situation and creates the habit of mind to access prior knowledge when encountering a new situation.

We have found this strategy fun and helpful as we go about our world. When scrolling through social media or reading the news, we can take any place, event, or problem of interest and think to ourselves, *What concepts live here?* This reflective step can propel our planning to new and unchartered territory. Rather than viewing our learning outcomes or standards as constraints that do not apply to different or relevant scenarios for our students, we can instead plan backward from real-world scenarios and see how they do indeed fit with our mandatory learning outcomes.

We believe this question can also be posed to students for them to analyze a novel scenario or real-world problem. Students can approach any task or learning experience with curiosity by asking themselves about the concepts or the conceptual relationships they see based on what they have learned prior to this moment. This simple question is a beautiful way to act as a catalyst for group brainstorming when contemplating any new context or lesson.

Transfer Strategy #2: Unlock and Refine

Once students build the habit of recognizing the concepts that apply in new situations, they should take it a step further by considering how the nuances of each new situation refines understanding. We do not want transfer to simply confirm student conceptual connections. Each new situation helps to refine our grasp of the organizational structure of our world. These four steps can be posted in the classroom to promote habitual reflection:

1. **Recognize the concepts that apply:** Which concepts are at play in this situation?

2. **Engage prior understanding of the conceptual relationship:** What do I already know to be true about the relationship among these concepts? What specific examples support my understanding?

3. **Determine the extent to which prior understanding applies:** What makes this new situation different from the situations I've seen in other learning

experiences? Does what I understand about the relationship between these concepts apply to this new situation? Which parts of my prior understanding transfer and which don't?

4. **Modify and refine understanding based on the new situation:** How has transferring to this situation refined or reshaped my thinking? (Stern et al., 2017)

Considering these questions as we begin planning or co-creating learning experiences helps to ensure we're creating the best environment possible for students to transfer their learning. Figure 8.25 illustrates how learning would ideally progress throughout a unit or series of learning experiences moving from simple to complex transfer. We want to intentionally move from academic to real-world transfer and from similar to dissimilar transfer through learning experiences toward real-world, dissimilar transfer.

Figure 8.25 **Leading to Innovation**

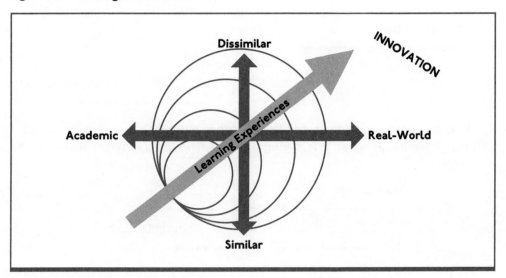

SOURCE: Adapted from Stern et al., 2017.

We are designing instruction to help students acquire, connect, and transfer their understanding of concepts and conceptual relationships across the Learning Transfer Spectrum. The strategies presented up to this point should be woven throughout learning experiences to help students explicitly share and refine their current thinking.

An additional strategy that promotes students learning transfer is debate. Debates increase engagement and promote transfer by providing relevant topics, encouraging diverse perspectives, and creating space for critical thinking and reasoning. One of our favorite debate strategies is known as Divide and Slide.

Transfer Strategy #3: Divide and Slide

This popular strategy is very simple to setup. Post a compelling question or statement that will elicit strong opinions of agreement or disagreement. The next set of steps demonstrate how to setup a Divide and Slide debate in the classroom.

1. Post a compelling, debatable question or statement and give students time to think silently about their stance. For example, you may ask the following:

   Should scientists be able to genetically engineer humans to have certain desirable traits?

2. Tell students to stand and line up along a spectrum of answers. If students were going to debate the question above, the answers could be "yes" and "no" or "strongly agree" and "strongly disagree." Ask students to stand on the line based on how strongly they feel about their stance. It's useful to do this along a piece of tape or against the wall so that students are in a straight line.

   Should scientists be able to genetically engineer humans to have certain desirable traits?

   Strongly Agree   Strongly Disagree

   ←――――――――――――――――――――――→

3. Divide the group of students in half and ask one side of the spectrum to take a large step forward.

4. Have <u>students</u> "slide" down toward the other half so they are in two parallel lines. Students should be across from someone who has a different stance on the question.

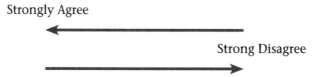

5. Ask students to share their stance on the question, reasoning behind it, and evidence to support their reasoning. Give a set amount of time for one side of the line to share, and their partner needs to not reply and only listen. This strategy teaches both the skill of providing evidence to justify reasoning but also active listening skills. Make sure to plan in time for both sides to share their stances and move about the line to listen for strong arguments or misconceptions.

6. Once the debate is over, ask students to return to their seats and reflect on the debatable question or statement. Encourage them to acknowledge both their stance and their partner's and if their thinking has changed as a result of the debate. (Stern et al., 2017)

Transfer Strategy #4: Deliberation in the Classroom

Unlike debate where students take a strong stance, deliberation is the act of careful consideration of multiple sides or perspectives related to a problem with the goal of shared understanding and developing a solution that works for everyone. With the complexity of issues in the media, changes happening in the world, and problems that are yet to be discovered, students must be able to weigh all sides pragmatically without impulsively jumping to conclusions. They must use ethics, logic, and reasoning rather than hearsay to formulate plans. Deliberating in a Democracy is an international program that teaches students how to deliberate controversial issues, and the process in Figure 8.26 has been adapted from their steps to fit all content areas.

When teaching for transfer, the quality of student thinking is dependent upon both using strategies to help students make sense of their learning and the quality of the contexts provided in the learning experiences. When we plan contexts, we purposefully share a problem, text, or scenario that will either clarify or complicate student thinking. These contexts can be teacher directed or based on student interest, but they must be meaningful and inspire students to want to understand the conceptual connections within them. The ultimate goal of learning is transfer, and we have failed our students if they fail to transfer. Our final two strategies of the chapter both incorporate critical thinking, empathy, and solving real-world problems. These are the Pro-Pro method and Design Thinking.

Figure 8.26 **Deliberation in the Classroom**

Step	What It Looks Like
Introduction	Introduce the compelling question or topic of deliberation.
	Explain the difference between debate and deliberate.
Lesson focus	Students view a text, data set, or simulation, for example.
	Students select three interesting facts or ideas.
Clarification	Check that students understood the lesson focus.
	Clarify understanding of new concepts.
	Ensure students understand the compelling question.
Presentation of Positions	Split students into groups of four, made of pairs A and B.
	Team A finds at least two reasons to say YES to the compelling question and Team B finds at least two reasons to say NO.
	Each team teaches the other their most compelling questions.
Reversal of Positions	Team A and B switch positions.
	Team B now finds reasons to say YES while Team A finds reasons to say NO.
	Each team teaches the most compelling reason from the other team and adds one more reason.
Free Discussion	Students now deliberate both sides of the compelling question in their small group.
	Students should reach a personal decision based on evidence provided and logic.
	The group identifies areas where they all agree and make a decision about the compelling question.
Whole Class Debrief	The class engages in discussion to gain deeper insight into the compelling question.
	As a group, they make a decision by voting in some way.
Student Reflection	Students now individually reflect on the compelling question and what they have learned throughout the process.

SOURCE: Adapted from Deliberating in a Democracy, www.deliberating.org/images/pdf/Deliberation_ Steps.pdf

Transfer Strategy #5: Pro-Pro Method

It's likely that you have heard or used a pro/con list to make a decision—it usually goes one of two ways: You compromise and choose the option with the least cons, or you stare at a list of equal pros and cons and feel no closer to an answer than when you started. The pro/con list is rarely the recipe for productive problem-solving, and never leads to new ideas.

Instead, if you want to work toward a better answer, try a Pro-Pro Chart. This thinking tool leaves the cons behind and just focuses on the positives (or pros!). Instead of choosing one of the options, at the expense of the other, a focus on the "pros" moves students to insights and new possibilities.

The Pro-Pro Chart—affectionately named by students—is part of the Integrative Thinking process. Integrative Thinking is a problem-solving methodology inspired by the insight that opposing models are an opportunity for innovation, instead of an obstacle to it. We lead with Integrative Thinking, and the Pro-Pro Chart as part of that process because we have seen it make significant impact on the thinking, problem-solving, and decision-making skills of students, teachers, and leadership teams (I-Think, personal communication, 2020).

I-Think is a nonprofit organization making real-world problem-solving core to every classroom. In ten years of research and application, they have worked directly with over 2,000 teachers and 950 school leaders; together they have created meaningful learning experiences that strengthened the problem-solving skills of over 100,000 students. Educators in the I-Think community have used the Pro-Pro Chart across K–12 classrooms in all subject areas. Figures 8.27 and 8.28 are but one example of the pro-pro strategy in the classroom.

The pro-pro process starts by identifying a problem to solve and the either/or choice at its heart. For example,

To hear from I-Think educators, including some of the stories below, visit the Hello I-Think webpage.

- When a kindergarten classroom is learning about nature, should they study nature in nature or should they disrupt nature by bringing it into the classroom?
- When city planners are designing an outdoor space, should they design a public park or a conservation area?
- When a community garden looks to high school students to solve stealing, should they allow access to the garden to meet community needs or limit access to ensure their program integrity?

Transfer Strategy #6: Design Thinking

"[We] forget that we can be playful and try wild ideas in the pursuit of academic learning . . ." (Ryder, 2016). **Design thinking** is a way to promote creative thinking and solution finding through an iterative five- (or six-) stage model, popularized by Stanford University's d.School. These stages—empathy, define, ideate, prototype, and test—have helped numerous individuals and businesses place their users at the center of the solution finding mission in order to create the best products or services possible.

Figure 8.27   Online Learning vs. Face to Face Learning

Pro-Pro Chart

Benefits of Virtual Online Education vs. In Person at School Education

In the chart below, you are going to roleplay a little bit. Think about and reflect on what benefits each of the stakeholders receives with this model.

Use this statement: *I like that this model gives me _____ because _____.*

**Replace the word "Stakeholder #1, 2, 3" with your chosen stakeholders. You should have at least three or four benefits per stakeholder.

Model #1: Virtual Online Learning			Model #2: In Person at School Learning		
Students	Teachers	Parents	Students	Teachers	Parents
I like that this model gives me flexibility Because I can do work whenever.	I like that this model gives me family time Because it gives me more time to myself and my family.	I like that this model gives me time Because I don't have to be working 24/7.	I like that this model gives me friendship Because it gives me the chance to talk to my friends.	I like that this model gives me interaction Because it gives me the chance to interact with students.	I like that this model gives me a routine Because it makes things structured.
I like that this model gives me freedom Because I can snack while doing work.	I like that this model gives me more time to mark work Because then I can mark work fairly.	I like that this model gives me time with my kids Because otherwise they are always at school.	I like that this model gives me motivation Because it makes me work harder.	I like that this model gives me the ability to see students work Because I will know if they are struggling.	I like that this model gives me time Because I don't have to take care of my kids all the time.
I like that this model gives me time Because I have more time to understand work.	I like that this model gives me more time to look for work online Because I can use parts of their work.	I like that this model gives me time Because I don't have to travel to work and back.	I like that this model gives me understanding Because I can talk and ask questions with the teacher a lot more.	I like that this model gives me assurance that kids won't cheat Because it is easy to cheat online.	I like that this model gives me security Because I don't have to worry about losing my job.

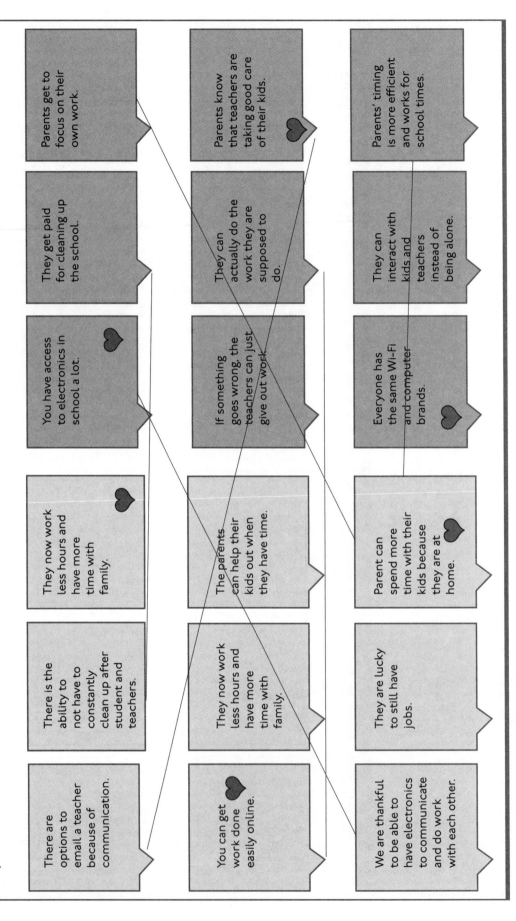

Figure 8.28 Examining the Models

Today you are going to look at both models (Virtual Online Education vs. In-Person Education). To examine the models, you are going to look at each model and draw connection lines (using the line tool in slides) between the models that are similar, or that are connected. You are then going to ♥ the benefits you and your group think are the most important (no more than three per side).

Cut your Pro-Pro Chart from above and paste it into this slide so you can make your connections.

Parents get to focus on their own work.

Parents know that teachers are taking good care of their kids.

Parents' timing is more efficient and works for school times.

They get paid for cleaning up the school.

They can actually do the work they are supposed to do.

They can interact with kids and teachers instead of being alone.

You have access to electronics in school a lot.

If something goes wrong, the teachers can just give out work

Everyone has the same Wi-Fi and computer brands.

They now work less hours and have more time with family.

The parents can help their kids out when they have time.

Parent can spend more time with their kids because they are at home.

There is the ability to not have to constantly clean up after student and teachers.

They now work less hours and have more time with family.

They are lucky to still have jobs.

There are options to email a teacher because of communication.

You can get work done easily online.

We are thankful to be able to have electronics to communicate and do work with each other.

SOURCE: Images courtesy of I-Think

252

We can draw upon this framework to help students craft meaningful learning experiences and find real-world solutions. The steps in Figure 8.29 apply the cycle of design thinking to the classroom (Ryder, 2016).

A pattern that hopefully has become apparent is our continuous return to metacognitive strategies. Without student reflection or continuous monitoring of their progress, the ACT model will fall short of its intended goals and purpose.

Figure 8.29   **Stages of Design Thinking in the Classroom**

DISCOVER

What do we need to know about _____ in order to solve _____?

Invite inquiry and curiosity into the environment. Bring a sense of wonder that causes students to want to know more.

EMPATHIZE

Who is your intended audience? Whose life will be impacted if this solution is found?

Identify the point of view of your intended audience. If possible, get to know this group through observation or interviews.

EXPERIMENT

How might we _____? What would happen if _____? Should we _____?

Play around with possible ideas. Conduct an uninhibited brainstorm where all ideas are possibilities that should be considered and put on the table.

PRODUCE

How will students receive feedback on their ideas, prototypes, or solutions?

Receive feedback to gain momentum. Once students produce a solution, learning is not over. Learning is iterative and relies upon specific feedback to propel even further.

REFLECT

How has your thinking evolved since _____? How have you changed as a result of _____?

Stop and reflect on how you or your thinking has changed as a result of this exploration.

SOURCE: Adapted from Ryder, 2016.

Transfer Strategy #7: What to Wow

The concluding strategy of the chapter is the What to Wow method, Figure 8.30, designed and shared by Matt Murrie (Stern & Aleo, 2020) in Episode 17 of *Conceptually Speaking*. Although it is being shared in the transfer section, this strategy can be used in all three phases of the ACT model. This process not only gives the teacher insight into what the student comprehends and understands about the concepts, conceptual relationships, or transfer contexts, but it also allows students the opportunity to safely reveal where they are confused or moments of revelation.

Figure 8.30   What to Wow

Who?	Who do these concepts, connections, or contexts affect?
What?	What is it? What are the critical attributes or problems at hand?
When?	When does it apply? When did it happen?
Where?	Where does it happen?
How?	How does it work?
Why?	Why is it important?
Huh?	Are you confused about any points? Is anything troubling you?
Wow!	What's awesome or amazing about these concepts, connections, or contexts?

SOURCE: Stern & Aleo, 2020, *Conceptually Speaking,* Episode 17.

DESIGNING INSTRUCTIONAL CALENDARS

Like many teachers, once we write our unit plan and have selected a few of our go-to instructional strategies, we like to sit with a calendar and make a rough sketch of the learning progression so that we can ensure cohesion and a strong through line between each learning experience. An instructional calendar creates a visual of the time spent in each phase of the learning process. This calendar essentially takes the unit storyboard and maps it out on an actual calendar.

Figure 8.31 shows a sample instructional calendar with some questions that we like to ask ourselves as we are planning the different learning experiences. This is not prescriptive and should be adjusted based on the conditions of each unit and situation. It acts as a guide to think through layering instruction in the ACT model.

Notice that most of the time in the calendar is spent in deeper levels of learning with students connecting concepts in relation to one another and transferring their understanding to new situations. We also set time aside for students to set goals, reflect, and monitor their learning as well as provide opportunities for student ownership, voice, and choice in the learning experiences.

It is essential to consider which phase of the learning journey we are in when selecting instructional strategies. We can't begin with a debate; it will probably not demonstrate a sophisticated level of knowledge or thought if students have not acquired understanding of important concepts. We also want to make sure that we are teaching for transfer, so we like to conduct one final check to ensure we are indeed moving our students toward increasingly dissimilar, real-world transfer.

The matrix in Figure 8.32 helps to evaluate where a context or learning experience might fall along the spectrum. We try to incorporate a variety of experiences so that students can feel success, have their thinking complicated, and reach for deeper levels of critical thought leading to innovation. This thinking prompt is useful to ensure we are moving our students toward dissimilar, real-world transfer.

DESIGN STEP

Create a rough sketch of our instructional calendar. Download the blank template and begin to plot our learning experiences in a calendar.

Figure 8.31 **Sample Instructional Calendar**

Monday	Tuesday	Wednesday	Thursday	Friday
Hook via Compelling Question: Share a big picture overview of the unit. Make **prior knowledge** of concepts visible. **Acquire** understanding of initial disciplinary lenses and/or anchoring concepts.		Share **conceptual questions** or support students in developing their own questions about the concepts and relationships between them. **Connect** concepts through inquiry into a simple context.		**Self-assess** current understanding of conceptual connections. **Set goals** for the remainder of the unit.

Cognitive Apprenticeship: Think aloud, give feedback on thinking. Are there experts in the community who can support student thinking and learning in this unit?

Are there **new concepts** that students need to acquire before applying to novel situations? Are there additional conceptual questions to pose?

Introduce additional contexts to help students **transfer** their understanding to novel situations. Increase sophistication of thinking by connecting inquiry back to the big picture.

Are there new concepts that students need to acquire understanding of before applying to novel situations? Are there additional conceptual questions to pose? What new contexts should students explore to deepen their thinking about the disciplinary lenses and anchoring concepts in the unit? **Transfer** to new contexts that move along the Learning Transfer Spectrum. **Refine thinking** with critical thinking tools and have students compare their thinking to the experts'.				**Self-assess** current understanding of concepts and questions posed this week. How has student thinking evolved or refined?

Performance Task: original application of thinking, knowledge and skills, rather than just routine use of facts and procedures. It also entails disciplined inquiry into the details of a particular problem and results in a product or presentation that has meaning or value beyond success in school: Transfer to novel situation, authentic audience, using concepts from multiple disciplines.

Reflect on unit and determine extent to which goals were met.

Record new insights about self as learner.

online resources Download template at www.learningthattransfers.com.

THINKING PROMPT

Looking at the contexts we've planned in the storyboard, we can determine if we are intentionally moving students toward innovation.

Figure 8.32   Context Transfer Matrix

Read through the criteria and place the context or learning experience into the most applicable spot.			
Dissimilar and appears completely foreign to other learning experiences. It is nothing like the original learning experience.			**INNOVATION**
Dissimilar to the original learning experience but students are able to see how concepts might apply.			
Similar learning experience to what students have been doing in class. It is not exactly the same.			
Academic, Similar Transfer	Only relevant or done in an academic or classroom setting. There is no authentic audience or impact.	Some real-world application. Students complete the task for a specific audience and the experience could potentially be impactful, but students do not see evidence of impact.	Completely real-world challenge— students present solutions to an authentic audience and can observe evidence of impact.

online resources ↖ Download at www.learningthattransfers.com.

DESIGNING LESSON PLANS

Now we can synthesize all of the ideas in this chapter and design a lesson. Figure 8.33 provides additional questions to gain clarity on the phase of the learning journey we are seeking to implement so that we may select an appropriate and powerful strategy to achieve our intent.

THINKING PROMPT

Figure 8.33   ACT Model Lesson Planning Brainstorm

ACQUIRE	Is the purpose to make meaning or consolidate understanding of concepts? Or both?
CONNECT	What connection(s) between concepts will students make? How will students document their growing thinking?
TRANSFER	Where does this experience fall on the Learning Transfer Spectrum? How does it compare to previous experiences? Do students need to acquire understanding of new concepts to navigate this new scenario?

Figure 8.34 provides a sample lesson planning template that helps to organize our thinking. We begin by listing the goals of the lesson across the top. Then we determine the purpose of the lesson, what strategies will be used, thinking tools or self-assessments for students to monitor their learning, additional resources for the specific contexts students will explore or notes they will take, and finally how we will formatively assess to ensure students understood the content and purpose of the lesson.

Find additional lesson planning frameworks aligned to other initiatives such as Project-Based Learning, Inquiry-Based Learning, personalized learning, International Baccalaureate, virtual learning, and more linked in the QR code.

Scan the QR code for additional Lesson Planning Frameworks.

DESIGN STEP

BUILD A LESSON PLAN

Figure 8.34 **Sample Lesson Planning Template**

Lesson Planner

Learning Intentions	Success Criteria	Conceptual Question(s)

MENTAL MODEL		
Phase (check all that apply): ☐ Acquire ☐ Connect ☐ Transfer ☐ Student Action		
Strategy(ies):		
Thinking Tool/Self-Assessment:		
Additional Resources:		
Formative Assessment:		

online resources ⏷ Download template at www.learningthattransfers.com.

Scan this QR code to access the companion website and download all templates.

CONCLUSION

In Chapter 2, we introduced many shifts that will need to occur in order to have a transfer-focused classroom. We hope the strategies and explanations in this chapter have added even greater clarity on how to make the shifts seen in Figure 8.35 become a reality.

Figure 8.35 **Student and Teacher Roles in a Transfer-Focused Classroom**

Student Role	Teacher Role
DIRECTOR of their own learning	**DESIGNER** of empowering lesson plans
DETECTIVE of their own thinking	**DETECTIVE** of student thinking
COLLABORATOR with peers and teachers	**EVALUATOR** of their own impact on learning
PATTERN-SEEKER through diverse ideas and experiences	**CURATOR** of diverse resources and experiences

Might look like

- Co-constructing success criteria
- Setting goals
- Monitoring their thinking
- Self-questioning
- Self-regulating
- Selecting among strategies
- Providing self- and peer feedback
- Applying feedback
- Deciding what to investigate next
- Adjusting learning behavior

Might look like

- Establishing a collaborative, safe culture
- Establishing credibility
- Making thinking routine
- Modeling thinking
- Modeling risk-taking
- Modeling learning from errors
- Cognitive coaching students
- Providing and soliciting feedback
- Adjusting instruction

There are an infinite number of instructional strategies that can be used to teach students how to make sense of our complex world. The key is to empower our students to become their own teachers. We do that through explicitly teaching them how to be conscious of their thinking and learning, to question their assumptions, to revisit what they previously understood, to make connections that help them understand how our world is organized, and to use their understanding to unlock new situations.

Imagine the possibilities if more and more students are able to do this type of complex learning independently. Imagine the type of communities we could enjoy if more and more adults begin to seek understanding before judgment. We all entered this profession to help young people go on to lead meaningful and successful lives. We need to abandon the idea that this is achieved through the mere accumulation of disconnected bits of knowledge. The ACT model is a way of thinking about how learning occurs to help students make sense of the complexities of our world, without oversimplifying it. We are cautiously optimistic about the power that this way of teaching and learning can have on our greater society.

Scan the QR code for video reflections from students and teachers.

THINKING PROMPT

Take a moment to reflect on your refined thinking in response to the following questions:

- What is the relationship between **intentionality**, **iteration**, **planning**, and the **ACT model**?
- What is the role of the **student** in a learning-transfer classroom? What is the role of the **teacher**?
- How does **classroom community** impact **student thinking**?
- How do **student independence**, **metacognition**, and the **ACT model** interact?

_____

_____

_____

_____

_____

Remaining Nimble

How Do We Continue to Evolve in an Unprecedented World?

It's the summer of 2020 and Julie is sitting in her backyard, trying to work a bit while her kids take pictures with their iPads. Her four-year-old says, "Julie Stern's iPhone." She hears the familiar beep of the airdrop feature and this picture pops up on her screen.

Figure 9.1 Photo Taken by Andrew Stern

PHOTO CREDIT: Andrew Stern, 4 years old.

Little Andrew had not yet entered pre-Kindergarten. He had learned letters and their sounds, but it was his first time actually reading words. He was motivated by technology. He took a stunning nature photo and figured out how to read in order to share the picture with his mom via the internet.

A few days later he and his older brother, Alex, who had just turned six years old, decided they would ride their pedal-powered bulldozer down the steep hill in front of their house. They would shout with glee as they took turns barreling down the hill at top speed. While Andrew was zooming down, Alex stood and watched from the side of the top of the hill. He mused, "Mommy, from this angle, it doesn't look that steep."

Shocked, she asked him where he learned those words, "angle" and "steep." He shrugged and replied, "YouTube." Whether we like it or not, technology is profoundly changing the way our children learn. Julie uses all the parental controls on their iPads and continues to be outsmarted by her four- and six-year-old children. They figured out that if they watch videos together on each other's iPads, they can "double" (they actually used that word) the amount of time they can watch before they reach their limits. When she made a screen-time exception for the camera app because of their love of nature photography, Alex started to use his iPad to record videos of TV shows playing on Andrew's iPad so that he could extend his video watching. She simultaneously felt both frustration and pride toward his creativity.

Our role as educators is changing and evolving right alongside everything else in our lives. COVID-19 only accelerated some of the changes happening due to technology. As a guest on our podcast, *Conceptually Speaking*, Professor Yong Zhao pointed out, many young people are already organizing worldwide around topics of interest. They are learning incredible content from videos and other multimedia—we see it with our own young children. Professor Zhao suggests that we let go of the notion of teachers as providers of knowledge and consider ourselves more as *curators* of learning and something like *advisors* to our students as we help them become self-determined learners (Stern & Aleo, 2020).

The ideas presented in this book provide the first steps toward education evolving to meet the needs of our changing world. A focus on learning that transfers is inherently motivating. It harnesses students' prior knowledge and interests in the service of deepening their learning, refining their thinking, and applying their knowledge to new situations. The ACT model teaches students how to be adaptable as they can apply it to any new field they encounter.

We hope that this book offers practical solutions that can be implemented within the context of standard-based curriculum that is organized around traditional subjects and age-based groupings of children. We hope that it has inspired readers to use the standards of learning in a meaningful way and that you have gained valuable tools to embrace an empowering way of teaching and learning.

At the same time, we need to keep our ears to the ground and our eyes ahead to determine what additional changes should be considered in the ways we go about formal education. For instance, we may need to consider shifting our whole notion of itemized standards of learning. What if curriculum committees of education experts considered the most important, transferable concepts and competencies of the 21st century, and these became the basis of the outcomes of learning? And what if we provided way more opportunity for students to explore areas of interest to them to increase their expertise and creativity at solving the world's greatest challenges?

Many calls for major reform of our curricular outcomes deserve attention by our greatest teachers and thought leaders. We need to acknowledge how much our world is changing and adapt accordingly. Super computers now calculate complex science and mathematics at speeds previously inconceivable. Yet we still teach students how to hand calculate scores of mathematical concepts that professionals no longer calculate in their careers. Meanwhile, fake news spreads six times faster on social media than true news (Rhodes, 2020). All of these new realities mean we need to teach our students how to transfer and revisit some of our curricular topics.

For instance, Professor Jo Boaler, esteemed mathematics teacher educator, has become well known recently for her call for action in terms of mathematics education reform. She explains that mathematics education—in its current state—is too procedurally focused. She asserts that mathematics is a conceptual language, and if students develop conceptual understanding of mathematics there is very little to memorize as the ideas continuously build on one another (Stanford SCOPE, 2013).

In addition to needing to change the way we approach mathematics instruction, we also need major reform in what we prioritize for mathematics content. In 2009, in a survey of *Freakonomics Radio* only 2 percent of listeners indicated they use calculus or trigonometry in their lives while 31 percent analyze and interpret data regularly and 66 percent need to use Excel to perform in their career (Boaler & Levitt, 2019). This data emphasizes that we need to shift from the traditional high school courses to an increased focus on data science and the use of technology to support flexibility in mathematical thinking.

Like Boaler, Conrad Wolfram (2020), author of *The Math(s) Fix: An Education Blueprint for the AI Age* and founder of computerbasedmath.org, stresses that students need to be able to reason about big data and increase their computational thinking skills. Wolfram's approach to mathematics also emphasizes being able to think conceptually by first defining real-world problems, abstracting mathematics from these problems, finding a solution, and then interpreting this solution to determine if it makes sense in context of the original problem. This process is only capable if we shift from having students doing calculations by hand and encourage them to use technology and computers to aid in making sense of the problems around them. According to Wolfram, "The computer fundamentally changes what it's possible to learn, the tools that you can use, and how you can understand and experience the world around you in a computational way" (Pearson North America, 2020). Rather than viewing technology as a short cut we need to view it as a portal to the world and deeper mathematical thinking. Both Boaler's and Wolfram's methods implore curriculum writers to prioritize reasoning over memorization and data science over complex calculus if we want to shift to more meaningful mathematics that students will actually use in their futures.

In the natural sciences, experts from dozens of fields are sounding the call about the irreversible effects of climate change and resulting ecological catastrophes that will follow. Meanwhile, science curriculum has become increasingly seen as a tool to serve the economy—dominated by discussions of STEM career paths and technological innovation while neglecting ethical considerations and environmental stewardship. As machines and robots continue to learn, mimicking human-like decisions, understanding deeper "why" questions and developing broader understanding of scientific principles and theories will be more useful than rote knowledge or decontextualized skills. Looking at current trends in American policy and public perception, it seems generating popular support and understanding of scientific issues might need to be re-prioritized in STEM curriculum and public discourse more broadly.

Updates to our curriculum should be addressed in the humanities as well. As we become an increasingly digital society and culture, multimodal forms of communication and representation will become essential for all. Print based literacy will continue to be necessary, but will it be sufficient to help students navigate the swirling world of text, images, video, and sound they're immersed in every day? A leader in writing instruction, author Angela Stockman, shared that some of her most talented students struggled to transfer their skills to contexts outside of print-based settings, while those who were able to interpret and create across modes are thriving in a variety of industries (Stern & Aleo, 2020).

There are also growing concerns around the types of texts that should be taught in classrooms, or even regarded as canon. More educators and parents are beginning to question whose voices are centered and whose are marginalized by the traditionally white, western, and male canon. The Great Books certainly merit a place in schools, but notions of creating top down cultural cohesion through curriculum feel anachronistic and misguided in our highly global, multicultural, and digital world. The National Council of Teachers of English has recently added a #DisruptTexts section of their journal named in honor of the hashtag started by Tricia Ebarvia, Lorena Germán, Kim Parker, and Julia Torres. The goals of #DisruptTexts capture the essence of wider trends in classrooms and scholarship to help foster critical literacy, empower students, and center Black, indigenous, and people of color in the English curriculum.

Similarly, we are facing social, political, and cultural unrest accelerated by a growing crisis around questions of truth and fact. Understanding these issues, as well as their historical roots, is the only way we can course correct our civic systems enough to weather these new threats. Thinkers like the Stanford History Education Group are already hard at work developing courses and curriculum that can be used to help improve student civic reasoning to help young people determine what is true and what is not on the web (Breakstone et al., 2018).

With everything happening across the world right now, a strong understanding of concepts and theories from the social sciences and history are more important than ever. Current and future generations of learners need to develop the capacity to be discerning about the increasingly complex forms of propaganda, manipulation, and fake news that have taken over our news feeds and television screens. Learning that transfers is essential in today's fast-paced world.

The introduction to this book outlined key drivers of change in today's world. Technological advances in artificial intelligence and other areas such as Blockchain are undoubtedly going to impact the course of humanity at a breathtaking pace that will dwarf today's changes. As a species, we are not ready for this. We need new competencies to help us to deal with these changes. And the pace of technological change is only one factor at play today. Calls to decolonize the curriculum and the questioning of biased and harmful assessment practices are twin forces that are going to reshape today's schools.

The question for us is, *How will we respond to these changes?* Will we ignore them and keep doing what we've always done? Or will we model the type of resilience, lifelong learning, and innovation that we so desperately want our students to gain? We are hopeful about the networks of passionate teachers and leaders from around the world who are willing to collaborate to design a better future.

The Institute for the Future offers 10 Skills for the Future, as listed in Figure 9.2, in response to the drivers of change. You will notice many, if not all of them, are explicitly or implicitly addressed throughout this book.

Figure 9.2   **Ten Skills Needed for the Future**

Skill	Description
Sense-Making	ability to determine the deeper meaning or significance of what is being expressed
Social Intelligence	ability to connect to others in a deep and direct way, to sense and stimulate reactions and desired interactions
Novel & Adaptive Thinking	proficiency at thinking and coming up with solutions and responses beyond that which is rote or rule based
Cross-Cultural Competency	ability to operate in different cultural settings
Computational Thinking	ability to translate vast amounts of data into abstract concepts and to understand data-based reasoning
New-Media Literacy	ability to critically assess and develop content that uses new media forms, and to leverage these media for persuasive communication
Transdisciplinarity	literacy in and ability to understand concepts across multiple disciplines
Design Mindset	ability to represent and develop tasks and work processes for desired outcomes
Cognitive Load Management	ability to discriminate and filter information for importance, and to understand how to maximize cognitive functioning using a variety of tools and techniques
Virtual Collaboration	ability to work productively, drive engagement, and demonstrate presence as a member of a virtual team

SOURCE: Adapted from Davies, A., Fidler, D., Gorbis, M., 2011.

No one person or organization holds all of the pieces to solving this puzzle. What is paramount is that we work together. That we check our egos and push for trust, generosity, and possibility. That we embrace risk and believe to our cores that the best is yet to come. This may mean letting go of some of our cherished practices to ensure that our students are prepared for an uncertain future.

Learning that transfers is the most certain path toward a brighter future. It is the way to ensure our students are prepared to lead meaningful lives, which is why we all entered this profession in the first place. Let's focus on what we can control and collaborate to make this vision a reality.

Learning That Matters

Yong Zhao

University of Melbourne
University of Kansas

As human beings, we cannot *not* learn. We are natural born learners. When we are born, our only survival skill is to continuously learn. We observe, we imitate, we create, and we apply. Whatever we learn is what makes us grow.

But there is so much to learn in the world. We become selective. There are things we want to learn and there are things that are of no interest to us. Gradually, we can make decisions on what we want to learn. We begin to focus on learning that matters.

When we go to school, learning changes. We are taught to learn what teachers teach. We are taught to learn for grades. We are taught to learn for rewards, however small they may be. We are taught to learn to avoid punishment. We begin to follow the teacher instead of our own heart. We begin to comply with school mandates instead of our passions. We learn not to ask why we learn.

Learning should be purposeful but not all school learning is. We come to school to learn things that matter to us, to others, and to the world. But we are often fed with content that is rarely related to us. We may be told that the content will be useful in the future, but we cannot see how. We may be told that the learning is in preparation for the future, but we never see the real connection.

It's a great pleasure to read *Learning That Transfers* by Julie Stern, Krista Ferraro, Kayla Duncan, and Trevor Aleo. The book argues that we need learning that transfers. That is, we need to have learning activities and processes that will result in the students' abilities to apply the learned knowledge and skills in different contexts in the future. The argument is not new and has been accepted generally in psychology and education. Very few people would make a counter argument.

Purposeful or intentional learning is what schools should offer students. Learning to transfer is purposeful and intentional. The world we live in is uncertain. Changes happen fast. We cannot teach knowledge that will exactly match the future problems our students will encounter. No knowledge is guaranteed to meet the needs of the unknown future. Our students need the ability and attitude that will help them develop new solutions to new problems that they have never encountered. In other words, the learning in schools is not memorization of existing solutions to existing problems.

While the argument is not new, the book offers a brilliant plan and strategies for teachers to make learning to transfer a reality. I have been deeply impressed with the thoughtfulness and comprehensiveness of the ideas offered in the book. Starting from a deep understanding of learning to transfer, which is fundamentally based on understanding of concepts, to the broad consideration of the foundations of learning to transfer that involves the changing roles of teachers, students, curriculum, and assessment, the book lays out the essentials for learning to transfer. Later on, the book paints a comprehensive picture of learning to transfer, offering research-based strategies and tactics teachers can use to deliver instructions that enable learning to transfer.

Learning to transfer is not easy but can be done. In many ways, all learning should be about transfer. If what we learn cannot be applicable to future situations, that learning is perhaps a waste of time. More important, learning that does not transfer can teach students a mindset that learning is for the immediate purpose of passing exams or learning is an artificial activity in schools. This mindset can become one of the most negative outcomes of education.

One of the purposes of education is about enhancing every student's abilities and cultivating a mindset they can always change and adapt. It is also about developing their strengths and passions. Thus teaching students to learn to transfer needs to consider the learners—their desire and passions, their strengths and weaknesses, and their capacity to take control of their own learning. In this book, Julie Stern, Krista Ferraro, Kayla Duncan, and Trevor Aleo show a great understanding of the importance of the learning. They place "fostering self-directed learning" as one of the fundamental roles teachers play.

There are many aspects of this book that I love. But the aspect that I love the most is the focus on the learner. Although it captures the entire process of teaching, the ultimate goal is about enhancing student learning. It respects the individual student as the driver of learning, with a clear understanding of "self-regulated learning" as the core basis of learning. It returns the foundation of teaching to the natural nature of learning. All teaching is about learning.

Ultimately, learning is a natural tendency of humanity. This tendency should not be suppressed. We can find ways to guide this tendency toward more productive outcomes. We can develop contexts in which students can explore their natural learning tendencies. We can also create opportunities for students to exercise this natural born tendency so they can get even better at what they learn. As educators, the best job we can do is to follow and support this tendency and work on creating learning that transfers!

Glossary

Academic transfer: Situations that are new to the students (not previously studied in class) and require students to apply their learning to more targeted and controlled settings and reflect more school-related tasks such as timed essays, standardized tests, etc.

ACT model: The process of acquiring, connecting, and transferring concepts and their relationships to new situations.

Anchoring concepts: The focus or building blocks of a unit of study; the essential conceptual elements of our content that span over an entire unit.

Backward design: Starting with the end in mind. First, establish goals of learning, then design assessment that will measure those goals, and then design learning experiences.

Concept: An organizing idea with distinct attributes that are shared across multiple examples.

Conceptual framework: The ways ideas are organized in the brain.

Conceptual knowledge: Grasping the larger structure of relationships among concepts (Anderson et al., 2001).

Conceptual relationship questions: Questions that direct students' attention to connecting concepts in relationship with one another. These connections reveal the structure of how the world is organized and are, therefore, critical to facilitating learning that transfers.

Contexts: Situations that illustrate how concepts and their connections work; they allow students to explore questions of conceptual relationship. Each new situation pushes us to reconsider our understanding, to examine concepts and their connections from all sides, and deepen our grasp of how the world works.

Curriculum Design: The process of taking our required standards or learning outcomes and turning them into course overviews, unit plans, assessments, instructional calendars, and lesson plans.

Disciplinary lenses: The highly transferable disciplinary ways of knowing and doing within the discipline itself that should be applied all the time, like a set of lenses that students put on when thinking like a practitioner in this field.

Disciplinary literacy: The specialized ways of knowing and doing that characterizes a particular field of study (Shanahan & Shanahan, 2012).

Dissimilar transfer: Applying learning to a completely new scenario that is very different from the original learning context.

Expansive framing: The ways that teachers and students integrate everyday experiences and different contexts into the main content of the curriculum.

Facts: Specific details or information that do not transfer easily beyond a narrow set of circumstances, such as mathematical facts or formulas, historical names, dates, or time periods, specific artistic styles.

Human Experience Concepts: The concepts that explore and acknowledge the enduring ideas that shape and inform our humanity.

Interdisciplinary: Learning experiences requiring analysis, synthesis, and harmonizing links between disciplines to create a new, coherent whole

Learning transfer: Using our previous learning to understand or unlock a completely new situation.

Mental models: A formulation—usually through words and visuals—that helps us to make visible the invisible, often subconscious frameworks that we use to think through complex situations.

Metacognition: Monitoring what we are thinking about as we move through the learning journey.

Metacognitive knowledge: Recognizing how thinking and learning works as well as monitoring one's own thinking (Anderson et al., 2001).

Modern Literacies: Countless programs, initiatives, philosophies, and pedagogies that all seek to bring in new ways of thinking, knowing, and doing into education and unites them under one conceptual umbrella.

Multidisciplinary: Learning experience requiring knowledge from several disciplines, but each stay within their boundaries.

Multimodalities: Includes more than one mode of communication, such as print, video, images, audio, and tactile.

Nonlinguistic representation: Ways of demonstrating knowing that do not use written words, such as drawing, charades, sculpting with modeling clay, etc.

Personalizable education: Students become creators of their learning experiences as opposed to choosing from a list curated by the teacher (Zhao, 2018).

Procedural knowledge: Knowing how to do something in a particular field of study (Anderson et al., 2001).

Real-world transfer: Situations that are new to the students (not previously studied in class) and require students to solve complex, real challenges, utilize concepts from multiple disciplines, present their findings to authentic audiences, and impact the world around them.

Schema: Patterns of interaction or networks of thoughts between concepts and ideas.

Similar transfer: Applying learning to a different, but quite similar situation to the original learning context.

Skills: Specific abilities for students to *do* something, such as follow a set of procedures, usually with an eye toward gaining automaticity or fluency with practice.

Subconcepts: Very discipline-specific concepts that allow students to navigate more specific contexts and examples and usually bring a sharper focus to the anchoring concepts and the disciplinary lenses.

Teacher credibility: Students' beliefs in the teacher as knowledgeable, trustworthy, enthusiastic, and accessible, has the power to significantly increase student learning (Fisher, Frey, & Smith, 2020).

Transdisciplinary: Learning experiences that transcend the traditional boundaries of several disciplines.

References

Achieve the Core. (2020). *CCSS where to focus grades K-8 mathematics*. Student Achievement Partners. https://achievethecore.org/category/774/mathematics-focus-by-grade-level

Agarwal, P. K. (2017, November 30). *Braindumps: A small strategy with big impact*. Retrieval Practice. https://www.retrievalpractice.org/strategies/2017/free-recall

Agarwal, P. K., & Bain, P. M. (2019). *Powerful teaching: Unleash the science of learning*. Jossey-Bass.

Ainsworth, L. (2010). *Rigorous curriculum design: How to create curricular units of study that align standards, instruction, and assessment*. The Leadership and Learning Center.

Alferi, L., Nokes-Malach, T. J., & Schunn, C. D. (2013). Learning through case comparisons: A meta-analytic review. *Educational Psychologist, 48*(2), 87–113.

Almarode, J., & Vandas, K. (2018) *Clarity for Learning*. Corwin.

Anderson, L. W. (Ed.), Krathwohl, D. R. (Ed.), Airasian, P. W., Cruikshank, K. A., Mayer, R. E., Pintrich, P. R., Raths, J., & Wittrock, M. C. (2001). *A taxonomy for learning, teaching, and assessing: A revision of Bloom's Taxonomy of Educational Objectives* (Complete edition). Longman. https://www.depauw.edu/files/resources/krathwohl.pdf

Archer, A. L., & Hughes, C. A. (2011). *Explicit instruction: Effective and efficient teaching*. Guildford Press.

Bandura, A. (1977). Self-efficacy: Toward a unifying theory of behavioral change. *Psychological Review, 84*(2), 191–215. https://doi.org/10.1037/0033-295X.84.2.191

Beghetto, R., Kaufman, J., & Baer, J. (2015). *Teaching for creativity in the Common Core classroom*. Teachers College Press.

Boaler, J., & Levitt, S. (2019). Are we teaching the wrong mathematics to high school students? *Youcubed*. https://www.youcubed.org/wp-content/uploads/2019/10/Are-we-teaching-the-wrong-math.pdf

Bostrom, N. (2019). The vulnerable world hypothesis. *Global Policy, 10*(4), 455–476 https://www.nickbostrom.com/papers/vulnerable.pdf

Bransford, J. D., Brown, A. L., & Cocking, R. R. (Eds.). (2000). *How people learn: brain, mind, experience, and school* (Expanded ed.). The National Academies Press. https://doi.org/10.17226/9853

Bray, B., & McClaskey, K. (2017). *How to personalize learning: A practical guide for getting started and going deeper*. Corwin.

Breakstone, J., McGrew, S., Smith, M., Ortega, T., & Wineburg, S. (2018). *Why we need a new approach to teaching digital literacy*. Phi Delta Kappan. http://kappanonline.org/breakstone-need-new-approach-teaching-digital-literacy/

Brookhart, S. M. (2010). *How to assess higher-order thinking skills in your classroom*. ASCD.

Bruner, J. (1977) *The process of education* (2nd ed.). Harvard University.

Bureau of Labor Statistics, U.S. Department of Labor (2019, September 4). *Fastest growing occupations* [Occupational Outlook Handbook]. https://www.bls.gov/ooh/fastest-growing.htm

Campione, J. C., & Brown, A. L. (1984). Learning ability and transfer propensity as sources of individual differences in intelligence. In P. H. Brooks, R. Sperber, & C. McCauley (Eds.), *Learning and cognition in the mentally retarded* (pp. 265–293). Erlbaum.

CASEL. (2017). *Core SEL competencies*. Collaborative for Academic, Social, and Emotional Learning. https://casel.org/core-competencies/

Cuban, L. (2008). *Hugging the middle: How teachers teach in an era of testing and accountability*. Teachers College Press.

Davies, A., Fidler, D., & Gorbis. D. (2011). *Future work skills 2020*. Institute for the Future for University of Phoenix Research Institute. https://www.iftf.org/uploads/media/SR-1382A_UPRI_future_work_skills_sm.pdf

d'Efilippo, V. & Ball, J. (2013). *The inforgraphic history of the world*. Collins.

Donovan, M. S., & Bransford, J. D. (Eds.). (2005). *How students learn: History, mathematics, and science in the classroom*. The National Academies Press. https://doi.org/10.17226/10126

Dweck, C. (2016). *Mindset: The new psychology of success*. Ballantine Books Trade.

Edmondson, A. (1999). Psychological safety and learning behavior in work teams. *Administrative Science Quarterly, 44*(2), 350–383. https://doi.org/10.2307/2666999

Emerich, P. (2020). *Reclaiming personalized learning: A pedagogy for restoring equity and humanity in our classrooms*. Corwin.

Engle, R., Lam, D., Meyer, X., & Nix, S. (2012). How does expansive framing promote transfer? Several proposed explanations and a research agenda for investigating Them. *Educational Psychologist, 47*(3), 215–231.

Engle, R., Nguyen, P. D., & Mendelson, A. (2011). The influence of framing on transfer: Initial evidence from a tutoring experiment. *Instructional Science, 39*(5), 603–628. https://doi.org/10.1007/s11251-010-9145-2

Epstein, D. (2019). *Range: Why generalists triumph in a specialized world.* Macmillan.

Erickson, H. L., & Lanning, L. A. (2014). *Transitioning to concept-based curriculum and instruction: How to bring content and process together.* Corwin.

Ficarra, L. (2016). *Health education standards modernization supplemental guidance document: Instructional resource packet for heroin and opioids.* New York State Education Department. http://www.nysed.gov/common/nysed/files/programs/curriculum-instruction/nysed-heroin-opioids-instructional-resource-packet6.17.pdf

Fisher, D., Frey, N., & Hattie, J. (2016). *Visible learning for literacy, grades K–12: Implementing the practices that work best to accelerate student learning.* Corwin.

Fisher, D., Frey, N., & Smith, D. (2020). *The teacher credibility and collective efficacy playbook.* Corwin.

Fluckiger, J. (2010) Single point rubric: A tool for responsible student self-assessment. *The Delta Kappa Gamma Bulletin, 76*(4), 18–25.

Frey, N., & Fisher, D. (2010). Modeling expert thinking. *Principal Leadership Magazine, 11*(3). https://www.bpi.edu/ourpages/auto/2014/2/24/53664572/Modeling%20Expert%20Thinking.pdf

Friedman, T. L. (2016). *Thank you for being late: An optimist's guide to thriving in the age of accelerations.* Farrar, Straus and Giroux.

Fullan, M., Quinn, J., & McEachen, J. (2018). *Deep learning: engage the world, change the world.* Corwin.

Gardner, H. (2006). *Five minds of the future.* Harvard Business School.

Gee, J. P. (2010). A situated-sociocultural approach to literacy and technology. In E. Baker (Ed.), *The new literacies: Multiple perspectives on research and practice* (pp. 165–193). Guilford.

Gee, J. P. (2014). *An introduction to discourse analysis: Theory and method* (4th ed.). Routledge.

Gentner, D. (2010). Bootstrapping the mind: Analogical processes and symbol systems. *Cognitive Science, 34*(5), 752–775. https://doi.org/10.1111/j.1551-6709.2010.01114.x

Georgia Standards of Excellence [GSE]. (2016). *Social studies Georgia Standards of Excellence: 7th grade* (SS7H1). Georgia Department of Education. https://lor2.gadoe.org/gadoe/file/75f1c375-0ca3-4431-b2a6-abc0f1b5d669/1/Social-Studies-7th-Grade-Georgia-Standards.pdf

Georgia Standards of Excellence [GSE]. (2017). *GSE high school physical science curriculum map.* Georgia Department of Education. https://www.georgiastandards.org/Georgia-Standards/Documents/Science-High-School-Physical-Science-Curriculum-Map.pdf

Georgia Standards of Excellence [GSE]. (2019). *Georgia Standards of Excellence curriculum map: GSE algebra 1* (MGSE9-12.F.LE.1, MGSE9-12.F.LE.1a-c, MGSE9-12.F.IF.1). Georgia Department of Education. https://www.georgiastandards.org/Georgia-Standards/Frameworks/Algebra-I-Curriculum-Map.pdf

Gick, M. L., & Holyoak, K. J. (1983). Schema induction and analogical transfer. *Cognitive Psychology, 15*(1), 1–38.

Gonzalez, J. (2015, October 15). *The big list of class discussion strategies.* Cult of Pedagogy. https://www.cultofpedagogy.com/speaking-listening-techniques/

Gray, D., Brown, S., & Macanufo, J. (2010). *Gamestorming: A rule book for innovators, rule breakers, and change makers.* O'Reilly Media.

Hammond, L., & Jackson, Y. (2015). *Culturally responsive teaching and the brain: Promoting authentic engagement and rigor among culturally and linguistically diverse students.* Corwin.

Harbour, K. E., Evanovich, L. L., Sweigart, C. A., & Hughes, L. E. (2015). A brief review of effective teaching practices that maximize student engagement. *Alternative Education for Children and Youth, 59*(1), 5–13. https://doi.org/10.1080/1045988X.2014.919136

Hattie, J. (2009). *Visible Learning.* Routledge.

Hattie, J. (2012). *Visible Learning for teachers.* Routledge.

Hattie, J. (2020). *Visible Learning MetaX.* https://www.visiblelearningmetax.com/research_methodology

Hattie, J., Fisher, D., & Frey, N. (2017). *Visible Learning for mathematics: What works best to optimize student learning.* Corwin.

Hattie, J., Stern, J., Fisher, D., & Frey, N. (2020). *Visible Learning for social studies: Designing student learning for conceptual understanding.* Corwin.

Hattie, J., & Timperley, H. (2007). The power of feedback. *Review of Educational Research, 77*(1), 81–112. https://doi.org/10.3102%2F003465430298487

Higgins, C. (2011). *The good life of teaching: An ethics of professional practice.* Wiley-Blackwell.

Higgins, R., Hartley, P., & Skelton, A. (2002). The conscientious consumer: Reconsidering the role of assessment feedback in student learning. *Studies in Higher Education, 27*(1), 53–64. https://doi.org/10.1080/03075070120099368

International Baccalaureate. (2013). *IB learner profile.* https://www.ibo.org/contentassets/fd82f70643ef4086b7d-3f292cc214962/learner-profile-en.pdf

ISTE. (2016). *ISTE standards for students.* International Society for Technology in Education. https://www.iste.org/standards/for-students

James, C., Weinstein, E., & Mendoza, K. (2019). *Teaching digital citizens in today's world: Research and insights behind the Common Sense K–12 Digital Citizenship Curriculum.* Common Sense Media.

Johansson, F. (2017). *The Medici effect: What elephants and epidemics can teach us about innovation.* Harvard Business Review Press.

Jones, B., & Idol, L. (Eds.). (1990). *Dimensions of thinking and cognitive instruction.* Erlbaum.

Kalantzis, M., & Cope, B. (2012). *New learning: Elements of a science of education* (2nd ed.). Cambridge University Press.

Kalantzis, M., & Cope, W. (2013). "Education is the new philosophy," to make a metadisciplinary claim for the learning sciences. In A. Reid, E. Hart, & M. Peters (Eds.), *A companion to research in education* (pp. 101–115). Springer, Dordrecht. https://doi.org/10.1007/978-94-007-6809-3_13

Kalantzis, M., Cope, B., Chan, E., & Dalley-Trim, L. (2016). *Literacies* (2nd ed.). Cambridge University Press.

Kane, T., & Staiger, D. (2012). *Gathering feedback for teaching: Combining high-quality observations with student surveys and achievement gains.* Bill and Melinda Gates Foundation. http://k12education.gatesfoundation.org/download/?Num=2680&filename=MET_Gathering_Feedback_Research_Paper1.pdf

Knight, J. (2013). *High impact instruction.* Corwin.

Lakoff, G., & Johnson M. (2008). *Metaphors we live by* (2nd ed.). University of Chicago Press.

Lam, D., Meyer, X. S., Engle, R. A., Goldwasser, L., Perez, S., Zheng, K., Clark, J., Naves, E., Rosas, H., & Tan, D. (2012). *A microgenetic analysis of how expansive framing led to transfer with one struggling student.* 10th International Conference of the Learning Sciences: The Future of Learning, ICLS 2012 – Proceedings, *1*, 40–47.

Lee, I. (2009). Ten mismatches between teachers' beliefs and written feedback practice, *ELT Journal, 63*(1), 13–22. https://doi.org/10.1093/elt/ccn010

Lobel, A. (1970–1979). *Frog and toad I can read stories.* HarperCollins.

Louis, A., Nokes-Malach, T. J, & Schunn, C. D. (2013). Learning through case comparisons: A meta-analytic review. *Educational Psychologist, 48*(2), 87–113. http://dx.doi.org/10.1080/00461520.2013.775712

Marzano, R. J. (2009). *Formative assessment & standards-based grading.* Marzano Resources.

Marzano, R., & Kendall, J. (1998). *Awash in a sea of standards.* McREL. https://cksraiders.org/UserFiles/Servers/Server_610718/File/Academics/Curriculum/5982IR_AwashInASea.pdf

Marzano, R. J., Norford, J. S., Finn, M., & Finn III, D., (2017). *A handbook for personalized competency-based education: Ensure all students master content by designing and implementing personalized competency-based education system.* Marzano Research.

Massachusetts Curriculum Framework for Science and Technology/Engineering. (2016). *Science and technology/engineering: Grades pre-kindergarten to 12 (PreK-ESS1-1).* Massachusetts Department of Education. http://www.doe.mass.edu/frameworks/scitech/2016-04.pdf

McCombs, B. (2010). *Developing responsible and autonomous learners: A key to motivating students.* American Psychological Association. https://www.apa.org/education/k12/learners

McKinzie, T. (2016) *Dive into inquiry.* EdTech Team Press.

McTighe, J., & Willis, J. (2019). *Upgrade your teaching: Understanding by Design meets neuroscience.* ASCD.

Mehta, J., & Fine, S. (2019). *In search of deeper learning: The quest to remake the American high school.* Harvard University.

Moje, E. B. (2007). Developing socially just subject-matter instruction: A review of the literature on disciplinary literacy teaching. *Review of Research in Education, 31*, 1–44.

Moje, E. B. (2015). Doing and teaching disciplinary literacy with adolescent learners: A social and cultural enterprise. *Harvard Educational Review, 85*, 254–278.

Muijs, D., & Bokhove, C. (2020). *Metacognition and self-regulation: Evidence review.* Education Endowment Foundation. https://educationendowmentfoundation.org.uk/evidence-summaries/evidence-reviews/metacognition-and-self-regulation-review/

Murphy, G. (2002). *The big book of concepts.* MIT Press.

National Research Council. (2012). *Education for life and work: Developing transferable knowledge and skills in the 21st century.* Committee on Defining Deeper Learning and 21st Century Skills, J. W. Pellegrino & M. L. Hilton (Eds.), Board on Testing and Assessment and Board on Science Education, Division of Behavioral and Social Sciences and Education. The National Academies Press

Newmann, F. M., Bryk, A. S., & Nagaoka, J. (2001). *Authentic intellectual work and standardized tests: Conflict or coexistence?* Consortium on Chicago School Research.

Nosich, G. (2005). *Learning to think things through: A guide to critical thinking across the curriculum* (2nd ed.). Prentice Hall.

Pace, D., & Middendorf, J. (2004). *Decoding the disciplines: Helping students learn disciplinary ways of thinking.* New Directions for Teaching and Learning. No 98. Summer 2004. Jossey-Bass.

Pankin, J. (2013). *Schema theory.* MIT. http://web.mit.edu/pankin/www/Schema_Theory_and_Concept_Formation.pdf

Paterson, M. (2019). *Pop-up studio.* Circularity Press.

Pellegrino, J. W., & Hilton, M. L. (Eds.). (2012). *Education for life and work: Developing transferable knowledge and skills in the 21st century.* The National Academies Press. https://doi.org/10.17226/13398

Pearson North America. (2020, May 18). *ICTCM 2020 virtual: Conrad Wolfram on the future of math* [Video]. YouTube. https://youtu.be/TvACkVWa3-Q

Perkins, D. N., & Salomon, G. (1988). Teaching for transfer. *Educational Leadership, 46*(1), 22–32. http://www.ascd.org/ASCD/pdf/journals/ed_lead/el_198809_perkins.pdf

Perkins, D. N., & Salomon, G. (1992). Transfer of learning. *International Encyclopedia of Education* (2nd ed.). Pergamon Press. http://learnweb.harvard.edu/alps/thinking/docs/traencyn.htm

Perna, M. (2018). *Answering why: Unleashing passion, purpose and performance in younger generations.* Greenleaf Book Club Press.

Potash, B. (2020, September 11). *Hexagonal thinking: A colorful tool for discussion.* Cult of Pedagogy. https://www.cultofpedagogy.com/hexagonal-thinking/

Reddy, M. (1993). The conduit metaphor: A case of frame conflict in our language about language. In A. Ortony (Ed.), *Metaphor and thought* (pp. 164–201). Cambridge University Press. https:10.1017/CBO9781139173865.012

Refsum Jensenius, A. (2012). *Disciplinarities: Intra, cross, multi, inter, trans.* https://www.arj.no/2012/03/12/disciplinarities-2/

Repko, A. (2008, Fall). Assessing interdisciplinary learning outcomes. *Academic Exchange Quarterly.* https://oakland.edu/Assets/upload/docs/AIS/Assessing_Interdisiplinary_Learning_Outcomes_(Allen_F._Repko).pdf

Retrieval Practice. (2019, January 4). *Three reasons why retrieval practice boosts learning* [Video]. YouTube. https://youtu.be/pYbbZJOQudk

Rhodes, L. (producer), & Orlowski, J. (director). (2020). *The Social Dilemma* [Video file]. https://www.netflix.com/title/81254224

Ritchhart, R., Church, M., & Morrison, K. (2011). *Making thinking visible: How to promote engagement, understanding, and independence for all learners* (1st ed.). Jossey-Bass.

Rothstein, D., & Santana, L. (2011). *Make just one change: Teach students to ask their own questions.* Harvard University Press.

Ryder, D. (2016, February 17). *How might we the content? Applying Design Thinking in a high school English classroom.* The Synapse. https://medium.com/synapse/how-might-we-the-content-applying-design-thinking-in-a-high-school-english-classroom-74f7c202b9bb

Schlechty, P. (2011). *Engaging students: The next level of working on the work.* Jossey-Bass.

Schneider, S., Nebel, S., Beege, M., & Rey, G. D. (2018). The autonomy-enhancing effects of choice on cognitive load, motivation and learning with digital media. *Learning and Instruction, 58,* 161–172. https://doi.org/10.1016/j.learninstruc.2018.06.006

Senge, P. M. (2010). *The necessary revolution: How individuals and organizations are working together to create a sustainable world.* Doubleday.

Shackleton-Jones, N. (2019). *How people learn: Designing education and training that works to improve performance.* Kogan Page.

Shanahan, T., & Shanahan, C. (2012). What is disciplinary literacy and why does it matter? *Topics in Language Disorders, 32*(1), 7–18. https://doi.org/10.1097/TLD.0b013e318244557a

Shatilovich, A. V., Tchesunov, A. V., Neretina, T. V., Grabarnik, I. P., Gubin, S. V., Vishnivetskaya, T. A., Onstott, T. C., & Rivkina, E. M. (2018). Viable nematods from late Pleistocene permafrost of the Kolyma River lowland. *Doklady Biological Sciences, 480,* 100–102. https://doi.org/10.1134/S0012496618030079

Soter, A., Wilkinson, I., Murphy, P., Rudge, L., Reninger, K., & Edwards, M. (2008). What the discourse tells us: Talk and indicators of high-level comprehension. *International Journal of Educational Research, 47*(6), 372–391. https://doi.org/10.1016/j.ijer.2009.01.001

Sousa, D. (2017). *How the brain learns* (5th ed.). Corwin.

Spencer, J., & Juliani, A. J. (2017). *Empower: What happens when students own their learning.*

Stanford SCOPE. (2013, February 25). *Jo Boaler on the good and bad of mathematics education* [Video]. YouTube. https://youtu.be/ZZrlk4NqaJ4

Stern, J., & Aleo, T. (Hosts). (2020a, June 23). *Adam Hansen talks innovation and metacognition.* Conceptually Speaking [Audio podcast]. https://www.buzzsprout.com/1073776/4285709-adam-hansen-talks-innovation-and-metacognition

Stern, J., & Aleo, T. (Hosts). (2020b, July 28). *Matthew Murrie talks curiosity and connection.* Conceptually Speaking [Audio podcast]. https://www.buzzsprout.com/1073776/4751195-matthew-murrie-talks-curiosity-and-connection

Stern, J., & Aleo, T. (Hosts). (2020c). *Angela Stockman talks equity, voice, and metaphorical thinking.* Conceptually Speaking [Audio podcast]. https://conceptuallyspeaking.buzzsprout.com/1073776/4102124-angela-stockman-talks-equity-voice-metaphorical-thinking

Stern, J., & Aleo, T. (Hosts). (2020d). *Yong Zhao talks Student autonomy and the future of education.* Conceptually Speaking [Audio podcast]. https://conceptuallyspeaking.buzzsprout.com/1073776/4846586-dr-yong-zhao-talks-student-autonomy-and-the-future-of-education

Stern, J., Ferraro, K., & Mohnkern, J. (2017). *Tools for teaching conceptual understanding: Designing lessons and assessments for deep learning.* Corwin.

Strauss, V. (2020, August 12). Three necessary things for young people who feel their future is unraveling. *The*

Washington Post. https://www.washingtonpost.com/education/2020/08/12/three-necessary-things-young-people-who-feel-their-future-is-unraveling/

Termaat, A., & Talbot, C. (2016). *Chemistry, MYP by Concept 4 & 5.* Hodder Education.

ten Berge, T., & van Hezewijk, R. (1999). Procedural and declarative knowledge: An evolutionary perspective. *Theory & Psychology, 9*(5), 605–624. https://doi.org/10.1177/0959354399095002

Twenge, J., Cooper, A., Joiner, T., Duffy, M., & Binau, S. (2019). Age, period, and cohort trends in mood disorder indicators and suicide-related outcomes in a nationally representative dataset, 2005–2017. *Journal of Abnormal Psychology, 128*(3), 185–199. http://dx.doi.org/10.1037/abn0000410

Unsworth, N., Redick, T. S., Heitz, R. P., Broadway, J. M., & Engle, R. W. (2009). Complex working memory span tasks and higher-order cognition: A latent-variable analysis of the relationship between processing and storage. *Memory, 17*(6), 635–654. https://doi.org/10.1080/09658210902998047

Vendetti, M. S., Matlen, B. J., Richland, L. E., & Bunge, S. A. (2015). Analogical reasoning in the classroom: Insights from cognitive science. *International Mind, Brain, and Education Society, 9*(2), 100–106. https://doi.org/10.1111/mbe.12080

Wagner, T. (2012). *Creating innovators: The making of young people who will change the world.* Scribner.

Weil, Z. (2016). *The world becomes what we teach: Educating a generation of solutionaries.* Lantern Books.

Wiggins, G., & McTighe, J. (2005). *Understanding by design* (2nd ed.).

Wiliam, D., & Leahy, S. (2015). *Embedding formative assessment.* Learning Sciences International.

Willingham, D. T. (2009). *Why don't students like school? A cognitive scientist answers questions about how the mind works and what it means for the classroom.* Jossey-Bass.

Willis, J. (2018, November 30). *Applying learning in multiple contexts.* Edutopia. https://www.edutopia.org/article/applying-learning-multiple-contexts

Wolfram, C. (2020). *The math(s) fix: An education blueprint for the AI age.* Wolfram Media.

Wormeli, R. (2018). *Fair isn't always equal* (2nd ed.). Stenhouse.

youcubed K–12 Data Science. (2020). *What's a "data-talk"? youcubed.* https://www.youcubed.org/wp-content/uploads/2020/05/What-is-a-Data-Talk-1.pdf

Zhao, Y. (2013). What works may hurt: Side effects in education. *Journal of Educational Change, 18*(3), 1–19.

Zhao, Y. (2018). *Reach for greatness: Personalizable education for all children.* Corwin.

Index

Confident Teachers, Inspired Learners

CAROL PELLETIER RADFORD

This vivid and inspirational guide offers educators practical strategies to promote their well-being and balance. Readers will find wisdom for a fulfilling career in education through teachers' stories of resilience, tips for mindful living, and podcast interviews with inspiring teachers and leaders.

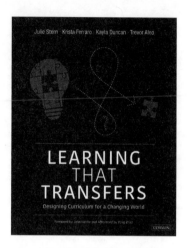

JULIE STERN, KRISTA FERRARO, KAYLA DUNCAN, TREVOR ALEO

This step-by-step guide walks educators through the process of identifying curricular goals, establishing assessment targets, and planning curriculum and instruction that facilitates the transfer of learning to new and challenging situations.

STEPAN MEKHITARIAN

Transition back to school by leveraging the best of distance learning and classroom instruction. Learn how to create a blended learning experience that fosters learning, collaboration, and engagement.

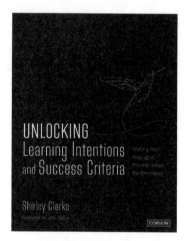

SHIRLEY CLARKE

Learning intentions and success criteria expert Shirley Clarke shows how to phrase learning intentions for students, create success criteria to match, and adapt and implement them across disciplines.

No matter where you are in your professional journey, Corwin aims to ease the many demands teachers face on a daily basis with accessible strategies that benefit ALL learners. Through research-based, high-quality content, we offer practical guidance on a wide range of topics, including curriculum planning, learning frameworks, classroom design and management, and much more. Our resources are developed by renowned educators and designed for easy implementation in order to provide tangible results for you and your students.

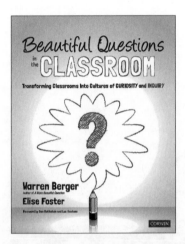

WARREN BERGER, ELISE FOSTER

Written to be both inspirational and practical, *Beautiful Questions in the Classroom* shows educators how they can transform their classrooms into cultures of curiosity.

ERIC M. ANDERMAN

Delve into the what, why, and how of motivation, its effects on learning, and your ability to spark that motivation using practical strategies to improve academic outcomes.

SERENA PARISER, EDWARD F. DEROCHE

Gain time in each day, reduce stress, and improve your classroom learning environment with 35 practical, teacher-proven strategies for managing time and setting personal boundaries.

CATLIN R. TUCKER

Balance With Blended Learning provides teachers with practical strategies to actively engage students in setting goals, monitoring development, reflecting on growth, using feedback, assessing work quality, and communicating their progress with parents.

CORWIN

A SAGE Publishing Company

Helping educators make the greatest impact

CORWIN HAS ONE MISSION: to enhance education through intentional professional learning.

We build long-term relationships with our authors, educators, clients, and associations who partner with us to develop and continuously improve the best evidence-based practices that establish and support lifelong learning.